confidence culture

confidence culture

shani orgad & rosalind gill

Duke University Press *Durham and London* 2022

Designed by Aimee C. Harrison
Typeset in Portrait Text and Canela Text
by Copperline Book Services

Library of Congress Cataloging-in-Publication Data
Names: Orgad, Shani, [date] author. | Gill, Rosalind
(Rosalind Clair), author.
Title: Confidence culture / Shani Orgad and Rosalind Gill.
Description: Durham : Duke University Press, 2022. |
Includes bibliographical references and index.
Identifiers: LCCN 2021019043 (print)
LCCN 2021019044 (ebook)
ISBN 9781478014539 (hardcover)
ISBN 9781478017608 (paperback)
ISBN 9781478021834 (ebook)
Subjects: LCSH: Self-esteem in women. | Self-confidence. | Women—
Psychology. | Women—Conduct of life. | Confidence. | Feminism. |
BISAC: SOCIAL SCIENCE / Women's Studies | SOCIAL SCIENCE /
Sociology / General
Classification: LCC HQ1206.O766 2022 (print) | LCC HQ1206 (ebook) |
DDC 155.3/3382—dc23
LC record available at https://lccn.loc.gov/2021019043
LC ebook record available at https://lccn.loc.gov/2021019044

Cover art by Asma Istwani

In memory of Sylvia Chant

contents

acknowledgments

We first had the idea for this book in 2015, when we created our "confidence basket," in which we started collecting the many examples of confidence messages, exhortations, and programs we kept encountering all around us. The basket quickly started overflowing, not least thanks to conversations with numerous colleagues, friends, and students, who shared with us their own examples, experiences, and ideas. Both the basket and our thinking about the phenomenon we call confidence culture developed out of these interactions. We also greatly benefited from presenting our ideas to different audiences around the world and discussing them with policymakers and journalists. The ideas that developed through all these interactions underscore our belief that the production of knowledge is a collective enterprise. While it would be impossible to individually thank each person, we would like to express our appreciation to the feminist community of which we are a part, which includes critical scholars of all kinds—in media and communications, cultural studies, sociology, psychosocial studies, critical race studies, LGBTQ+, and gender and sexuality studies. The friendship, solidarity, and critical challenges from all these fields have been vital and formative.

Lisa Adkins and Maryanne Dever gave us our first opportunity to publish on the confidence cult(ure) in an article we wrote for *Australian Feminist Studies* in 2015. We are immensely grateful for the space the journal provides as a key site of feminist debate and collegiality. An article about the relationship between the promotion of individual women's self-confidence and the neoliberalization of feminism was published in a special issue of *New Formations* in 2017, and we would like to thank Sara Farris and Catherine Rottenberg for the opportunity to contribute to this important and stimulating collection, as well as for their helpful feedback. Kim Allen and Anna Bull also deserve special thanks for including our paper on "the amazing bounce-backable woman" in their special issue of *Sociological Research Online* on the "turn to character." The intellectually generative and enjoyable events they set up around this theme at King's College London and at Goldsmiths, University of London, brought together a range of colleagues interested—like us—in the "psychological turn" in neoliberalism. We were honored that the resulting article, in which we focus on resilience, won the 2019 British Sociological Association/Sociological Research Online prize. Finally, we thank Mehita Iqani and Katlego Disemelo, who invited us to contribute a paper to their special issue of *Cultural Politics* on joy and consumer culture and inspired us to write about "getting unstuck" and confidence coaching in the context of COVID-19.

We are very lucky to be part of a feminist community of staff and students in London. Over the last few years this community has resisted the insularity, managerialism, and competitiveness of universities and set up joint events, held in different places, including London School of Economics and Political Science (LSE), King's College, City University, and Goldsmiths, and most recently via Zoom. Thanks to everyone involved for keeping this community alive, vibrant, and supportive, especially during the pandemic of the last year.

Our shared feminist friendship group has been an invaluable source of intellectual sustenance, inspiration, support, and fun while writing this book. Sarah Banet-Weiser, Sara de Benedictis, Bridget Conor, Jo Littler, Rachel O'Neill, Catherine Rottenberg, and Christina Scharff: you are the most awesome and inspiring women—visionary intellectuals, kind and supportive friends, passionate feminists, and individuals whose multiple talents include baking, cultivating plants, and karaoke. It is a pleasure and a privilege to know you, and we look forward to a time—after the pandemic—when we can get together around a table and share food and wine again.

We would also like to express our great appreciation to Hannah Curran-Troop, who read and copyedited the entire manuscript for this book, as well as doing literature searches and myriad other tasks with unfailingly good spirits. Thank you, Hannah: you are a pleasure to work with.

Thank you also to Courtney Berger, Sandra Korn, Barbie Halaby, and Liz Smith at Duke for being super-professional, insightful, and eagle-eyed. We could not have hoped for a more incredible team and are very grateful for your enthusiasm about our project and all your hard work. We are immensely grateful to Asma Istwani and Aimee Harrison for designing the wonderful book cover, and to Elli Cartwright for introducing us to Asma and her incredible work. Many thanks to Paula Durbin-Westby for her very careful and professional indexing.

In addition, Shani would like to thank the Department of Media and Communications at LSE for supporting the writing of this book, and especially Sarah Banet-Weiser: I could not have asked for a more supportive colleague and wonderful head of department. Thanks also to my colleagues Omar Al-Ghazzi, Simidele Dosekun, and Sonia Livingstone for their advice on research for some of the chapters in the book. Leo Beattie, James Deeley, Silas Scott, and Lwam Tesfay have all provided much-appreciated support and helped in publicizing the research for this book. We have a wonderful community of PhD students in the department, and I had the pleasure of discussing ideas in the book with some of them.

Our department's collaboration with Northwestern University has been intellectually fruitful and introduced me to Kate Baldwin and Jan Radway (my longtime heroine since the publication of *Reading the Romance*)—two incredible women and scholars who have since also become friends. I am grateful to both for their intellectual generosity that has contributed to this book. I also appreciate Radha Hegde and Dafna Lemish for their inspiring ideas and encouragement. I want to express my gratitude to Cynthia Little and Catherine Rottenberg for their help with editing some of the book's chapters. Personal thanks to Maya Becker, Avital Shaal, Hila Shkolnik-Brenner, Sagit Schneider, Reima Yosif Shakeir, and my beloved family, Assaf, Yoav, Amnon, Atalya, Nechemya, Kobi, and Itamar. Special thanks to Eileen Aird for her ongoing encouragement and guidance. All of you are the fabric of my own private "confidence net," as we call it in Hebrew. Finally (for Shani), this book is the labor of a precious friendship and a unique intellectual partnership with Ros: I am so incredibly fortunate to have had the privilege of writing this book with you.

Rosalind would like to thank City, University of London, for research leave that facilitated the writing of this book. In particular, thanks to my colleagues in the Department of Sociology, the Centre for Culture and Creative

Industries, and the Gender and Sexualities Research Centre. Special thanks to Jo Littler, colleague, friend, and partner in crime at City, and to our many wonderful PhD students with whom I've discussed the ideas in this book. Thanks also to the University of Newcastle, New South Wales, for a professorial fellowship, which gave me the opportunity to present my work on body confidence and which offered the chance to collaborate with brilliant scholars from the Youth Studies Network and the Gender and Education group, including on Australia Research Council applications and grants. Thank you to all, especially to Julia Coffey, with whom I'm delighted to work on shared interests.

Four colleagues who are also now friends and coauthors on topics directly related to this book are Ana Elias, Laura Favaro, Akane Kanai, and Kirsten Kohrs. Our collaborations have been such a pleasure, and I have loved thinking and writing together about topics and issues such as compulsory positivity, love your body advertising, and "woke capitalism." Thank you.

Personal thanks also to Meg-John Barker, Beverley Dean, Simidele Dosekun, Ngaire Donaghue, Najiba Feroz, Roisin Flood, Veronica Forwood, Laura Harvey, Elizabeth Hess, Lesley Hoggart, Sue Jackson, Gail Lewis, Lia Litosseliti, Ann Phoenix, Andy Pratt, and especially Jude Willetts. The hugest thanks of all to Shani for making this project such a joy and a pleasure. Shani, you have an extraordinary way of combining intellectual brilliance, practical generosity, and extraordinary support and friendship: thank you.

This book was completed shortly after the untimely death of my beloved friend Sylvia Chant, who was also Shani's colleague at LSE. Sylvia was a feminist geographer, an inspiring teacher, an activist for social justice, and an absolutely amazing friend to me for twenty-five years. I'm still trying to work out how to live without her. This book is dedicated to Sylvia's passion, joie de vivre, and commitment to creating a fairer world.

introduction
the confidence imperative

TO BE SELF-CONFIDENT is the imperative of our time. As gender, racial, and class inequalities deepen, women are increasingly called on to *believe in themselves*. This paradox is manifest across a wide range of apparently disparate domains and contexts. At the same time that women are subjected to intensifying appearance pressures and unrealistic body ideals, beauty brands are hiring "confidence ambassadors," women's magazines are promoting a "confidence revolution," and the fashion industry is telling women "confidence is the best thing you can wear." Advertising, notorious for its reliance on and reproduction of sexist, racist, ageist, and ableist stereotypes, is being reinvented as "femvertising," or "woke branding," organized around positive affirmations and confidence commandments.

While pressures to be perfect continue to proliferate and have devastating effects on young people's mental health, more and more female celebrities advocate body positivity and self-love. Examples include chart-topping popular songs such as Demi Lovato's "Confident" and "Sorry Not Sorry"; the self-confidence and self-love hit "Truth Hurts" by the 2020 Grammys' top-nominated artist, Lizzo; and Bomba Estéreo's self-love anthem "Soy Yo," which propelled Latina teen Sarai Gonzalez to global fame. Even US congresswoman Alexandria Ocasio-Cortez produced a video with *Vogue* where she shares her beauty secrets and makeup routine, celebrating female self-confidence.[1] "The one foundation of everything," Ocasio-Cortez tells her viewers as she puts the finishing touch to her makeup, is "loving yourself." Meanwhile, a burgeoning number of sites and blogs are promoting body positivity, self-esteem, and confidence, with established hashtags such as #MotivationMonday, #WellnessWednesday, and #SelfLoveSunday. Inspirational mantras and affirmations are endlessly trafficked between girls and women across Instagram, Facebook, Pinterest, and other social media such as TikTok and Tumblr, mostly advocating self-belief and positivity.

Similarly, at the same time as women suffer profound inequality at work, including significant pay gaps, workplace schemes designed to promote gender equality respond by offering "confidence training" courses for women, and confidence coaches promote workshops and training programs advising women how to appear "virtually confident" when using videoconferencing technologies. As societal policies following the recession and austerity and now COVID-19 hit women hard, topping the best-seller lists are books that place female self-confidence at their argumentative heart: from Sheryl Sandberg's 2013 international best seller *Lean In* to Katty Kay and Claire Shipman's 2014 *The Confidence Code,* Jen Sincero's 2018 *You Are a Badass* to Rachel Hollis's 2019 best seller *Girl, Stop Apologizing,* and thousands of other self-help books promising confidence, self-esteem, and happiness.[2] Mindfulness and self-care apps are promoted as an individualized solution offering confidence-building and anxiety-reduction techniques for women, even as the current mental health crisis is known to impact women and other disadvantaged groups disproportionately.

We began to notice the rise of imperatives to confidence in the early 2010s and wrote several articles about the way that confidence—and related dispositions such as resilience—were taking on a new cultural prominence across many apparently unrelated spheres of life: in the welfare system, in consumer culture, in the workplace, in sex and relationship advice, and even in international development initiatives.[3] We expected that this might be a short-term trend; that confidence might just be "having a moment." But several years later, our culture's obsession with confidence—particularly women's self-confidence—shows no sign of diminishing. Indeed, it seems to be ramping up, partly as a result of the new visibility of popular feminism.[4] Even the military has gotten in on the act: as we write, the British army's 2020 recruitment campaign centers on addressing potential female soldiers with the message that joining the forces will give them deep and lasting confidence. The campaign's images contrast the superficiality of the pseudoconfidence that "can be reapplied every morning" (like makeup or false eyelashes) with the confidence that comes from being in the military—which "can last a lifetime" (fig. I.1).[5]

These exhortations have become ubiquitous across so many different domains of social and cultural life, and with such striking homogeneity, that they have come to constitute a kind of unquestioned common sense. The self-evident value of confidence—and particularly female self-confidence—has been placed beyond debate, treated as an unexamined cultural good that is

I.1 British army 2020 recruitment campaign "Army confidence lasts a lifetime"

CONFIDENCE
CAN BE
REAPPLIED
EVERY
MORNING

OR IT CAN
LAST A
LIFETIME

rarely, if ever, interrogated. In this way, a belief in confidence has come to suffuse contemporary culture, like an article of faith.

At the same time, in recent years there has been a seemingly contradictory move, which we call the vulnerability turn.[6] We are witnessing more and more expressions and encouragements for women to express publicly their weaknesses, insecurities, and self-doubt. Indeed, many of the champions of the confidence cult—such as female celebrities Meghan Markle, Serena Williams, Melinda Gates, Michelle Obama, Demi Lovato, and even the "queen" of self-love, Lizzo—have confessed across various media their self-doubts, experience of impostor syndrome, and emotional and physical struggles. Similarly, exhortations to women to be confident frequently encourage them to "embrace" and display their vulnerability. Such messages have gained particular prominence and visibility in the wake of the global COVID-19 pandemic and the dramatic reinvigoration of protests for racial justice, most prominently of Black Lives Matter. For example, in March 2020, the self-help guru Brené Brown launched *Unlocking Us*, dubbed by many as the perfect podcast series for our times. Each episode in this series reiterates Brown's mantras of embracing vulnerability and negative emotions. On the professional network LinkedIn, where members commonly promote their polished professional selves, there has been an outpouring of posts by individuals confessing their struggles, burnout, pain, and anxieties in the wake of George Floyd's death and the pandemic. Meanwhile, hashtags such as #Vulnerability, #BeVulnerable, #SelfCompassion, #LettingGo, #RadicalAcceptance, and #VulnerabilityIsStrength are increasingly trafficked on Instagram, TikTok, Twitter, and Tumblr. However, although the focus on vulnerability might seem to challenge some of the characteristics of the confidence imperative, we show that ultimately it reinforces and props up the confidence cult(ure). Vulnerability, we argue, has become almost mandatory and authorizes the individualistic psychologized confidence imperative.

Interrogating Confidence Culture

In this book we take this new common sense to task. Our aim is not to argue "against" confidence in some straightforward way—after all, who could possibly be *against* confidence? Would anyone genuinely want to position themselves against making young women feel more comfortable in their own skins, endowing mothers with self-esteem, or helping older women feel confident in the workplace? Of course not. Instead, we interrogate *the cultural prominence of confidence*: What ideas, discourses, images, and practices make up the confidence culture? Why has the cult(ure) of confidence emerged and proliferated across so many areas of life at this particular moment? Who does the confidence cult(ure) address, and how are its subjects called upon to act? And crucially, what does the contemporary cultural preoccupation with confidence *do*—both at an individual level for those addressed as needing greater confidence and on a wider social and political scale?

We theorize confidence as both *culture* and *cult*. It is an arena where meanings about women's bodies, psyches, and behavior are produced, circulated, negotiated, and resisted through different discourses, processes, and practices. Concurrently, it is an assemblage of discourses, institutions, and regulatory modes and measures that is systematic, patterned, and directed toward a desired and desirable goal: confidence. The notion of "cult" captures the sense in which confidence has become an unquestioned article of faith while simultaneously spreading across culture. We examine what the confidence cult opens up and closes down, what possibilities for thinking, change, and action it facilitates, and, conversely, what it renders unintelligible.

The book shows that contemporary confidence discourses disproportionately address women, calling on them to recognize themselves as lacking confidence or having a confidence deficit. We use "women'" here in an inclusive sense to include all who identify as such, including trans and gender nonconforming individuals, while noting that the confidence cult(ure) as a technology of self is disproportionately addressed to cisgender women. More than this, self-confidence is frequently mobilized as an explanatory framework wherever there is talk of gender inequality or injustice. Whatever the problems or injustices faced by women or girls, the implied "diagnosis" offered is often the same: she lacks confidence, to which the proffered solution is to promote female self-confidence. Inequality in the workplace? Women need to lean in and become more confident (check). Eating disorders and poor body image? Girls' confidence programs are the solution (check). Parenting problems? Let's make moms feel more confident so they can raise confident kids (check). Sex life in a rut? Well, confidence is "the new sexy"! (check). What is striking is not only the similarity of the discourses, programs, and interventions proposed across diverse domains of social life but also the way in which features of an unequal society are systematically (re)framed by the confidence cult(ure) as individual psychological problems, requiring us to change women, not the world.

The contemporary prominence of female confidence is—at least in part—a result of the force and influence of feminist discourses over several decades. Indeed, confidence can be seen as part of a progressive political project designed to create a more just society. Without feminism, the inequalities to which confidence initiatives are addressed would not even be recognized, nor would efforts be expended on improving women's self-confidence. Yet we contend that the versions of feminism deployed in confidence cult(ure) are troublingly individualistic, turning away from structural inequalities and wider social injustices to accounts that foreground *psychological change* rather than social transformation. As we show in this book, the confidence cult(ure) operates to exculpate the institutions and structures of contemporary life, not holding them to account for unfairness. Instead, it often—implicitly or explicitly—blames women for their difficulties or subordinate positions, frequently through everyday unexamined phrases such as "sometimes you're your own worst enemy" or "your lack of confidence is holding you back." Above all, in locating the cause of social injustice in a confidence deficit, it calls for women to undertake intensive work on the self, from changing the way they look, communicate, and occupy space to psychological work on building a more confident inner life through practices of gratitude, affirmations, self-friending, and more. The confidence cult(ure) becomes part of an "obligated freedom," in which not achieving the required change is framed as moral and psychological failure.[7] In the process, confidence plays a pivotal role in both the neoliberalizing of subjectivity and the remaking of feminism along neoliberal lines.[8]

Postfeminism, Postrace, Postqueer

The confidence cult(ure) is deeply gendered. It is not that men are never addressed by confidence discourses; they are. From dating websites to shows such as *Queer Eye* to advertising campaigns for Viagra, incitements to men to feel more confident are evident. However, the language used to address men is very different. A sponsored ad for male coaching that came up at the top in our Google search for men and confidence exemplifies this. The coach is described as a "No Bullsh*t Confidence Coach."[9] He promises to teach men to "perform at your highest level," "gain total clarity," "become a remarkable leader," "have unstoppable confidence," and "reach social mastery." The "wins" of confidence are framed competitively in greater status and top performance. By contrast, confidence in women is frequently framed in terms of overcoming deeply rooted internal obstacles and correcting a psychological deficit. Even financial confidence may be sold to women as a variant of indulgent "me time" and self-care, as in a magazine article that promises "5 ways to make managing your money an act of self-love."[10] The practices enjoined are different, too, with a focus on turning inward, keeping a journal, or practicing gratitude rarely seen in confidence messages directed at men.

Perhaps most significantly, confidence programs for women are frequently framed as feminist interventions, positioned as a way of overcoming inequality. Conversely, a more troubling historical root of "confidence" is the "confidence man" and his "confidence games."[11] As Alison Hearn, Jack Bratich, and Sarah Banet-Weiser observe, the mid-nineteenth-century book *The Confidence Man: A Masquerade* and "confidence tricks" provide the blueprint for the type of masculinity championed by contemporary political leaders from Donald Trump to Jair Bolsonaro and which is advocated by pickup artists advising heterosexual men how to seduce women. This masculinity relies on "the investment of trust, the taking of confidence, to achieve its own ends, forming an interpersonal relationship via swindling."[12] Rachel O'Neill's stunning analysis of the seduction "community-industry" shows vividly how the acquisition of dating confidence in these spaces is also shaped by highly competitive homosocial relations among men.[13]

The confidence cult(ure) is entangled in complicated ways with other axes of power and identity, including race, class, age, sexuality, and disability. As we demonstrate throughout the book, confidence imperatives can be seen to recognize and respect differences between and among women—for example, in body confidence campaigns that center on brown skin, curly hair, or fat bodies, which often have a defiant and celebratory tone. Yet at the same time, the specificity of oppressions faced by women of different races, ages, classes, sexual orientations, body sizes, cultural locations, or (dis)abilities is glossed over. The proposed response to social and economic injuries is nearly always exactly the same: to work on increasing one's self-confidence. In this way the confidence cult(ure) opens up the promise of a more intersectional address that is attentive to power and difference, only to close this down, returning us to a "one-size-fits-all" message.

Thus, the confidence cult(ure) is imbricated in, and contributes to, a novel sensibility that is both feminist and postfeminist, postrace, postqueer, and postclass, in which "differences" are recognized only to be emptied of their history, context, and effectivity. These "post" discourses all signal a sense of society having "moved on" from painful historical power relations to a situation in which individual psychological change is required rather than social transformation.

A postfeminist sensibility is one in which feminist ideas are said to have been "taken into account" already, obviating the need for radical social transformation along gender lines.[14] In recent years this has mutated from outright repudiation of feminism into something more subtle: a sense of the "obviousness" of the importance of feminism, alongside its reconstruction in purely individual terms that stress choice, empowerment, and competition.[15]

Postrace discourses, too, hold that race is no longer a live and active political force in contemporary culture.[16] They perform crucial work in "neoliberalizing race," shoring up fresh instantiations of structural racisms, and cutting off some subjects from entitlement to subjecthood while authorizing others to wealth and power.[17] In turn, neoliberalism underwrites postracial ideologies, "moving racialization beyond, and away from, the logics of power and phenotype."[18] "Recognizing some racial differences while disavowing others, it confers privilege on some racial subjects (the white liberal, the multicultural American, the fully assimilable Black, the racial entrepreneur)"—and, we might add, the young Black woman striving for greater confidence in order to succeed in a white beauty culture or to fit into corporate environments—"while stigmatizing others."[19] Since 2016, and in particular since the reinvigoration of antiracist activism after the murder of George Floyd in May 2020, discourses of race have taken on new forms in consumer culture as brands have sought to harness the cultural energy of this movement for change and to claim "woke" credentials. Though numerous examples of the hollow and cynical appropriation of Black Lives Matter exist (discussed more fully in chapter 1), there are also novel and more positive iterations that have gained widespread praise. For example, Rihanna's brand, Fenty, has been lauded for hiring diverse models and influencers and for contributing to conversations about social justice by centering the young, Black, sexually confident woman.

Similarly, "postqueer" has become a way to talk about the new visibility of lesbians and gay men in the media, but in a way that is not disruptive to heteronormative assumptions and institutions and indeed may work to underwrite them.[20] The privileging of the femme lesbian and the erasure of the butch is one example of this, which also has classed dimensions, as is the hypervisibility of the gay wedding compared with other far less visible aspects of queer identity and cultural practice. The confidence cult(ure) interpellates LGBTQ+ people as potentially having particular problems with confidence. However, rather than exploring how this may be related to a homophobic, biphobic, transphobic society—and the ways this might be transformed—the emphasis is on developing the personal psychological resources to survive. Such injunctions can be deeply moving, as in the extraordinarily powerful letter Irish journalist Lyra McKee, murdered by the Irish Republican Army (IRA) in 2019, wrote to her fourteen-year-old self. She writes of the cruel ho-

8

mophobic bullying she received: "It's horrible. They make your life hell, they whisper about you and call you names." But she encourages her teenage self to endure it and be brave—"It will take courage but you will do it"—and to come to realize that "it won't always be like this. It's going to get better."[21] We do not underestimate the importance of this, particularly in the light of the disproportionate mental health issues suffered by LGBTQ+ young people. However, as with the "it gets better" movement, the emphases on developing bravery, resilience, and self-confidence often displace other actions to *change* or *end* the causes of this unhappiness, implying that collective struggle is either unnecessary or impossible.

Finally, a related dynamic is seen in depictions of disability in the confidence cult(ure). These representations often privilege the psychological over material struggles. They suggest that self-doubt and insecurity are more significant challenges than benefit cuts, poverty, or a built environment that systematically favors young, healthy, and nondisabled people. Alison Kafer characterizes this kind of contemporary practice for representing disabled people as "billboard liberation": individualistic, depoliticizing, and often structured through celebrity "superhumans" such as Christopher Reeve, Michael J. Fox, or para-Olympians.[22] Too often confidence cult(ure) messages are culpable in this, presenting disability as an individual obstacle to be overcome through character strengths such as determination, confidence, and resilience and obscuring how different forms of disability are a product of and response to neoliberalism.[23]

Ambivalent Critique

The confidence cult(ure) is powerful and seductive, and we do not exist outside this. As feminist scholars of media and culture and psychosocial studies, we are profoundly aware that power does not just exist "out there" in the world; it also exists "in here"—it shapes our ways of relating to ourselves and others. Inspired by Black, feminist, and postcolonial scholars from Fanon to Said to hooks and Butler, we recognize the *psychic force* of diverse forms of oppression, the terrifying ways in which subordination and social injustice operate not simply through dispossession and discrimination, but by taking up residence in our own heads and hearts. In this respect, it seems clear that patriarchal society can—perhaps inevitably *must*—be seriously damaging to a woman's health, and to nonbinary and genderqueer people too. Indeed, living in a society that is gendered by design and systematically undervalues and attacks women and minorities, it would almost be surprising if there were *not* an impact on women's sense of confidence, entitlement, and well-being. Yet we remain deeply uncomfortable about the way the confidence cult(ure) is framed as the solution, formulating inequality and injustice in individualistic terms and shifting the blame and responsibility for gender inequality away from institutional and structural injustices to assumed "deficits" in women.

To critique our culture's focus on confidence is to break a powerful contemporary taboo. It is one that operates very often through secrecy and silence, in unspoken feelings and experiences. An expert blog post on the *Psychologies* magazine website is typical in this respect: discussing "improving your social confidence," Dawn Breslin notes that a client was "glamorous" and "sociable" and "doesn't seem shy, but she's absolutely terrified. She's worried that people will find her dull and boring, or that she'll get something wrong."[24] In this way, lack of confidence is presented as a pathology that may be hidden, unspeakable, yet still exerts crippling effects.

Furthermore, the invisibility of what is constructed as a confidence deficit is allied to a prevailing sense of the *work of confidence* never being done.[25] As part of our research for this book we each undertook the "confidence test" provided online by the authors of the best-selling book *The Confidence Code* (which we discuss in chapter 2). We recognize that we were fortunate—and privileged—to score highly on this test, each achieving the grade "confident." Yet in giving us feedback the website immediately warned that this did not mean we could relax. Rather, ongoing vigilance was necessary, since "even those who are fairly confident often experience periods of self-doubt. Or perhaps you feel confident in most areas but still feel more nervous than you would like" in some situations, such as public speaking.[26] Confidence can thus never be understood as assured or complete but is always a work in progress, requiring continual introspection and labor.

It is easy to critique this "sell": like horoscopes or crude marketing tools it always gives you the "right answer"—guess what, you need more confidence! Yet as women (who are daughters, sisters, mothers, teachers, and friends) we are not inured to the affective force of the confidence culture. We have found ourselves moved to tears by accounts like that on the *Psychologies* site, by "love your body" campaigns, by apps that instill a sense of well-being and self-belief, by equality and diversity programs that seem genuinely to celebrate women's achievements. What's more, we are ourselves active—if ambivalent—participants in the confidence cult(ure), for example, repeatedly encouraging our female students to be bold and take up more space in the world, and not to apologize for themselves or preface their remarks with "I'm just" or "I'm no expert."

The cult(ure) of confidence thus resonates powerfully with both our intellectual commitments and our own everyday lives and experiences. Indeed, it is the very simplicity, ubiquity, and seductiveness of the confidence message which makes it so appealing and powerful. But that is also why it deserves critical scrutiny from a feminist perspective, and this is what *Confidence Culture* sets out to contribute.

With our broad argument and our own ambivalent locations in relation to the confidence cult(ure) briefly outlined, the remainder of this introduction is divided into three main sections. In the first we contextualize the emergence of the confidence cult(ure), locating it in relation to the particular neoliberal moment of capitalism in which we exist, specifically: the pervasiveness of therapeutic discourse and the extension of psychological self-help ideas across social and cultural life. In the second section we set out the theoretical resources that inform our account of the confidence cult(ure) and add a brief note about our methods. Drawing on Foucault's notion of technologies of self, we explicate our expansive reading of the confidence culture as a discursive, visual, and affective regime and as social practice. Finally, we close by introducing the structure of the book.

Contextualizing Confidence Culture

Why has the cult(ure) of confidence emerged at this time? What historical and contemporary features have shaped current preoccupations with female self-confidence? In this section we briefly situate its emergence in the context of therapeutic cultures and contemporary models of selfhood, the media's growing emphasis on self-transformation, and neoliberalism's construction of enterprising and "responsibilized" subjects called on to take full responsibility for their lives no matter what constraints they may face.

Therapeutic Cultures

Any account of the rise of the confidence cult must begin with "the psychological century"—the twentieth century—and the therapeutic turn to which today's emphasis on self-worth, self-confidence, and self-esteem belongs. Freud coined the term "psychoanalysis" in 1896, formulating a dramatically new language for conceptualizing the self, which not only helped to make sense of some of the major changes at the time he was writing—shifts in relation to gender, sexuality, and the family—but, more importantly, itself became part of the cultural matrix through which we make sense of our lives, with notions like repression and denial becoming part of everyday language. The subsequent "triumph" of the "psy complex,"[27] and of psychological discourse, is even more well-established today, furnishing taken-for-granted ideas about the individual's wants, drives, and desires and attempts to know and control them. As Eva Illouz argues, therapeutic notions of the self have been diffused throughout and across Western societies, moving far beyond the consulting room, and have come to shape workplaces, schools, universities, the military, the welfare state, the carceral system, and many other spheres, part of a remaking of capitalism along more therapeutic or emotional lines.[28] Confidence is part of this trend that involves the mainstreaming of psychological discourse for making sense of ourselves and others.

Radical reformulations of the self have occupied new domains and taken distinct forms over the last century. The humanistic psychology articulated in the late 1950s and early 1960s by Abraham Maslow and Carl Rogers was very different from psychoanalysis, but it further underscored the idea of *working on the self* and augmented the dissemination of therapeutic ideas across social life. This idea, we will demonstrate, clearly informs confidence imperatives and their focus on personal growth and self-fulfillment. Maslow popularized the notion of "self-actualization" to describe an aspired-for state in which individuals who were self-motivating and self-directed work to achieve their fullest life possible. According to Maslow's famous "hierarchy of needs," individuals could only achieve full self-actualization when their other basic needs (such as safety, security, food, and shelter) were met. As Micki McGee argues, it was a notion that "fused religious and psychological discourses. . . . Work on the self—the quest for a path, the invention of a life, or the search for authenticity—is offered as an antidote to the anxiety-provoking uncertainties of a new economic and social order.[29] McGee calls the subject that is produced by these discourses the "belabored self."

One clear precursor of the confidence cult(ure) was the trend for "assertiveness training," which sought to replace passive and aggressive modes of communication with assertive ones. Courses and training programs for women proliferated in the 1980s, often featuring exercises and role plays, such as practicing how to say "no" or to engage in a difficult conversation without apologizing. However, compared with today's confidence culture, assertiveness training back then was more focused on surface behavior and on language rather than remaking the whole self. It was also, arguably, more bounded in certain domains and less widely taken up—e.g., not institutionalized in workplaces or schools or advertising.

These ideas clearly resonated with wider countercultural trends of the time, such as sexual liberation, LGBTQ+ activism, antiracism and civil rights, antiwar, environmental, and animal rights movements, and, of course, feminism. As many scholars have noted, feminism as a political movement helped to foster the conditions of possibility for the dramatic expansion of therapeutic culture and notions of the self.[30] This was effected partly through feminism's reflexive project and its emphasis on personal life as ineluctably political.

The field of positive psychology represents another, more contemporary iteration of therapeutic culture that is central to the confidence cult(ure). Coming to prominence since the late 1990s, positive psychology represents a dramatic shift away from "problems" and psychopathology toward a focus instead on how "positive" psychological states such as happiness, resilience, and confidence can be fostered. It calls forth a self-motivating subject who possesses the ability to "*choose* happiness over unhappiness, success over failure, and even health over illness"—and confidence over insecurity, we might add![31] "Education of the spirit" is proposed as a priority by advocates of positive psychology such as Martin Seligman and Richard Layard.[32] Nationally and globally there are now multiple indexes and governmental programs that measure and promote happiness. Like confidence, happiness is seen as something to be called into being through the efforts of individuals working on themselves, rather than through social interventions concerned with public health, greater social support, or reduction of poverty.

The Rise of Self-Help

The rise of self-help—itself part of therapeutic culture—is also central to understanding how confidence as a gendered ideal has come to such extraordinary prominence today. Yet as we show throughout this book, the confidence cult(ure) is by no means limited to self-help; rather, it materializes across education, workplaces, policy discourses, and media.

Self-help is disproportionately addressed to women, and femininity has long been marked as a "problematic object in need of change."[33] Elaine Showalter and Lisa Appignanesi are among the leading feminist scholars who have eloquently analyzed associations between women's bodies, female sexuality, and madness.[34] Cultural constructions of the figure of Ophelia are one prominent site where this is evident, indexing fragility and inability to control or contain emotions.[35] Such depictions are also profoundly classed, racialized, and heteronormative in ways that privilege whiteness, middle-classness, and heterosexuality.[36] In her erudite analysis in *Self-Help, Inc.*, Micki McGee argues that Helen Gurley Brown and Betty Friedan were key exponents of a kind of early feminist self-help, centering both financial and economic independence.[37] McGee's analysis of their impact suggests such figures as potential precursors of the contemporary importance of confidence in their foregrounding of female autonomy and satisfaction. Yet looking back on the final decades of the twentieth century, McGee contends: "In less than thirty years, 'self-help'—once synonymous with mutual aid—has come to be understood not only as distinct from collective action but actually as its opposite. . . . The self (of self-help) is imagined as increasingly isolated, and 'self-help,' with some exceptions, is represented as a largely individual undertaking."[38] This resonates with many other feminist engagements with self-help critiquing the way in which such literature offers a "re-privatization" of problems and challenges faced by women in an unjust society.[39] As Janice Peck puts it, "therapeutic discourse translates the political into the psychological—problems are personal (or familial) and have no origin or target outside one's own psychic processes."[40]

More recently, Meg Henderson and Anthea Taylor discussed the "neoliberalization" of self-help (considered further below).[41] In this iteration the feminist ideals of the 1980s and 1990s are transformed with even greater individualism and more emphasis on producing subjects "better adjusted to neoliberalism." They chart how a focus on feminist consciousness-raising has "mutated" in postfeminist conduct texts into something less angry and less political.[42] For example, "sisterhood" has morphed into "friendship" and "rage" into "passion." Meanwhile, "equality" has been substituted by "empowerment" (and, as we will show, also by "diversity" and "inclusivity"), and "revolution/liberation" is now figured in terms of "success."[43] A related argument is made by Sarah Riley et al., noting the "postfeminization" of self-help, particularly as it relates to increasingly salient discourses of self-acceptance. This "marries seemingly pro-feminist sentiments of body positivity and self-acceptance with appearance concerns that tie women's value back to their bodies, the consumption of products, and the blurring of economic and psychological language."[44]

Crucially, self-help has not simply proliferated as a form or genre across multiple sites or problems—e.g., work, sex and relationships, dieting, parenting. It has also, paradoxically, refocused on remaking the self across *all spheres of life* with *general* injunctions to positive thinking, resilience, and, of course, confidence. The neoliberalization of self-help is marked, too, by a particular affective tone in these texts directed at women. Its emphasis is on optimism, boldness, the right mindset, feeling good, developing the right attitude, do(ing) what you love, and so on. Having the right "emotional style" becomes formulated as an imperative: feel this and you can change your life; dream big; take control; make a choice; and "be confident!"[45]

Lifestyle Media and Psychological Transformation

Self-help is no longer confined to books or articles but is a global multimillion-dollar industrial complex that has spread out to include a vast lifestyle media whose aim is to offer up different models of living and to inspire self-transformation. In the context of what some social theorists regard as the "unfixing" or "untethering" of the self in late modern capitalist societies, such media reframe decisions about "how to live" through a dazzling array of individual lifestyle choices. Stuart Hall, Doreen Massey, and Mike Rustin argue that the fantasies of success, individualization of identity, and endless refashioning of the self seen in lifestyle media are "soft forms of power" that are every bit as "effective in changing social attitudes" as more obvious hard forms of control or governance.[46] Katherine Sender locates lifestyle media as guides in navigating the difficulties and possibilities of a world in which everything seems to rest on individual "choice."[47] Lifestyle media center on exhortations to remodel the self and interior life—not simply to become thinner, be better groomed, or have more successful dates, but to make over one's psychic life or subjectivity to become a "better" version of oneself, that is, confident, happier, more resilient.

Aiding in this process, Sam Binkley argues, is a new stratum of "everyday experts of subjectivity"—diet experts, confidence trainers, life coaches, therapists, wellness mentors, influencers, and mindfulness gurus—who "mediate becoming," bringing the psychologically upgraded subject into being.[48] Indeed, perhaps the most significant force of lifestyle media is the way it systematically refigures individuals as *self-governing subjects*, "as the agents of their destinies, who achieve goals of health, happiness, productivity, security and wellbeing through their individual choices and self-care practices."[49] Working on one's own self-confidence is, for women, precisely one of these self-care practices, and a means by which they are made responsible for their own success or failure—understood not through accounts of structural inequality or social injustice but in personal, psychological terms.

Finally, the emergence of the confidence cult(ure) is intrinsically connected to the enduring and pervasive impact of neoliberalism as an organizing force in contemporary Western societies. Neoliberalism is classically understood as "a theory of political economic practices that proposes that human wellbeing can best be advanced by liberating entrepreneurial freedoms and skills within an institutional framework characterized by strong private property rights, free markets and free trade."[50] It is regarded as a distinctive phase of contemporary capitalism, marked by privatization, deregulation, and the "small state," alongside a profound shift of responsibility onto individuals. But as well as an economic and political program, it is a social and cultural project, an *everyday sensibility* and rationality underpinned by ideas of choice, entrepreneurialism, competition, and meritocracy. Neoliberalism has insinuated itself into "the nooks and crannies of everyday life" to become a hegemonic, quotidian sensibility.[51]

Under neoliberalism, a market ethic works to reconstitute subjectivities, calling into being subjects who are self-motivating and entrepreneurial, who will make sense of their lives through discourses of freedom, responsibility, and choice—no matter how constrained the latter may be (e.g., by poverty or racism).[52] Conducting life through an entrepreneurial spirit, the neoliberal self is said to be hailed by rules that emphasize ambition, calculation, competition, self-optimization, and personal responsibility.

While we concur with this emphasis on neoliberalism's operation across social life—what Wendy Brown calls its "stealth revolution" across the entire demos—we depart from accounts that regard the self called forth by neoliberalism as *purely* rational and calculating.[53] To this we want to add an understanding of its dynamics at *an affective or emotional level*, the extent to which neoliberalism incites particular qualities, dispositions, and feelings—among them confidence. Barbara Cruikshank's work on the "state of esteem" is crucial in this respect, arguing that the cultural prominence of self-esteem is "not an escape from politics but a sign that the political has been reconstructed at the level of the self." It is, she asserts, "a practical technology for the production of particular kinds of selves."[54] Christina Scharff vividly shows this in her study of how neoliberal features of the "entrepreneurial subjectivity," such as embracing risks, resilience, and positive thinking, permeated the hearts and minds of the female creative workers she interviewed as they recounted their attempts to succeed in a competitive field.[55] Akane Kanai discerns similar trends in her analysis of young women's social media representations, in which difficulties are presented through "humorous, upbeat quips" and in which pain and struggle must be rendered into "safe, funny, 'girl-friendly' anecdotes."[56]

These and other studies demonstrate how "being able to use psychological language to reflect on the self is a core requirement of neoliberal subjectivity."[57] Moreover, a focus on "positive mental attitude" is increasingly central to contemporary culture. As Barbara Ehrenreich has argued, "positive thinking . . . has made itself useful as an apology for the crueller aspects of the market economy."[58] "Happiness" and "wellness" are related imperatives, underpinned by entire industries, bodies of expertise, and cultural programs.[59]

More generally there is a "turn to character" in neoliberal societies, which centers qualities such as passion, "grit," confidence, and resilience.[60] They serve as contemporary regulatory ideals that have flourished in the context of austerity and worsening inequality.[61] For example, Lynne Friedli and Robert Stearn demonstrate how these dispositions are used in the British welfare system, enacting a new form of "deserving poor" who are compelled to be "positive" in order to get payments.[62] Discourses of resilience call on people to be adaptable and positive, "bounce back" from adversity, and embrace a mindset in which negative experiences must be reframed in upbeat terms. Incitements to resilience have been shown to be gendered and classed, seen in many areas of public policy such as health and welfare, and also adapted in schools and workplaces as a means to train people to cope with the stress, bullying, overwork, and precariousness that are endemic features of contemporary social life.[63]

If neoliberal culture requires subjects who work on their characters and psychic dispositions, then it also works by attempting to shape what and how people are enabled to *feel*—and how their emotional states should be displayed. This is part of a wider entanglement between neoliberal capitalism and feelings that Eva Illouz has dubbed "emotional capitalism."[64] We contend that neoliberalism not only shapes culture, conduct, and psychic life but also produces a distinctive "structure of feeling" in which women are called on to disavow a whole range of experiences and emotions—including insecurity, neediness, anger, and complaint—while displaying others such as "positive mental attitude" or "inspiration."[65] Throughout this book, we demonstrate how confidence has become part of the cultural, discursive, and affective scaffolding of neoliberalism.

Theoretical and Methodological Approach:
Confidence as a Technology of Self

How, then, should we make sense of the new cultural prominence accorded to confidence? What theoretical resources are useful for exploring and examining it? The confidence cult(ure) could be considered in various ways: a "turn" to confidence, a confidence "movement," a new zeitgeist, or "confidence chic."[66] We consider it as a *cultural formation* or *dispositif*—a set of knowledges, apparatuses, and regulatory modes that systematically call forth a novel *technology of self*. Foucault developed the notion of technology of self in his later work as a way to overcome what he saw as the limitations of his own theorizing of power and to move beyond the notion of individuals as docile, passive, and disciplined subjects.[67] Technology of self became, for Foucault, a key term for fashioning an understanding of the link between wider discourses and regimes of truth and the creativity and agency of individual subjects: "Technologies of self . . . permit individuals to effect by their own means or with the help of others a certain number of operations on their own bodies and souls, thoughts, conduct and way of being, so as to transform themselves in order to attain a state of happiness, purity, wisdom, perfection or immortality."[68]

For us the notion is valuable for four reasons. First, it offers a way to think about the relation between culture and subjectivity that is not reductive, deterministic, or conspiratorial but nevertheless insists on holding together work on the self with a wider appreciation of power. As Foucault puts it, technologies of self are "the way in which the subject constitutes himself [*sic*] in an active fashion, by the practices of the self, [but] these practices are nevertheless *not something that the individual invents by himself* [*sic*]."[69] They are not random, then, nor individually or idiosyncratically produced, but are historically and culturally specific—as we will show in relation to the cult(ure) of confidence.

Second, this notion highlights the way in which the confidence cult(ure) relies on a self that is apparently independent of—or ontologically separate from—itself.[70] That is, a self is posited who is reflexive, somehow able to reflect upon and act upon itself, and whose responsibility—indeed ethical obligation—this task of self-reflection is. The notion allows us to access the reflexiveness of the confidence cult, then, to see how it requires a self-monitoring individual attuned to practicing and increasing their confidence.

Third, this later work by Foucault opened up a space for theorizing agency (not just domination), as well as for considering "the psychic life of power."[71] As such, it refuses a view that would regard the confidence cult(ure) as mere "false consciousness." While we seek to engage critically with the contemporary proliferation and force of confidence messages, our critique is not based on a *dismissal* of those advocating female self-confidence, nor of those many millions to whom the confidence cult(ure) is addressed. On the contrary, we argue that the confidence cult(ure) has taken hold so powerfully precisely *because* of its ability to connect meaningfully with many women's lived experiences— troubled relationships with their bodies, struggles in parenting, difficult experiences in the workplace, and so on. Our critique, then, proposes not to "take down" confidence as an idea or ideal but rather to look at what the confidence cult *does*: how it operates performatively, what it brings into being and renders visible, and what it obscures or makes unintelligible.

The fourth valuable feature of "technology of self" is the way that it allows us to examine how the confidence cult "sensitizes" those to whom its exhortations are addressed, making its individualistic and psychological prescriptions appear self-evident rather than one particular way of framing the issues.

There have been numerous productive feminist attempts to use Foucault's focus on technologies of selfhood—among them the work of Susan Bordo, Judith Butler, Teresa de Lauretis, Angela McRobbie, Hilary Radner, Adrienne Evans, and Sarah Riley—and our work contributes to this broader theoretical project.[72] We see the confidence cult(ure) as a gendered technology of self, which not only is primarily addressed to women but also acts on gender relations, reframing critical accounts of gender power in individual and psychological terms.

In our feminist critique of the confidence cult(ure) we want to push at and develop Foucault's term "technology of self" in several key ways. Foucault's primary interest was in the discursive—conceived broadly. To be sure, the cult(ure) of confidence works through and mobilizes a range of different yet patterned discourses. Indeed, time and again while researching this book, we have been struck not simply by the proliferation of different areas of life that the confidence cult addresses but also by the way in which the same ideas and even the same words and phrases would recur over and over in apparently distinct domains and genres, from advertising to policy documents to self-help. Yet confidence as a technology of self also materializes as a visual regime, in affect and feeling rules, and in a huge variety of different practices—ranging from advice on how to generate confidence by holding your body in a particular way to quizzes to measure your "confidence quotient." In the next section we look briefly at each realm in turn to offer a rich and expansive understanding of confidence as a gendered technology of self.

Confidence Culture as a Visual Regime

Over the past two decades, and particularly in the last few years, a relatively stable set of images has been developed to convey messages about female autonomy, power, and capacity. As many scholars have noted, this was partly demanded by significant changes in demographics (e.g., more women working outside the household than ever before), in combination with media producers' recognition of the power of feminism. In our examination of the confidence cult(ure) as a visual regime, we draw on critics who highlight how the feminist ideas and specifically images are appropriated and incorporated, offered back to women in depoliticized ways.

Robert Goldman, Deborah Heath, and Sharon Smith's work in the early 1990s examined how advertisers sought to distill a kind of "commodity feminism," in which they could harness the power and excitement of feminism as a movement while emptying it of its radical politics.[73] This analysis is significant in its attempt to analyze how advertisers sought to present feminism as *visual style* built around a slim, toned body, an assertive posture, the holding of the gaze, and particular clothes (e.g., a tailored business suit, sharp bag, and high heels) as indicators of female self-confidence, sutured with more conventional markers of femininity to ward off the potential threats posed by this new construction. A few years later Susan Douglas commented that advertising agencies have "figured out how to make feminism—and anti-feminism—work for them. . . . the appropriation of feminist desires and feminist rhetoric by Revlon, Lancôme and other major corporations was nothing short of spectacular. Women's liberation metamorphosed into female narcissism unchained as political concepts like liberation and equality were collapsed into distinctly personal, private desires."[74]

More recently, digital visual archives such as the Lean In Collection—a collaboration between Sheryl Sandberg's LeanIn.org and Getty Images that was launched in 2014—have become key loci of images of "confident" women and a vehicle for their dissemination. Claiming to show "real women doing real things," the Lean In Collection seeks to confront the media industry's "image gender gap"—notably the ubiquity of clichéd and stereotypical images of women and men across visual culture—and intervene in the visual landscape to promote gender equality, on the basis that, as Sandberg puts it, "you can't be what you can't see."[75] The collection has been criticized for its lack of diversity (although it is significantly more diverse in terms of age, race, and body type than Getty Images) and its foregrounding of white, privileged women whose "empowerment is heavily premised upon ideals of corporate success."[76] It replaces an earlier genre of images of women balancing mother-hood and work at immense cost—dubbed by Jessica Valenti "Sad White Babies with Mean Feminist Mommies"—with a new romanticized stereotype in which happy and high-achieving women work productively while beatific infants gurgle in playpens next to their desks.[77] Thus, though the Lean In Collection offers novel images of confident and successful women, as Caroline West notes, it "underscores the internalization of neoliberal rationality" via a fantasy of ease and privilege and without any challenge to capitalism—a theme we develop in the following chapters.[78]

Reevaluating Goffman's *Gender Advertisements*, Kirsten Kohrs and Rosalind Gill identify a style they dub "confident appearing," evident in an analysis of a corpus of two hundred advertisements in upmarket women's magazines.[79] The visual elements of this style involve several repeated features: head held high, face turned forward, eyes meeting the gaze of the viewer and looking directly back at them. When women are pictured alone, smiling is rare, and sometimes the gaze has an almost defiant aspect. These visual motifs are anchored by the linguistic elements, which highlight female independence, empowerment, self-belief, and entitlement. A good example is Clinique's 2020 advertisement for skincare products. Using the face of US feminist Tavi Gevinson, known for founding the online feminist magazine *Rookie* while a teenager, the ad declares "FACE FORWARD" (fig. I.2). Facing forward, like facing the world, is a synonym for confidence. Gevinson's visage, made up in a naturalistic style, with her hair swept away from her face and tucked behind her ears, exemplifies this idea: her "bare" face looks straight at us with a neutral expression. The confidence message is underscored by the written text, which declares: "Dress for yourself. Dream big. Find your voice. And put it out there."

Other tropes in the visual construction of "confident appearing" involve control and movement, for example, with the figure of the woman striding confidently forward through an urban landscape, echoing the image of the "woman with the flying hair" that dominated the visual landscape in the 1980s. As Hochschild writes, "She has that working-mother look as she strides forward, briefcase in one hand, smiling child in the other. Literally and figuratively, she is moving ahead. . . . She is confident, active, 'liberated.'"[80] In such representations the stride is typically exaggerated to highlight a sense of a forward-moving woman.[81]

Dress for yourself. Dream big.
Find your voice. And put it out there.
Tavi Gevinson #faceforward

CLINIQUE

I.2 Clinique ad "Face Forward"

Confidence as an Affective Regime

The confidence cult(ure) is also an *affective technology of self*: it operates in and through emotions, feelings, and desires. Injunctions to female self-confidence are not simply exhortations to speak differently or behave differently; they are calls to *feel differently about oneself*, even though this is regarded as the hardest shift to make, and women are often exhorted, in the meantime, to *act*—or "fake it till you make it." The idea is that repeated *performance* of external confidence markers such as assertive posture or speech will, eventually, generate the longed-for *internal* shift—something that is "explained" via various loosely formulated means such as "hormones" or neurotransmitters, for example, testosterone, dopamine, or serotonin (frequently referred to in dumbed-down language as "the feel-good hormone" or "the cuddle chemical").

Confidence messages are attempts to produce particular feelings or dispositions—such as boldness, pride, joy, or self-love. As we show throughout this book, the confidence cult exhorts women to "love your body," to believe one is worthy of being loved, to feel more entitled and take up more space in the workplace, to experience pride as a mother and to instill similar pride in one's children, and so much else. We demonstrate that much of the force of the confidence cult derives from its attempts to inculcate and shape our emotional lives, through what Arlie Hochschild dubbed "feeling rules."[82] Through this analysis of the confidence cult(ure) as a feeling-producing technology, our work makes a contribution to thinking about the current conjuncture not simply in economic or social or political terms but also in affective terms.

The last two decades have seen an extraordinary "turn to affect" across contemporary theory, as scholars have sought to understand the way that emotions such as rage, envy, and melancholia shape social life.[83] A growing body of research interrogates public moods and atmospheres that are understood as intersubjective and widely shared, theorizing affect as social or public.[84] Sara Ahmed's work asks what emotions *do*, exploring how they "circulate between bodies," sticking to some and passing over others.[85] In turn, Imogen Tyler analyzes how processes of "social abjection" operate by mobilizing affects such as anger or disgust toward particular groups.[86] And on a broader scale still, Kirsten Forkert, John Clarke, and Larry Grossberg read contemporary culture through the lenses of "public mood," loss, and affective landscape.[87]

While the confidence cult(ure) might be illuminated by any and all of these perspectives, the perspective we have found most compelling is Margaret Wetherell's affective-discursive approach.[88] Frustrated by the often vague articulations of affect theory with their emphasis on sensations and intensities that are said to precede or exist outside of the social, Wetherell has offered a thoroughly social rereading of affect. It rejects the idea that affect is a "pre-personal and extra-discursive force hitting and shaping bodies" and argues that affect is social, patterned, and implicated in power relations.[89] Importantly, this makes it amenable to rigorous analysis and empirical study—through research that examines affects and discourses together, using the notion of affective-discursive practices.[90]

Confidence Culture as Practice

As we have argued, confidence is a technology of self that operates discursively, visually, and affectively. Confidence ideals and imperatives exist in language, they can be seen in distinctive visual constructions, and they also materialize as exhortations to feel differently. More than this, it is clear that the confidence cult designs and offers a huge variety of *practices* for generating self-worth and self-esteem. It is organized through a multiplicity of techniques, knowledges, and affective apparatuses designed to measure, assess, market, inspire, and manufacture self-confidence. As we show throughout this book, these practices include different ways of speaking, of writing, of dressing, of holding one's body. They are called forth in physical exercises, in affirmations of self-worth, in injunctions to be one's own friend, in cautions against perfectionism, in gratitude diaries, and in self-coaching. The confidence cult has entered the marketplace, the workplace, the home, the bedroom; it is located in our most intimate relations with ourselves and others, and it is found at the widest level of global development. And as it traverses sites, a range of experts, programs, and discourses are invested in establishing women's lack of confidence as the fundamental obstacle to women's success, achievement, and happiness and in promoting the acquisition or development of self-confidence as its ultimate solution.

The theory of media practice seems pertinent in this context, for many of the confidence practices that women are called on to engage in are oriented around and toward media: from online and print quizzes and forms of self-evaluation to self-tracking technologies, photographic filters, and confidence apps.[91] The ostensible aim of these media practices is to induce and cultivate in women confidence as the prime practice, what Ann Swidler would call the practice at the top of the hierarchy that anchors all other practices.[92] As we will show, the confidence culture is geared toward manufacturing confidence in how women act in the world across all domains, in the myriad of the practices in their lives. And while in this book we do not investigate whether and how individuals take up the confidence practices on offer, we use the concept of practice to underscore the potential force of the confidence culture in shaping what women *do*.

A Brief Note on Methods

Finally, we want to make a brief note about our methods and the scope of this study. As indicated already, our geographical focus is predominantly on the United Kingdom and United States, with other examples drawn from Australia, New Zealand, and various parts of mainland Europe. Chapter 5 is the exception here in being attentive to the "export" of confidence discourses to the global South. Yet we eschew a universalizing discourse and locate the contemporary preoccupation with confidence primarily as a Northern and

Western phenomenon. Our temporal focus, in turn, is, as much as possible, on the contemporary. Notwithstanding that, as we have demonstrated already in this introduction, the confidence cult(ure) did not emerge out of nowhere but has clear historical roots and antecedents. As academics we have been tracking this over several years, and our examples include early iterations of confidence messages—such as Dove's Campaign for Real Beauty, which was launched in 2004—alongside case studies that we encountered as the book was going to press, during a global pandemic, at a time of revitalized antiracist activism, and in an election year in the US.

Cultural analysis is a "craft skill" and it is not always easy to lay bare with precision the manner in which analyses proceeded—though such transparency and clarity is, in our view, a laudable aim. Broadly speaking, our approach to analyzing examples is rooted both in a media and cultural studies tradition and in a particular attentiveness to discourse. As we have indicated above, we do not regard discourse purely in terms of language but as inhering in images, affective states, and practices, which we examine in the book. Our work has also been influenced by the ethnographic focus on "following the object"—in this case, constructions of self-confidence.[93] We have attempted to track confidence imperatives across multiple sites, topics, and practices—reading, analyzing, and experiencing them, keeping careful records, and attempting to practice the reflexiveness that is a hallmark of feminist research.

We have amassed a significant "confidence archive" during research for this book. Yet, as scholars with rigorous methodological training, we have been (appropriately) wary of "confirmation bias," that is, of seeking out only examples that would support our argument about the force of the confidence cult(ure). As discourse analysts have argued, there are many ways for qualitative researchers to ensure the reliability and validity of their readings, including examining participants' understandings, using triangulation, and, of course, studying reception and readings of the phenomenon under study.[94] These have informed our approach, though a reception study was beyond the scope of this project. In addition, a crucial strategy for ensuring rigor is "deviant case analysis," in which researchers actively seek out cases that do not seem to fit the pattern being identified. One example of this is the attention that we now give to vulnerability. The relatively recent visibility of vulnerability as a cultural phenomenon at first seemed to challenge what we understood to be a cultural valorization of confidence.[95] Rather than ignore this—or, worse, seek to suppress it—we turned our attention to manifestations of the "vulnerable heroine" and, as a result, came to see vulnerability not as a repudiation of the confidence cult but as something intimately and dynamically entangled with it. This is an example of how attentiveness to principled scholarship materially contributed new insights to the research.

Structure of the Book

The book is structured thematically, tracking the iterations of the confidence cult(ure) across five distinct spheres: body confidence, workplace, relationships, motherhood, and international development. Each chapter focuses on one of the five domains, highlighting different features of contemporary imperatives to confidence.

In chapter 1, we examine the proliferation of body confidence messages targeted at women. We argue that body confidence has come to prominence as an issue through a multiplicity of different actors: activists, NGOs, national governments and transnational organizations, and—perhaps most visibly— the "love your body" (LYB) messages of contemporary advertising for brands like Dove, Always, and Gillette. Taking advertising as our main case study, we argue that increasingly ubiquitous commercial LYB messages underscore the idea that low self-esteem and poor body image are essentially trivial issues for which women are themselves responsible. These messages suggest that such issues can be quickly overcome through injections of positive thinking (and purchase of the right products). We show how some body confidence advertising expands the range of representations of diverse women (in terms of body size, race, religion, disability, and cis/transgender) yet at the same time hollows out these differences as if they were merely aesthetic. We demonstrate that while body confidence messages often have a warm and affirmative glow, they work to instill a new layer of discipline for women—a discipline that involves making over subjectivity to become an upgraded confident subject.

Chapter 2 moves on to look at confidence discourses in the workplace. We focus on two key sites where exhortations to confidence are made repeatedly to women in the context of work: advice literature on building and managing a career and other popular discussions about women and work. Specifically, we look at best sellers that appeared in the Anglo-American cultural landscape during the last ten years, including *Lean In* (2013) and *The Confidence Code* (2014), *Girl, Stop Apologizing* (2019), *A Good Time to Be a Girl* (2018), and *Option B: Facing Adversity, Building Resilience and Finding Joy* (2019), as well as at public appearances of successful businesswomen, workplace advice, work-related TED talks, and career-related apps. We show how these cultural texts promote ideas about women's obligation to work on themselves to overcome their confidence deficit and how the turn to confidence has been instrumental in putting workplace gender inequality on the agenda. At the same time, we demonstrate how the confidence culture calls on women to turn inward to tackle their "inner" obstacles and turns away from critiques of work cultures and the broader structures which produce women's self-doubt and stand in the way of their progress and success in the workplace.

Chapter 3 shifts the focus to confidence in relationships, showing how the confidence cult is shaping contemporary advice to women. We examine a range of different media, including magazines, smartphone apps, and best-selling books, demonstrating that confidence is presented as an essential quality, without which dating and intimacy will inevitably founder. We track a shift in sex and relationship guides aimed at heterosexual women: from "pleasing your man" to "being confident for yourself." We also examine the increasing attention being paid to one's own intimate relationship with oneself, exploring how confidence is entangled in broader incitements to self-belief and self-love—alongside seemingly paradoxical injunctions to embrace vulnerability and failure and to defy perfectionism.

In chapter 4 we explore how the confidence cult(ure) is refiguring motherhood in the context of discourses of intensive parenting, alongside increasing insecurity and precarity. Through attention to best-selling books, advertising, policy documents and campaigns, and social media sites, we interrogate the cultural landscape of confident mothering, showing how it operates with a "double whammy": exhorting women to be confident mothers while also calling on them to instill confidence and resilience in their children, particularly daughters.

Most of the book examines examples from the US, UK, Europe, and Australasia. In chapter 5, however, we discuss how the confidence cult(ure) is spreading out transnationally and, in particular, how confidence is increasingly mobilized in discourses about humanitarianism and international development. Tracing shifts in contemporary policies and practices of international aid, we demonstrate that a focus on girls' and young women's confidence has become central to what some call the "posthumanitarian" environment, marked by a shift from public to private actors and the increasing visibility of celebrities in "philanthrocapitalism." We consider how brands and NGOs promote female self-confidence as a unifying strategy that apparently benefits and empowers girls and women in the global South, while also endowing their Northern "sisters" with pride and entrepreneurial skills. This obscures obdurate inequalities and power relations steeped in colonialism and economic exploitation.

The conclusion draws together the threads of our argument across these multiple topics, domains, and cultural forms. We show that across disparate aspects of life—the body, the workplace, motherhood and other intimate relationships, and even international development initiatives, confidence has come to be a coherent *dispositif*—built on technologies of self that require women to work on and remodel their subjectivity and experience. This is materialized through remarkably similar practices of introspection, vigilance, and labor. We argue that the confidence cult(ure) operates to do nothing less than transform women's sense of self in a manner that exculpates social structures and institutions from responsibility for gender injustice, laying it squarely at women's door. In the process, we suggest, the confidence cult(ure) is implicated in making over feminism along individualistic and neoliberal lines. But how could this be otherwise? How might it be possible to rethink confidence as a collective project—not an individual woman's obligation? Or even to move beyond confidence? In concluding the book, we explore some alternative formulations and the ways that they might open up, rather than close down, possibilities to work toward a more just world, beyond (if not completely outside) confidence.

body confidence

IN THE 2018 COMEDY *I Feel Pretty* (dir. Abby Kohn and Marc Silverstein), Amy Schumer plays Renee Bennett, a lovable "girl next door" who is struggling at work, in romantic relationships, and above all with body dissatisfaction. What must it feel like "to be just undeniably pretty" she wonders, while bemoaning her lack of dates ("no one even looks at the profile, they only care about the picture and I'm *sick* of it!"); enduring chilly put-downs from haughty sales assistants ("er, you could probably find your size online"); and suffering a host of small humiliations that range from not being served in a bar to having babies scream when she smiles at them. All this, it is implied, is because she is *not beautiful enough.* "I have a crazy idea," Renee says, in a scene in which she is shown looking in the mirror at her average- rather than model-size body: "Let's be honest for a minute. No matter how many times we hear 'it's what's on the inside that matters,' women know deep down it's what's on the outside that the whole world judges."

Renee duly sets out to discipline her body, showing up at SoulCycle to pedal furiously while casting furtive embarrassed and envious looks at other women. She is motivated, but the task is hard: she is body-shamed for having "wide feet"; the seat on her bike collapses, resulting in injury to her vagina; and then, in the film's defining moment, she falls during a spin class, sustaining a brutal blow to the head. When she regains consciousness, she has undergone a dramatic psychological transformation. Suddenly she feels great about herself: "Oh my god," she exclaims looking in the changing-room mirror after coming round, "I'm *beautiful!*" With her newfound confidence her life quickly improves: she is promoted at work, moving from a dingy basement to the cosmetics company's gleaming Bryant Park offices; she flirts and goes on dates, finally winning the love of one who adores that "you are just so yourself"; and she is shown being the life and soul of the party, talking to anyone, dancing wildly, and even spontaneously entering a bikini contest.

I Feel Pretty was almost universally disparaged by the critics. Yet as a contemporary confidence fairy tale it clearly struck a chord. By the end of the film, Renee comes to understand that her body is the same as it was before the accident but that what has changed is *the way she sees herself.* The rewards she believed she had accrued through beauty were actually the benefits of greater confidence. When you believe in yourself, the film suggests, you can achieve anything—the only thing holding women back is lack of confidence. This take-home message was widely endorsed in social media comments with accounts of the powerful recognition and identification the film generated among many women, as well as appreciation for its upbeat feel-good philosophy. "Confidence means you can do anything," posters wrote below the trailer on YouTube. "Believe in yourself and anything is possible," opined others, while yet more comments offered variants of the argument that "you've got to love yourself if you want to be loved."

In this chapter we unpack this nexus of issues concerning appearance, body image, and self-esteem, with a focus on the media's contemporary love affair with body confidence. Feminists have always been interested in the body—in abortion rights, in sex work, in transgender, and in beauty politics—indeed, the very foundational myth of second-wave feminism in the United States centers around a protest against objectification and commodification of the female body in a beauty pageant.[1] What is striking today is the way in which these diverse struggles—intersecting too with issues of racism, ageism, and disableism—have transmuted, and in some cases condensed, into a central focus on self-confidence. Why has the injunction to "love your body" become so prominent in contemporary culture? How has feeling good about one's appearance come to occupy such a central position? What ideological or discursive work is performed by this insistence that body confidence is now *the* issue? What is the confidence cult doing to the way we think about ourselves and the way in which we practice politics?

Here we will address these issues looking across a range of media, discussing television, social media, magazines, self-help, and smartphone apps, but focusing in particular on "love your body" (LYB) advertising or "femvertising." The chapter is divided into eight parts, beginning with the making of body confidence as an issue and its establishment as what we might call "the body confidence industrial complex." This is followed by a discussion that critiques commercial body confidence messages, interrogates their representational strategies, shows how they present diverse women through a postracial aesthetic and "wokewashing," and examines the way they are implicated in maintaining toxic beauty standards. The final sections show how the confidence cult(ure) works to trivialize and individualize appearance pressure, to blame women for low body confidence, and to enroll women into new disciplinary regimes in which they must not only work on the body but also make over their mindset and sense of self.

Making "Body Confidence" the Issue

Discourses about female self-confidence in relation to the body have become ubiquitous in the twenty-first century. Advertisers tell us to "forget foundation, choose confidence," suggest we bid "goodbye resolutions, hello empowerment," and pronounce that "confidence is the new sexy."[2] Magazine covers assert that "confidence is more important than beauty" and urge women to "love your body," while fashion spreads embrace "kick-ass curves" and an end to body-shaming. Daily news is suffused with stories about the dangers of a female self-confidence deficit, with reports from medical foundations concerned about increasing rates of self-harm or eating disorders, and news of celebrities' diets, feuds, and triumphant returns to "pre-pregnancy shape" and resultant confidence. Reality TV shows focus on the confidence boost of style makeovers or, conversely, become the object of confidence concerns—as when the UK show *Love Island* was indicted for contributing to a crisis of body confidence among young viewers.[3] And on social media body confidence materializes in quite literally millions of hashtags, from the motivational messages of influencers to activists to individuals documenting their own struggles. Body confidence is everywhere—it has become a structuring idea shaping the way people, organizations, and businesses think about themselves and others.

Alongside and increasingly entangled with commercial enterprises are a multiplicity of organizations championing body positivity—activist groups centered on queer, fat, trans, or disabled visibility; nongovernmental organizations (NGOs) working with young people or lobbying on mental health; national governments concerned with "the epidemic of low self-esteem" among young women; and transnational organizations like the UN that draw connections between media images, low self-confidence, and global gender inequality. A conviction in the centrality of confidence is proliferating across sites, domains, and topics and intensifying in its force as a regulatory ideal. There is nothing, it would appear, that self-confidence cannot solve—or at the very least ameliorate. As we noted in the introduction, it has become one of a very few "cheer words"—placed beyond debate as an unquestioned good and invested with almost magical properties.

The current focus on body confidence has multiple determinants. Feminist activism has been central to its new prominence, with decades of research and protest countering the narrow and restrictive ideals of female bodily perfection on offer in fashion, beauty, and media—including the advertising and music industries. Antiracist, LGBTQ+, and disability organizations have also contributed a trenchant critique of the exclusionary normative ideals for bodily acceptability and respectability over many decades. Fat activists in turn have played a key role in calling out the body-shaming of people who do not fit society's current ideals of size and shape. All these struggles have been immensely important in relation to body confidence by both expanding the range and diversity of bodies represented in contemporary cultural forms and drawing attention to the devastating impact on self-confidence of living in a world in which many bodies are symbolically annihilated—either invisibilized or stigmatized.

Resistance to this has developed in many different ways. It can be seen in critical academic research, in interventions with young people, in demonstrations and campaigns. It can also be seen on social media as posts proclaim the value and beauty of particular bodies and identities—articulating painful stories, bold entitlements to be valued, and yearnings to feel confident. Leah Vernon, for example, posts as a "Fat, Black Muslim" offering cogent critiques of the racist, misogynist, colorist, and fat-phobic aesthetics of Instagram, through posts that interrogate both wider US culture and the thin, light-skinned, "pastel" posts of most hijabi fashion bloggers. While her style is brightly colored and eye-catching, a central motif in her posts concerns her struggle for self-acceptance and confidence.[4] Similarly, disability pride and crip activist movements refuse both body-shaming and neuro-shaming.

"My fibromyalgia-slow-cane-using body is not something I'm going to hate," asserts Leah Lakshmi Piepzna-Samarasinha, author of *Care Work: Dreaming Disability Justice*.[5] This represents a shift from what Andrew Pulrang calls a "self-help" perspective that has the subtext "the only disability in life is a bad attitude," which is focused on "individual effort and personal growth," to a social justice orientation rooted in social or postmodern models of disability.[6] Often these interventions have explicitly intersectional agendas, such as the Twitter hashtag #DisabilityTooWhite, started by Vilissa Thompson, and the Disability Visibility Project, created by Alice Wong, who also established #CripTheVote, which played a key role as a site of political engagement in both the 2016 and 2020 US elections.[7]

Body confidence—or lack of it—has emerged also as a central public health concern in the last two decades, increasingly shown to be connected to anxiety, depression, eating disorders, and poor physical and mental health more broadly. In 2000, the concern was catapulted to the status of a major political issue in the UK when the government held a "summit" at 10 Downing Street (the prime minister's office)—something usually reserved for national issues of state relating to the economy or security—in response to growing public worry about the impact on young women of the use of extremely thin models in advertisements and magazines. Shortly before the summit, research had revealed that more than half of all twelve- to fifteen-year-old girls considered appearance to be the biggest concern in their lives.[8] The British Medical Association, which published research designed to coincide with this political meeting, criticized the harmful effects of the cult of "bodily perfection," calling for broadcasters and editors to take a "more responsible attitude" and for schools to launch media literacy campaigns to encourage more critical viewing of such images.[9] While there was criticism of what some—particularly in fashion and media and in some sections of academia—saw as oversimplification and scapegoating of the media, along with inappropriate intervention by the "nanny state," what is crucial is the way in which the summit established questions of self-esteem and confidence as matters of significant political and public concern.

This has also been the case elsewhere. In Australia and Canada, for example, body confidence has moved up the political agenda dramatically in recent years,[10] and in the US more than one hundred gender equality organizations have empowerment and confidence at their heart. Body Positive is one such example. It seeks to "create a lively, healing community that offers freedom from suffocating societal messages that keep people in a perpetual struggle with their bodies."[11]

Social media have significantly intensified the focus on confidence in several ways. On the one hand, they have foregrounded the visibility and traction of vulnerability—for example, in the thousands of YouTube videos based on the anxious solicitation "am I pretty or am I ugly?" On the other hand, confidence has increasingly emerged as a psychic requirement in the context of online hate, "ebile," and trolling.[12] Electronic communications have become the medium par excellence for sharing corporate confidence messages—popular viral ads by the cosmetics brand Dove, for example, have been viewed on YouTube tens of millions of times (we discuss these in more detail later). Furthermore, social media have become important sites for resistance to beauty norms and body-shaming. Indeed, it is striking to see how plus-size bloggers modeling their "Outfit of the Day" (OOTD) have impacted the magazine and fashion industries, expanding the range of body shapes that are represented. This is just one example of the way in which "resistant" practices may be taken up by mainstream culture—although not necessarily without problems, as we discuss later in this chapter.

The Body Confidence Industrial Complex

What is clear, then, is the way that body confidence has come to the fore from many directions and multiple actors—activists, academics, charities and NGOs, youth organizations, governments, and corporations have all been involved, often with ideas that are in tension. Yet from these different sites a veritable body confidence complex—or assemblage—has developed in which there are increasingly blurred lines and significant entanglements between actors. Consider, for example, the way that L'Oréal has paired with the UK's the Prince's Trust to roll out body confidence workshops that help "vulnerable" young people with education and employment (more on this campaign later in the chapter).[13] Weight Watchers, too, has recently rebranded as WW, using the alliteration to create new sets of meanings and programs—its points scheme, for instance, is now called WellnessWins.[14]

Perhaps the example par excellence, however, is Dove, which has teamed with research organizations, school boards, and national governments to become utterly enmeshed at multiple levels with body confidence as a project. Its website offers research reports and resources, campaigning tools, and free media literacy training programs for use in schools.[15] It funds authoritative research and links with respected academics and psychotherapists. It has located itself at the center of pedagogical projects designed to create a citizen-consumer who is critical of marketing of harmful or unrealistic norms but who is "invited to develop this narrative in conjunction with corporate culture."[16]

The work of Dove as a brand is emblematic of the dynamism and flexibility of the confidence culture and its ability to change and mutate to accommodate (or some would say appropriate) current trends. Early ads for Dove's self-esteem projects took as their targets the beauty industry and the associated worlds of photography and marketing. *Onslaught*, released by Ogilvy and Mather in 2007, shows a young white girl child, dressed simply and with no makeup, and proceeds over the course of eighty seconds against the soundtrack of "La Breeze" by Simian to show the veritable bombardment she is about to face from cosmetics companies, the diet industry, and surgery clinics. The force of the ad is intensified by its sped-up nature, which manages to distill years of hostile advertising messages about women's bodies, represented with proliferating makeup sets, skincare regimes, and yo-yo dieting, and to point to the amping up of appearance pressures via graphic images of the surgical marking of skin and injections. At the end of the ad the little girl is shown once again, with the tagline "Talk to your daughter before the beauty industry does." This represents what we call in chapter 2 the "double whammy" of the confidence culture's address to women, in its focus on the need for parents (usually mothers) to warn and protect their daughters; but it is striking that in this ad (and in others of the time, such as *Evolution*) a trenchant critique of the beauty-industrial complex is leveled. By the early 2010s this had given way to a focus on women's internal deficits and their difficulties with the manufacture of self-confidence. The latter part of that decade in turn saw Dove link this to broader visibility and social justice themes, particularly around race and body size, reaching its recent apotheosis in the brand's sponsorship of the CROWN Act, passed already in several US states, which seeks to outlaw "race-based hair discrimination."[17] This latest example of "commodity activism" or "cause marketing" sees the pantheon of confidence videos on Dove.com joined by a new statement of Dove's commitment to ending racism so that "all of our beauty" can be "welcome in all places and institutions." "We're in this fight together," declares the brand, pledging (yet more) programs "in the Dove Self-Esteem Project to help empower the next generation."[18]

As well as being thoroughly enmeshed in market (and governmental) logics, body confidence is intimately entangled with individualist and neoliberal values. It becomes positioned as a choice and a commodity—something one can pledge as if it were entirely a matter of will: "Today I pledge to be confident," as Dove's Be Real campaign advocates. Typically, as in anxieties about "sexualization," a particular racialized and classed subject is identified in these discourses—as white teenage girls become the privileged site of concerns about lack of self-confidence—though this changed somewhat in 2020–21, as the brand supports the CROWN Act, refuses the word "normal," and offers a pledge against systemic racism.[19] Multiple injustices are enacted in this process—both in who is recognized as/allowed to be "vulnerable" and who is not, in terms of the resources and products designed for and invested in such subjects, and in the everyday banal forms of violence that are perpetuated in assumptions about whose feelings matter, or indeed who is seen to *feel*.[20]

In what follows we focus mostly on one particular subset of body confidence messages, namely those found in advertising, while noting both the dissonances *and* the entanglements with other discourses about body confidence—such as those from governments or think tanks. The examples we examine here have become known as "love your body" advertising or "femvertising." These LYB discourses are positive, affirmative, seemingly feminist-inflected messages, targeted predominantly at girls and women, that exhort them to believe they are beautiful, incredible, and powerful. Calling on women to "feel comfortable in your own skin" and "feel sexy at any size," they encourage a belief in self-esteem and body positivity, with an emphasis on self-determination and individual beauty standards. At the heart of these discourses is the production of positive affect. If many media discourses about women's bodies are characterized by a focus on what is *wrong* (e.g., "dull, lifeless hair") or how it can be improved ("get smoother-looking, softer skin"), then LYB discourses constitute a dramatic—apparently counterhegemonic—interruption. They tell women that they are "worth it" and should feel appreciative and confident about their bodies. In the words of a well-known spoof on femvertising, body confidence advertising represents a shift from "exploiting women's insecurities to empowering their incredibilities."[21]

Examples are legion—and we discuss many here—including campaigns by Dove, Nike, Verizon, L'Oréal, Pantene, Olay, Always, and Weight Watchers. It might even be said that exhortations to body confidence—to feeling good in your skin, to rejecting "perfection" and believing in oneself—now constitute the dominant form of address to women in advertising, and one that, while superficially positive, demands our critical interrogation.

A Confidence Trick: Commercial LYB

One of the criticisms most often levied at commercial body confidence messages is that they are "fake."[22] Many of the companies adopting the iconography of "natural," "unfiltered," "real" beauty, and claiming their ads as empowering, authentic, and confidence-boosting, have been demonstrated to use precisely the techniques they claim to reject, such as photographic retouching. For instance, there has been discussion of the "visual fraud" of Dove Pro-Age texts which revealed the company's espousal of the very same battery of visual effects (cosmetic and technological) of which it has been critical.[23] Several years into its makeover as a body confidence organization, Dove was exposed placing a call in New York City's Craigslist searching for "flawless" non-models for the next commercial. The Craigslist ad stated, "Beautiful arms and legs and face . . . naturally fit, not too curvy or athletic . . . Beautiful hair and skin is a must." An article in *The Week*, commenting on this, noted that Dove's "come as you are" campaign has an "if you're flawless, that is" clause attached.

Another common critique of such advertising indicts it for hypocrisy. It is striking to note that many of the companies that have been particularly invested in promoting body dissatisfaction among women—such as those selling diet products or anti-aging creams—are precisely the ones that buy into the confidence cult most ardently. Weight Watchers, for example, would have us "awaken your incredible," while Lean Cuisine will apparently "feed your phenomenal." Sometimes LYB discourses rely on and reinforce the idea of the female body as inherently "difficult to love."[24] In doing so they "re-cite" hateful discourse about women's bodies that depend on their normalized cultural pathologization—as we see in an advertisement for diet brand Special K, which calls on women to "shut down fat talk"—in the process recirculating pernicious messages about big thighs, cellulite, and so forth.[25]

More broadly, the charge of "faux feminism" has been directed at companies whose feminist confidence messages are not matched by the makeup of their boardrooms, profile on equal pay, or gender equality records more generally. Katie Martell cites KPMG and Audi among many companies whose attachment to female empowerment is said to constitute jumping on the "femvertising bandwagon" rather than a genuine commitment to change.[26] Thinx and Nasty Gal have both had their "She E O" challenged on similar grounds, while LuluLemon found itself the subject of an article by a former employee titled "My Life in an Exploitative Libertarian Happiness Cult."[27] Martell recommends asking a battery of questions of brands about hiring practices, unconscious bias training, percentage of women on the board, and the like. Their score will place them on her continuum from "lip service" to "legit."[28]

It is not only feminism that may be said to be "faux" in LYB advertising. We also note that in most cases the apparent "diversification" of bodies shown represents only a small shift from the normative ideal of female attractiveness seen in most advertisements—what has been referred to as the "diversity paradox" or "a mediated ritual of rebellion."[29] Nike's and Dove's early LYB ads established the template for this type of imagery. While we were cued to read them as showing a diversity of different women, in practice they featured women who were cisgender, non-disabled, slim, young, and conventionally attractive. They were also disproportionately white or light-skinned. This kind of representation persists as a representational trope of "body diversity," even when it shows nothing of the sort. A look at Getty's top sixty stock photos using the search term "body diversity" captures this vividly, revealing image after image of slim, attractive, femme, mainly Caucasian models smiling or hugging, depicted against spare or neutral backgrounds.

There are signs that things may be changing through the influence of activists, social media, and commercial interests. In 2019 the UK's baby and maternity products retailer Mothercare launched its Body Proud Mums campaign to "encourage mothers to feel confident about their bodies."[30] Research by the brand revealed that body confidence is low after giving birth, with 90 percent of UK mothers comparing their own bodies unfavorably with images of celebrities or others they see on social media. The resultant advertising images are striking for showing loose flesh, stretch marks, and swollen breasts, representing a decisive shift in images of the postnatal body in the contemporary mediascape. The campaign's photographer, Sophie Mayanne, expressed the aim that women would identify with the images "and feel more confident with their imperfections."[31]

British fashion brand Missguided has also been significant in expanding the range of models depicted in its ads, particularly in its #InYourOwnSkin campaign, which features six models, all of whom have visible skin conditions such as scars, albinism, and psoriasis. A press release for the campaign called it "a bold and fearless move as the brand continues to build upon its globally empowering KeepOnBeingYou movement" (fig. 1.1).[32] It starts from "inspiring a strong self-empowered message; to embrace your flaws and to not strive for what the world perceives as perfection. Because f*** perfection, it doesn't exist."[33]

However, all too often these messages of resistance to and defiance against beauty norms do not stand up to scrutiny. Missguided's campaign featured only one plus-size model and one, very light-skinned, woman of color, and while the others had obvious skin conditions, they were slim and exceptionally attractive, fitting well within traditional images of model beauty. Likewise, the hyperbolic reaction that greeted the news that NikeTown in London was to feature a women's floor with "plus-size and para mannequins" was not matched by the reality.[34] Indeed, even the publicity shots showed only a single "larger than typical" mannequin—approximating to average female body size.[35] Furthermore, when Mattel launched its "curvy Barbie" to great acclaim—a sign of how far body confidence ideas have taken hold—it is worth noting that its dimensions, scaled up, were equivalent to a UK size 6–8 and a US size 2–4. Most importantly, these developments fail to disrupt the fundamental gendered link between appearance and self-worth. That is, women are invited to feel good about themselves even if their look slightly deviates from the most valued norm, but the basis for these affective experiences is still predicated on how they look.

Hyperbolic claims about how "bold," "brave," "different," and "radical" current advertising campaigns or fashion spreads are provide evidence of how *tightly* normative beauty standards are policed, so that even a minute departure or deviation attracts the label "fierce" or "badass," such as the commentary on the "no-makeup selfie," which depicts it as a real act of daring.[36] This idea was captured in some reactions to *I Feel Pretty*: "Amy Schumer is blonde, white, able-bodied, femme and yes, thin," tweeted comedian Sofie Hagens. "She IS society's beauty ideal"—so why present her as some sort of failure?[37] A similar dynamic can also be seen in the "feminist gloss" TV se-

1.1 *Missguided* website: "Keep On Being You"

KEEP ON BEING YOU

AT MISSGUIDED WE'RE ON A MISSION TO INSPIRE YOU, OUR BABES, TO FEEL UNASHAMEDLY CONFIDENT IN BEING YOURSELF. IT'S ALL ABOUT EMBRACING YOUR FLAWS, IGNORING THE HATERS, CELEBRATING WHAT MAKES YOU UNIQUE, AND ALWAYS STRIVING TO BE THAT LITTLE BIT EXTRA. BECAUSE F**K BEING PERFECT, JUST BE YOU BABE.

IT'S A REALLY GREAT LOOK

SHOP PARTYWEAR   MEET THE CAST

ries *The Bold Type* about fashion magazine *Scarlet*.[38] In one episode (season 2, episode 3) the three young, thin, beautiful twenty-something co-stars propose, without a shred of irony, that *they* should feature in the "body positivity" issue. The sequence filmed is hard-pressed to find any "flaws" but shows freckles, a scar, a tiny pimple. Yet, in tune with the times, the characters talk about how amazing and empowering it will be for readers to see their bodies represented: "I wish I'd seen something like this when I was growing up," says one of the characters, as if their normatively beautiful, conventionally feminine bodies represented a challenge to the dominant visual habitat of images.

Hollow Diversity and "Wokewashing"

At times, commercial body confidence messages do not simply overstate the diversity they represent but actually undercut it entirely. Dove's campaigns have been repeatedly indicted for racism in campaigns that repeat the tropes of some of the most notoriously racist and colonialist advertising of earlier eras. Rather like the infamous Pears soap ads of the late nineteenth century in which soap was portrayed as part of an imperial "civilizing" mission and darker skins were "dirty," Unilever has placed ads for body wash and body lotion in which Black women have been shown becoming white through use of Dove products.[39] In 2017 an ad posted by the company on Facebook garnered three thousand critical comments before Dove took it down, posting a lackluster apology: "An image we recently posted on Facebook missed the mark in representing women of color thoughtfully. We deeply regret the offense it caused."[40] The trivialization implied by "missed the mark" and other comments about "tone deafness" were widely perceived as adding to the injuries caused by the ad, by not taking seriously the charge of racism. It represented a spectacular failure for the company—the more so because it repeated a similar incident only six years earlier which had used a before-and-after sequence in which (again) a Black woman transitioned to whiteness via a Dove product. There are important questions to be asked about how such campaigns came to be made and posted—so crude and crass do they appear.

As disturbing as these examples of racism are, two more common, and in some ways more insidious, patterns of representation relate to what we understand as "postrace racism" and "wokewashing."[41] Postracial discourses hold that race is no longer a live and active political force in contemporary culture. The confidence cult(ure) *selectively* draws on the significance of race and remakes it in a highly specific fashion. Race is flexibly dissociated from the continuing power of historical structures and material resources

Chapter One

1.2 L'Oréal and the Prince's Trust All Worth It campaign

in order to offer "inclusion" or "visibility" within resolutely neoliberal paradigms. Many body confidence messages seem to operate in this postracial space—which is also a site in which sexuality, disability, and gender are seen as features like any other that can be freely interacted and transacted.[42] Visibility becomes an end in itself—a marker of progress and inclusion, which signifies that nothing has to change, since the politics *is* the visibility—a point we return to in relation to "wokewashing."[43] Some vivid examples of postrace representation can be seen in a series of L'Oréal ads from 2017 onward, which publicize a new partnership between the company and a British charity—the Prince's Trust—founded by Prince Charles in 1976 to help young people struggling with employment and mental health issues. The partnership itself is interesting for the way that it foregrounds the interpenetration of brands with charitable and other organizations (as discussed earlier), making neat distinctions impossible. Indeed, the central motif of the Prince's Trust ad is to be found in L'Oréal's longtime slogan "Because you're worth it," which is pastiched to make a new hashtag, #AllWorthIt, and used to advertise the collaboration (fig. 1.2).

All the advertisements feature a range of youthful, attractive celebrity speakers who vary in age, body shape, race, gender, sexuality, and ability but are all beautifully groomed and presented.[44] They are located in a stripped-back, monochrome space that is characteristic of LYB advertising. In the first ad the speakers greet us with L'Oreal's brand messages: "I'm worth it," "you're worth it, we're all worth it." Actress Helen Mirren is then shown striding onto the set saying, "Famous words I know. But L'Oréal Paris has always believed that *everyone* is worth it." The others take up the script: L'Oréal is "championing inclusivity and diversity because what makes us different is what makes us beautiful. And when we feel our most beautiful, it gives us the confidence to strive to be the best that we can be so that we can accomplish almost *anything*" (italics represent emphasis in the spoken voice).[45]

The participants are then shown laughing and smiling as they take up the "all worth it" message, finally using graffiti to scrub out the words "self-doubt" and replace them with "self-worth." This ad and subsequent iterations in the campaign are striking for having a diverse cast, which includes a lingerie model who is a wheelchair user, a white model who was scarred in an acid attack, a Muslim beauty blogger, a Black soccer player, a pregnant celebrity, a plus-size model, and a woman of color TV presenter with a strong regional accent. It does not represent fake diversity so much as hollow diversity in which differences are *aestheticized* and imbued with a feel-good factor rather than erased. The beautiful, gleaming participants each represent one form of "difference"—in a campaign held together by the immaculate white femininity of English actress Helen Mirren. It is an example of a contemporary corporate love affair with difference, in which all kinds of identities may be represented as long as their presence is "safe" and not disruptive to corporate interests. An identical dynamic is seen in the 2020 advert for the Marc Jacobs fragrance Perfect in which women of diverse ethnicities, shapes, sizes, and styles face the camera and intone, "I'm perfect."[46] As Roopali Mukherjee has argued, postrace re-envisions "the scriptures of colour blindness by firmly acknowledging a specified range of racial differences that serve to disavow any vestige of their *consequence* for anyone—of any race—who can fashion themselves as properly neoliberal subjects." One of the moves that postracial discourses make, then, is in severing identity from history and in the process erasing any sense of race as a "central organizing principle of American society."[47]

In the L'Oréal/Prince's Trust ads this is extended beyond race to other forms of difference, including religion, sexuality, and disability. The ads are striking in making these forms of difference visible—and, in the case of classed regional accents (e.g., north of England), "hearable"—but the effectivity and specificity of any particular identity is not addressed. Instead, paradoxically, the very differences that are foregrounded are also hollowed and homogenized through a combination of aesthetic means (makeup, clothes, stylization) and affective means (an upbeat emphasis on self-worth and confidence) that renders everyone the same and suggests that the interventions needed are uniform psychological programs (e.g., confidence training programs) rather than material, political, cultural, or economic changes. For example, in a 2019 series of advertisements for L'Oréal, the emphasis is on affirmations. It starts with examples of the negative voices we hear in our heads and instructs us to change them with "positive words we say to ourselves." "I am my own role model," declares Iska Lawrence; "I am brave enough to be me," intones AJ Odudu.[48] "Say it with me," says Katie Piper, a British model and TV presenter who was seriously injured when her ex-partner attacked her, throwing sulfuric acid in her face, "my future is what I make it." Piper's personal courage and resilience, in the face of disfiguring injury that left her blind in one eye and necessitated multiple surgeries, is also co-opted in a Pantene ad launched in 2019. In it she is shown confidently stepping out, with her long newly blonde hair bouncing on her shoulders as she explains, "My hair means so much more than just hair to me: it was my expressions when I couldn't make any, my curtain when I wanted to hide. So having smooth hair that I can actually control makes me feel empowered, more like myself. . . . Today I don't want to hide my face; I want to frame it. I'm Katie Piper and this is my bounce-back hair."[49] While undoubtedly moving, in this ad (as in so many others) the response to a patterned form of social injustice and abuse—in this case domestic violence—becomes to work on the self and buy products that make you feel good, now treated as synonymous with confident, empowered, and in control.

What we see in LYB confidence messages, then, is something more complicated than fake or pseudo-diversity. Rather, it is an attempt to use and strategically deploy images of minoritized groups (people of color, disabled people, Muslims, queer people) in commercial culture to "take diversity into account" only to *empty* any particular differences of their meaning and social significance. As Anandi Ramamurthy and Kalpana Wilson have argued in relation to other advertisements, this is demonstrably both a way of responding to activisms and social justice movements around race (and also class, sexuality, and disability) while at the same time not requiring any of the changes that such activist movements require.[50]

Intimately connected with this postracial culture, an intensification of corporate confidence messages has arisen in the last few years that is explicitly entangled with affirmations of support for social justice movements, including feminism, LGBTQ+ activism, and Black Lives Matter. Cosmetics companies nod to trans and nonbinary social movements with ads promoting "Generation Fluid"; women's athleisure brands bid "Goodbye resolutions, hello empowerment"; and numerous companies from banks to airlines celebrate sexual diversity with "GAYTMs" and rainbow branding. This practice has become known as "wokewashing," taking its place in a lexicon that also includes "greenwashing" by oil companies and fast-food chains and "carewashing" by numerous corporations that, throughout the COVID-19 crisis, sought to persuade consumers that they "have our backs" or that "we are all in this together."[51]

Common to these trends is the attempt to enlist the cultural energy of movements for change, and to strategically extract value from them, by seeking to persuade customers that brands are "allies" in struggles for climate justice, queer and trans rights, or antiracism. Of course, expressions of corporate "wokeness" have dramatically increased in the wake of the killing of George Floyd in May 2020 and the subsequent revitalization of Black Lives Matter activism, but as a trend it has a longer history, with similarities to "commodity feminism" and "queer chic" as marketing strategies.[52] One way of reading this kind of advertising, then, is as a form of cultural appropriation of radical and progressive movements, and indeed of particular identities that garner value as "cool" in a particular moment. In relation to the politics of race this has broader force as part of a growing tendency for individuals and corporations to selectively appropriate aspects of Black appearance or culture, in such a way as to empty out its significance. In this context, Wanna Thompson's notion of "Blackfishing" refers to the way that influencers appropriate the hairstyles, "glow," and other phenotypical attributes of African American identity as something that can be taken on or off at will, like a kind of "digital Blackface."[53] In turn, Alisha Gaines discusses it in terms of being *Black for a Day*, hollowed out and stripped of history and of consequences.[54]

Furthermore, too often the corporate practices of brands championing Black Lives Matter, feminist movements, or LGBTQ+ activism limit their interventions to the level of representation, without any kind of followthrough in terms of changes at a material or structural level such as pay, opportunity, or workplace equality. The fashion and beauty company ASOS's proclamations of "Unity, Acceptance, Equality," for example, were somewhat undercut when, in 2020, it was accused of mistreating its workers with humiliating body searches, the use of security guards in the bathrooms, and punishing "flexi shifts."[55] Likewise, fast-fashion brand Boohoo's dedication to body positivity and female self-confidence, as well as its supposedly inspiring messages of hope and togetherness during the pandemic, was called into question in mid-2020 in light of revelations of its operation of dehumanizing sweatshops with predominantly female migrant workers paid a fraction of the legal minimum wage.[56]

Undoubtedly many people welcome the new visibility "woke" advertising endows groups and constituencies that were previously marginalized or invisibilized, and also derive pleasure from its affirmative emphasis on the need for change. In a recent UK study, conducted during the COVID-19 crisis and at the peak of global BLM protests in 2020, young people were astute critics of the way that brands "jumped on the bandwagon" of antiracist activism, seeing it as self-serving and cynical, yet *at the same time* they expressed the view that it was nevertheless important to see the cultural discourse changing.[57] Indeed, "*invisibility*, in the failure to be visually represented by brands and *included* in this imagery, is framed as one of the primary wrongs of consumer citizenship, thus reinstating the importance of capitalist attention economies and the 'leadership' of brands."[58] What requires further scrutiny in relation to corporate wokeness is the *conditions* under which and ways in which historically marginalized bodies are accorded visibility. Too often, as Sarah Banet-Weiser argues about popular feminism, economies of visibility "fundamentally shift politics of visibility so that visibility becomes the end rather than a means to an end"; in short "the [feminist] T-shirt *is* the politics."[59]

These new branded and brandable visibilities are clearly complicated. Demands for visibility and representation are and have been central to almost all social justice movements. Today that has a new significance at a time when the secret algorithms of media giants like Google, YouTube, or Instagram quite literally erase or invisibilize certain subjects or bodies while promoting and rendering hypervisible others.[60] The practice of "shadowbanning" is one way in which subordinated groups are systematically "disappeared" from social media sites, as well as differential ratings, which render some material much harder to find than others (e.g., LGBTQ+ posts that may arbitrarily be dubbed "adult material").[61] These tendencies are further exacerbated by striking inequalities in financial reward that particular groups attract. For example, Black influencers are likely to be underpaid by brands relative to their white counterparts undertaking identical promotional labor.[62]

Toxic Beauty Standards

Another deeply troubling feature of many of the circulating LYB messages is that they are based on the lie that looks do not matter and that the only thing holding women back is their own negative self-beliefs. This is the myth that the film *I Feel Pretty* ostensibly set out to challenge but ended up endorsing:

when you feel confident, you can do anything. While this might be a desirable state of affairs—like a world in which race does not matter or in which gender is not so rigidly policed—to claim it as reality is monstrously disingenuous. In fact, the pressures on women are intensifying. It is a moment in which patriarchy is said to have "re-territorialized" in the fashion-beauty complex, pressurizing women to meet hitherto unprecedented appearance norms and inciting an ongoing—and never-ending—quest for perfection.[63]

The power of the beauty-industrial complex is undoubtedly amplifying—whether assessed in terms of its economic scale, its interconnections with other fields and industries (such as genetics, new technologies, food, and wellness), or the force with which it acts on consumers. Beauty standards, and the policing of them, now operate more intensely than ever. If in the early 2000s "surveillance of women's bodies constituted perhaps the largest type of media content across all genres and media forms," then today this is operating at ever finer-grained levels, becoming forensic in its gaze.[64] Indeed, it is striking that microscopes, telescopic gunsights, peepholes, calipers, and set squares have become ubiquitous in beauty advertising. Images of cameras and of perfect "photo beauty" or "HD-ready" skin also proliferate. Most common of all are the motifs of the tape measure (often around the upper thigh) and the magnifying glass, used to scrutinize pores, sun damage, or broken capillaries, but—more importantly at a meta-level—underscoring the idea of women's appearance as under constant (magnified) surveillance.[65]

Recent research shows that this surveillance imperative does not simply exist at the level of advertising or media images but is increasingly experienced in everyday life and practiced on the self and others.[66] Katharine Morton found an extraordinary level of visual literacy in relation to aging-related changes in appearance in her research. "Everyone is talking about the face," she argued, struck by the detail her respondents went into about fine lines, wrinkles, pigmentation, lack of elasticity, dehydration, and dullness.[67] They seemed to have a "clinical gaze" upon their own appearance, she notes—and one that is informed by what Susan Bordo famously described as a "pedagogy of defect."[68] Kristin Denise Rowe notes how in online spaces dedicated to promoting the "natural hair movement" among African American women in the United States, Black women's hair in its natural state is regularly described as "misbehaving" and something that should be "controlled" and "trained."[69] Ana Elias talks about the "nano surveillance" her twenty-something participants practiced.[70] Women's self-examination—often mediated by smartphones—routinely involved careful scrutiny of eyebrows, magnification of pores, and submission of selfies to apps that measure and deliver a score of facial symmetry.[71] The latest survey by the Be Real: Body Confidence for Everyone campaign supports this, finding that three-quarters of seventeen- to twenty-four-year-old women spend time carefully editing and filtering their images before posting them—with nearly a quarter spending at least five minutes per photo.[72]

Brands are clearly involved in both creating and capitalizing on the new visual literacies, for example, by expanding everyday skin care and makeup sets dramatically, fueled also by social media influencers and the proliferation of beauty apps.[73] As we were writing this chapter, we watched a video of actress Liv Tyler explaining her "no makeup routine," which involved twenty-five separate steps, fourteen of which were to prepare the skin *before* the application of makeup—with oils, mists, creams, serums, masks, massages, and a drop of CBD oil.[74] This marks an extraordinary shift from the beauty advice of an earlier era, which in the 1980s and 1990s was summed up in the magazine mantra "cleanse, tone, moisturize." What is striking today is that Liv Tyler's claims to have a "really, really simple" "everyday" makeup regime are actually plausible—if eye-wateringly expensive and time-consuming—so inflated and intensified have beauty requirements become in an age of contouring, highlighting, eyebrow definition, false eyelashes, and so on and so forth.

Ever new beauty standards are also proliferating for different parts of the body: from upper-arm definition to sexy armpits, from the thigh gap to the vajazzle. Jenna Drenten and Lauren Gurrieri track the new feminine ideal of the "bikini bridge"—"the space between the bikini and the lower abdomen when bather bottoms are suspended between the two hip bones," analyzing over ten thousand social media posts that used the term and helped establish it as "a thing."[75] In turn, the "thigh brow," "hot dog legs," and "underboob" have recently become new body ideals, extensively promoted on social media and now widely disseminated via fashion and beauty industries. "Instagram has spoken. Cleavage is out, underboob is in," reported the media.[76]

The requirement to "look good" is also extending to new temporalities in women's lives that might previously have been considered "outside" or beyond beauty pressures. It has shifted deeper into childhood, as media and cosmetics and fashion companies have moved in on younger age groups with beauty-focused teen magazines and product ranges. Clarins's 2019 slogan "Beautiful at every age" includes the pull quote "In beauty it is never too early and never too late"—prompting questions about when *is* too early for children to engage with skin care involving acid peels and retinol. The other end of life is also comprehensively colonized; indeed, mobilizations of fear and anxiety about aging are the beating heart of the beauty-industrial complex.[77] Moreover, if at one point pregnancy represented, for some women, an escape from or relaxation of the demands of beauty, this is no longer the case, at least in the West.[78] In fact, getting back to your pre-baby weight is increasingly represented in the media as a far greater achievement than giving birth or parenting.[79]

Individualizing and Trivializing Appearance Pressures

Against this context, the suggestion that beauty is simply "a state of mind" deserves skepticism. It trivializes the force of beauty norms and the impact they clearly have on many women and girls, and it systematically encourages us to see the issue in individualistic terms.[80] Confidence cult discourses about the body are notable for making visible and intelligible—and *relatable*—some of the pain associated with feeling fat or ugly or otherwise dissatisfied and unhappy with one's appearance in a looks-obsessed world, only to minimize this and displace/replace it with the Panglossian contention that "you are more beautiful than you think." Love Your Body discourses are affectively powerful precisely because they offer some recognition of the injuries inflicted on women in a patriarchal society, but these must be only momentarily acknowledged before they are overcome, triumphed over.

Because LYB discourses circulate (among other ways) in videos featuring "ordinary women," these glimpses of suffering are impossible to conceal. Indeed, part of the power is in revealing the pain, the shame, the insecurity—before it can be decisively "dealt with" by confidence technologies. This is vividly illustrated in Dove's "Real Beauty Sketches" in which a forensic artist draws two pictures of the same woman—one based on her self-description, the other (consistently more attractive) based on what another woman says of her.[81] As viewers we see the images juxtaposed and hear the tearful catches in the throats of the women as they attempt to describe their reactions to the dual portraits—"[this] one looks more open. Friendly and happy." In so doing the ads make available to us as viewers a glimpse of the pain and vulnerability they have endured as a result of not identifying themselves as this more appealing subject, of living with a more diminished sense of themselves. But in allowing itself to be witnessed, this injury must rapidly be overcome, with the certainty or conviction that comes from knowing that "the power is in your hands" or "beauty is a state of mind." Here the tagline, and the promise of the transformative effects of the product, aim culturally and psychically to "resolve" the tensions generated by witnessing women's distress.

A particularly vivid and egregious example is to be found in Dove's film *Patches*.[82] It follows an apparent "research study" in which a psychology professor from Columbia University sets up an experiment to test the effectiveness of a new "revolutionary product": the beauty patch. Women are recruited and asked to wear the patch (which resembles a hormone or nicotine patch) for twelve hours a day for two weeks and to make a video diary each day to report on how they are feeling about themselves. Edited clips from the women's videos are duly shown, intercut with interviews with the women, reporting on any changes they have undergone since donning the patches. They start off somewhat skeptical ("not really feeling any more beautiful today") but quickly report significant transformations. Most appear to have experienced real shifts and are shown talking about how the patch has made them feel more confident, helped them feel able to show parts of their bodies they would usually hide, and attract compliments from others. It has been, according to one participant, a truly "life-altering experience." The "big reveal" in the film comes when the women meet once again with the psychologist who recruited them. Has the patch changed their life?, they are asked. "Yes," reply the women shown. Would they buy it? Yes. Do they have any interest in knowing what is in it? the psychologist asks. Well yes, of course! They are then handed a brand-new patch and asked to turn it over. There, on the reverse, is one word: "NOTHING."

Various reactions greet this revelation, but we are shown barely any expressions of anger about this humiliation enacted upon the women. Most women instead seem to express the desired messages that "it's all in my head," "the key is me," and "I have the power to change the way I feel about myself"— a move that presents pressures to conform to particular templates of normative femininity as entirely an individual and personal matter. One woman becomes visibly upset at the revelation—whether because of the deliberate manipulation or because she believed the patch had worked and was some kind of answer for her, we do not know—but does quickly reach the desired teaching moment: "I don't need the patch." Together the reactions underscore the message that a lack of (body) confidence is all in our heads. The brutal effectivity of patriarchal culture with its normalized yet punitive judgment of women's bodies is instantly erased, and female body insecurity is resolutely cast as an individual phenomenon, a silly piece of self-sabotage with no foundation in reality. What's more, the film implies, women are clearly easily suggestible (rather than strong-minded) if a patch containing *nothing* can so dramatically change the way they feel about themselves. By contrast, the brand positions itself as knowledgeable and protective—better able to know and look after women's interests than they are themselves.

Blaming Women

As well as individualizing, trivializing, and repudiating the injurious nature of patriarchal culture, some body confidence messages go further in implicitly or explicitly blaming women for being held back in the workplace or society more generally. Such a position is the logical extension of the ideas discussed above: if the hurt or damage is so essentially trivial or superficial and can so easily be avoided or repaired by individual women, then it is not a stretch to suggest that women must be partly responsible via their current behavior. A commercial for Special K mentioned earlier in this chapter offers an example of this. The film opens with shots of tweets in which women have putatively said things such as "My face is so fat. Gross" or "I just wish I was skinnier"—each accompanied by a derogatory hashtag. The narrator's voice comes in over these images: "93% of women fat talk. We believe it is a barrier to managing their weight. It happens everywhere. Especially when shopping for clothes. To show how damaging words can be we created a store with actual fat talk." The film then cuts to an upscale clothes store called SHHH in which "fat talk" is reproduced on labels and posters on prominent display: "I'm feeling so disgusted about my figure at the moment," says one. "Cellulite is in my DNA," asserts another. The (apparently unwitting) female customers respond with horror: "What?!" "That's *awful*!" "What is this?" And then dawns the recognition: "I've said these things about myself." Suddenly the voices stop and the music changes as the following sentences are flashed on screen as if in a movie from the silent era: "You wouldn't talk this way to anyone else." Fresh screen: "So why do it to yourself." We cut back to the store and the women are now laughing and hugging each other: "I can't talk about myself that way anymore" and "we need to shut it down," they say, each mouthing "shhh." A final screen comes up: "LET'S SHHHHUT DOWN FAT TALK. Join us at fightfattalk.com."

This film, like so many other commercial body confidence messages discussed in this chapter, offers an acknowledgment of how widespread negative evaluations of women's appearance are and how shocking and painful they can be for women. In this advertisement, though, there is twist: all these hostile statements have been collected from women themselves, and moreover, they are things that women have said about *themselves* rather than others. Lest viewers have not understood the message, the voiceover spells it out for us unequivocally: "I do this to myself," "it's like bullying myself." Bullying may be bad behavior, but bullies are individuals, not structures or cultural forces. This is not a corporate conspiracy or a wider social or cultural problem, the ad seems to be saying—it is about women themselves being their own worst enemies, needing to "shhhh." The blame is resolutely located in women themselves and the gaze is turned away from a wider injurious culture—not to mention from the diet industry of which Special K forms a part.

This example is interesting for its attempt—seemingly—to critique "fat talk" as a form of discourse that hurts and harms women. For a diet cereal brand, it seems a staggeringly audacious move. However, rather than take on fat-shaming as a social or political issue, it upturns the critique in such a way as to foreground women's own role in "bullying" themselves. Fat-phobic discourse is not, it turns out, connected to a multibillion-dollar diet industry; it is something that women do to themselves. In such a way the ad trades on "feminist feeling," framing the brand as the feminist "activist" while actually blaming women for the problem.

Another attempt to enter this "political" terrain is Pantene's "Sorry Not Sorry" commercial, which builds on critiques of the differences in the way that women and men communicate.[83] Google's add-on "Just Not Sorry" is one example of an attempt to engage this issue: it works by flagging unassertive or apologetic phrases, using the familiar red squiggly underline to highlight the ways in which people (read women) undermine themselves in emails and presentations through unassertive and apologetic constructions (I'm just, I'm sorry, I'm no expert, etc.). The Pantene ad works the same territory, using a choppy documentary style to depict women in a range of different home and office situations, starting their sentences with "sorry": "Sorry, do you have a minute?," "Sorry, can I ask a stupid question?," saying sorry when someone bumps into them, and so on. Halfway through the ad, the footage stops and the following screen is displayed with bold black font on a white background: "DON'T BE SORRY." Then the upbeat music starts, just piano at first but becoming more rousing, and Pantene's brand colors and font appear with the words "Be strong and shine." As the music reaches its climax the original footage is replayed, but this time without the women apologizing. In the final scenes a young African American woman is shown pulling the duvet so she has most of it while sleepily saying, "Sorry not sorry" to her male partner, who accepts this with a smile, snuggling closer. The implication is clear: women can have so much more; it is not institutional structures in the workplace that prevent this, let alone men—on the contrary they would welcome it—but women whose own behavior and patterns (e.g., over-apologizing) holds them back from more power at work and equal relations within the home.

Disciplining Women

The final critical point we want to make concerns the new forms of discipline incited by the confidence cult. Consumer culture has always been intimately involved with the disciplining of women's bodies—whether fashion or advertising or magazines exhorting women to shape up, work out, and do better in everything from appearance to parenting to sexual techniques. What is striking, then, is the way that LYB messages operate as an apparent rupture with punitive appearance and standards, with an exhortation to self-love and self-care and to believe in one's own value no matter what. These commercial messages seem to represent a loosening of the grip of "the perfect"[84]—indeed an outright repudiation of perfection is a mainstay of such advertising, as we saw earlier in the chapter—for example in Missguided's campaigns and in Marc Jacobs's commercial for the perfume Perfect in which a range of models with different appearances implicitly reject the notion of singular perfection. It is not surprising, then, that such messages might be greeted with relief by consumers used to scrutiny, judgment, and a drive to be better. But how much do LYB campaigns really offer a break from discipline?

As an oblique way into addressing this question it is worth considering the distinctive tone of LYB advertising and the affects that it foregrounds. Vulnerability is central—one might say almost compulsory, as it authorizes the confidences messages and the implication that a self who hurts less is within reach. As we have noted, expressions of pain and insecurity are key features of commercial body confidence messages—to be glimpsed only briefly before a defiant riposte is blazoned: "My beauty. My say" (Dove); "From self-doubt to self-worth" (L'Oréal); "My can't stop me now hair" (Pantene). The list goes on. The tone is strikingly similar across brands and campaigns, drawing attention to vulnerability or insecurity—or at least its potential—to be replaced by defiant individualism. The target for this defiance is not specified—indeed the linguistic formulations are tightly scripted to impugn no particular actor or industry but rather to ask rhetorical questions such as "where is it written that" or "who says women can't be" or to simply claim that "things have changed," "this is now," or "this girl can." Despite the attempt to address a particular demographic, the messages are constructed in entirely individualistic terms, with foregrounding of the idea that this is about individual women rewriting their own rules, celebrating their own skin, their own body, their own hair—e.g., "My skin. My way" (Gillette Venus).

Launching a profound shift in its advertising to women and men in 2018, Gillette promoted the ideas behind its new campaign in a way that is emblematic:

> Remember these old Venus ads with one version of beautiful skin and one white bikini. Well, things have changed. It's time to do things a new way. Your way. Without conforming to conventions. So that your skin writes the rules. Because no one gets an opinion on how you live your life or why you shave. So we're shaving the hair that you have in all the places it grows. And we're bringing it to life with a female-led team in front of and behind the camera. We're celebrating every woman and her skin. You're in control of your skin—how it looks and how it feels. My skin, my way.[85]

Many of the lexical features of body confidence messages are here—choice, freedom, rewriting the rules, defying conventions—with images that reinforce these and a soundtrack of the song "Venus" (I'm your fire at your desire). Yet it is striking that Gillette is not trying to free women from pressures to remove body hair but rather attempting to *expand* the range of sites women normatively shave. As the voiceover declares, "We're shaving the hair you have in all the places it grows," we see a woman using a Venus razor to closely shave her forearm, revealing her sleeve tattoo. Here, then, signifiers of unconventional femininity are brought together with a strong sense of personal autonomy to adopt a practice that some would argue has been deeply symbolic of social control of women's bodies: removing body hair.[86] In this way a normative practice of femininity is being repackaged as rebellion—not challenged as a form of bodily discipline.

Indeed, LYB messages rarely represent a loosening of pressures around female bodily appearance, despite their defiant tone and apparent rejection of conventions and norms. Yet more troublingly still they also instigate an *additional* form of discipline—a psychological one in which there is pressure to be confident, empowered, and positive. This represents a move of discipline to women's psychic lives—you are exhorted not only to look good and "be your best self" in terms of outward appearance and self-presentation, but also to present as a happy, confident subject—"ready, steady, glow," as one skincare brand puts it.[87]

That is, body confidence messages require a transformation, and this time not only a physical "makeover." As we noted in the introduction to the book, the transformation imperative extends to subjectivity, to inner life, to the mindset and feelings of individuals addressed. Interestingly this "mental makeover" is offered as a promise of happiness and also as a corrective, a solution to "harmful" ways of relating to the female body. Yet it also requires rigorous self-discipline involving repression of negative feelings or reformulation of negative thoughts, affirmations of self-worth, and various practices of gratitude. We discuss these practices in more detail in chapter 3. It is worth noting how they have spread out across contemporary culture—for example, in fitness culture, with the hippest exercise spaces promoting euphoric feelings of self-love and capacity as you cycle, jog, or train.[88] "What problem did you bring to this class?" asks trainer/emcee Jono at 1Rebel gym. "What's the one thing stopping you being the best you can be?"[89] You "train" your body, but you also make over your mind and leave the class not only stronger and fitter but happier and more confident as well.

Conclusion

In this chapter we have looked at the growth of body confidence messages targeted at women, inciting feelings of self-worth and self-esteem. Arguing that body confidence is an assemblage or complex involving diverse kinds of actors—individuals, activists, charities, and NGOs, as well as governments and corporations—we have focused primarily on LYB advertising to raise some critical questions about the cult of body confidence. Love Your Body messages underscore neoliberal sensibilities around individualism, personal responsibility, and blame. This ubiquitous set of meanings suggests that low self-esteem and negative body image are trivial self-generated issues that can be easily overcome through injections of positive thinking (and purchase of a confidence-boosting product). The wider society is exculpated as women are exhorted to see any insecurities as their own problem—nothing to do with a cultural context that tells women they can never be pretty enough, thin enough, perfect enough.

This chapter has looked at charges of racism and fake diversity in relation to these commercial body confidence messages, while also noting the degree to which the visual habitat of representations is genuinely being expanded—to include people of different sizes and body shapes, those with visible disabilities, trans people, religious minorities, and women of color in wider representation. Unexpected benefits, alongside an exhilarating sense of the possibilities for change, may come from these new visibilities, yet at the same time we have shown how much of the newer postracial and woke campaigns come at the cost of hollowing out the meaning of these differences—as if they were simply individual variations rather than identities heavily freighted with power relations.[90]

Above all we have argued that these body confidence messages, while ostensibly warm, defiant, and positive, work to instill a new layer of discipline for women: a focus on making over subjectivity to become an upgraded confident subject. This task becomes a new responsibility, requiring an extensive array of psychological techniques and labor on the self. In the next chapter we turn to these as they relate to the world of work.

confidence at work

IN THE 2019 WORKPLACE COMEDY *Late Night*, the protagonist Molly (Mindy Kaling, who also wrote the screenplay), a young woman of Indian heritage, realizes her dream of working with the legendary Katherine Newbury (Emma Thompson), whose once popular show is losing ratings and is now threatened with being taken off the air. When she enters her new office, the first thing eager Molly does is to paste up a poster of a sunset with the inspirational caption "Never Give Up." Despite her male colleagues' dismissal of her as a "diversity hire," and in spite of the discrimination and humiliation she faces repeatedly, Molly transforms herself, by dint of extremely hard work, positive attitude, effervescent optimism, and determination, from an unglamorous chemical plant worker into a highly successful, confident, and admired screenwriter.

Molly is just one example of the proliferating iterations of a contemporary ideal circulating in popular culture, self-help literature, and workplace-related discourses: the resilient and confident professional woman who defies adversity by springing back from any crisis or challenge that she is forced to confront. The premise underpinning this ideal is that women suffer from an internal "defect," namely a "confidence gap," which holds them back in the world of work. Fixing this (supposed) internal barrier in women is constructed as key to their self-transformation and empowerment and to tackling gender inequality in the workplace more broadly. From the gender pay gap and the underrepresentation of women, particularly women of color, on company boards or in political parties, to the discrimination against women in hiring and promotion and the "leaky pipeline"—a popular metaphor used to describe women's dropping out of the workplace, and specifically in science, technology, engineering, and mathematics (STEM) fields—women's lack of confidence is frequently cited as the main contributor and addressing this deficit as the crucial solution. For example, gathering "ten years of insights into gender diversity," the 2017 *Women Matter* report issued by the global management consulting firm McKinsey highlights women's lack of confidence as one of the major obstacles to their success and progression and advocates the building of women's confidence as an urgent task for companies.[1] Indeed, self-confidence and resilience have become terms du jour in discussions about gender diversity (the term often favored over "equality") in the workplace.

As we show in this chapter, the turn to confidence has been instrumental in putting workplace gender inequality on the agenda and, as such, is to be welcomed. At the same time, however, it calls on women to turn inward to tackle their "inner" obstacles and turns away from critiques of work cultures and the broader structures that produce women's self-doubt and stand in the way of their progress and success in the workplace.

In what follows, we focus on two principal sites where exhortations to confidence are made repeatedly to women in the context of work: (1) advice literature on building and managing a career and (2) other contemporary discussions about women and work, for example in public appearances of successful businesswomen, in workplace advice, in work-related TED talks, and in career-related apps. We start the discussion by examining two of the women-and-work best sellers that appeared in the Anglo-American cultural landscape during the last ten years, which have been formative for the debate on workplace gender equality and confidence: Sheryl Sandberg's 2013 *Lean In* and the 2014 *New York Times* best seller *The Confidence Code*, authored by BBC World News America presenter Katty Kay and ABC News reporter Claire Shipman.[2] We show how these books promote ideas about women's obligation to work on themselves to overcome their confidence deficit, and how these ideas resonate in contemporary discussions about women and work, for example in media interviews with successful businesswomen, in official workplace communications, or in advice circulated during the COVID-19 pandemic in the wake of its dire impact on women's employment. We examine how a similar set of ideas is developed and transmuted in some more recent "feminist" advice best sellers and how these ideas have achieved the status of common sense with the proliferation of advice forums and outlets for women in the workplace. We highlight how, alongside exhortations about confidence at work, there are calls to embrace vulnerability in the workplace. However, we show that although a focus on vulnerability might appear to challenge some of the characteristics of the confidence imperative, ultimately it reinforces and props up the confidence cult, becoming its raison d'être.

Lean In and *The Confidence Code*:
Internalizing the Revolution, Blame, and Self-Work

In 2013, Facebook's chief operations officer (COO) Sheryl Sandberg published *Lean In: Women, Work, and the Will to Lead*—a business manual–style book that instantaneously topped the best-seller lists in both the US and Europe. This book, which to date has sold more than 4.2 million copies in thirty languages, played a pivotal role in revitalizing discussion about gendered power relations, the obstacles faced by women in the workplace, and why women still find it difficult to enjoy successful careers while raising children. Sandberg used the book as a launchpad for LeanIn.org, a nonprofit foundation that partners with corporations to provide advice and support strategies for women's empowerment and professional advancement. *Lean In*'s core ideas have been adopted widely by corporations (e.g., KPMG, McKinsey, PwC) to justify entire strategies, programs, and approaches geared toward "gender diversity" in the workplace, and individuals and groups both within and outside the workplace have appropriated Sandberg's feminist manifesto, as evidenced, for example, by the proliferation of "Lean In" circles and similar women's groups across the world.[3]

Lean In's ideas and terminology also reverberate in many popular representations of professional women who are shown to "kick ass" (e.g., *The Good Wife*'s lead character Alicia Florrick, *Scandal*'s Olivia Pope) and to "sit at the table," as Sandberg's much-cited metaphor promulgates.[4] Even in Disney's 2016 box office record-breaker *Zootopia* (*Zootropolis* in the UK), the lead character Judy Hopps literally climbs up the table to get herself noticed and asserts herself to work on resolving a major case of fourteen missing mammals. Similarly, in the 2019 film *Late Night* mentioned at the start of this chapter, at the first writers' meeting there is no seat for the new "diversity hire" Molly, so she has to squat on an upturned trash can—claiming in a stereotypically female self-belittling and apologetic fashion, "It's more comfortable than a chair!" However, by the end of the film, Molly is Sandberg's ideal Leaner In, occupying a prominent seat at the table.

Drawing extensively on her personal experience as a successful professional woman and mother, and interweaving personal anecdotes with positive psychology and cognitive science studies, in Lean In Sandberg seeks to spotlight the "external barriers erected by society" impeding women's success and progress in the workplace.[5] She discusses how women's work and family decisions are influenced by social norms, pressures, familial expectations, and workplace norms. For example, Sandberg highlights the need to design and implement organizational changes aimed at enhancing gender diversity in the workplace and to challenge gender stereotypes and develop alternative images of female success.[6] Relatedly, in 2014, LeanIn.org partnered with Getty Images to curate the "Lean In Collection," an online gallery that "set out to establish a new visual paradigm for women, work, and the family across media and advertising."[7]

However, although Lean In discusses some structural issues such as childcare costs, the pay gap, and gender stereotypes that need to be tackled, as implied by its title and as has been pointed out by various critics, Sandberg's book is fundamentally a call to middle-class white women as individuals to "forge a path through the obstacles, and achieve their full potential," by asserting themselves and making themselves noticeable.[8] Crucially, the ultimate onus is on women as individuals to change their thinking, feelings, and behavior. As Catherine Rottenberg notes, drawing on Sara Ahmed, Lean In advocates individualistic definitions of progress and success, which are inseparable from the historic privileging of heterosexual conduct, whiteness, and middle-classness.[9] This is manifested vividly in the visual gallery "Lean In Collection." Caroline West discusses how most of the photographs in the collection depict individual women, in predominantly corporate settings, happily and seamlessly combining mothering and paid work.[10] The photos, West argues, idealize a concept of female empowerment that is steeped in neoliberal rationality, focusing almost exclusively on "undertaking strategies of self-investment and entrepreneurship for thriving and surviving."[11]

Fundamentally, Lean In calls on women to "internalize the revolution" (the title of the book's first chapter), that is, to internalize the political project of challenging gender inequality in the workplace by treating both the problem and its solutions as personal, individualized, and psychologically based.

Thus, for example, Sandberg admits in the book to having suffered a "distorted" view of herself and struggled "to shake [off] feelings of self-doubt."[12] She then shows how they were resolved through a behavioral program geared toward overcoming self-doubt and "impostor syndrome" and through the building of self-belief, confidence, and assertiveness.[13] Although elsewhere in the book Sandberg refers to men's confidence as unjust(ified), she does not suggest how it could or should be challenged. It is women and women only who are positioned as responsible for both the act of distortion—self-damage that derives from doubting their ability—and its correction.

Ideas about women's self-doubt and low self-esteem, and the urgent need to address these problems via individualized programs and strategies, have gained huge traction in workplace-related discussions in recent years.[14] For instance, on the World Economic Forum's website, American investment banker Kathleen Murphy writes: "Too often, women have a confidence gap that makes them pause and slow down while men dive in and learn as they go. Just go for it!" Meanwhile, Cathy Engelbert, CEO of Deloitte, exhorts women to "raise your hand, take risks, and don't fear failure—it's one of the biggest impediments to success."[15] Various programs and initiatives designed to train women to overcome their impostor syndrome and low self-esteem are being recommended for and rolled out by corporations and organizations as part of their gender diversity programs.[16] Notably, exhortations to women to boost their confidence at work became particularly popular in the wake of COVID-19's devastating impact on women's economic security and mental health. "As the pandemic continues to overburden women and negatively impact their self-esteem, there are fortunately some simple steps that can go a long way for providing a boost of confidence in these dark times," reads one article, followed by a list of individualized tips such as "practice self-compassion" and "show resilience."[17] "Do deep belly breathing," "listen to a meditation or hypnosis audio on confidence," and make "a confidence-boosting, stress-busting audio to listen to before bed,"[18] reads another article counseling women on how to regain their confidence and calm after losing their jobs or when managing the pressures of working from home while caring for children. The emphasis in these and similar examples is exclusively on the harnessing of individual resources to overcome stress, inequality, and injustice, not on challenging the conditions that created them, such as workplaces' and governments' lack of or limited support during the pandemic. Confidence coaching, which before the pandemic was already a booming global industry with numerous coaches, practices, and training enterprises, became a popular source of advice for women on how to regain or boost their confidence during the pandemic.[19] The UK Life Coach Directory, for example, has noted a 74 percent increase in users searching for information on "confidence" since the onset of working from home in March 2020. "Have you thought how you would like to emerge from the pandemic?" asks one confidence coach on LinkedIn, acknowledging that women have been disproportionately affected by COVID-19 and offering prospective clients training that will help them build their confidence and credibility in the post-pandemic world.[20] While many of these programs and texts nod at some of the structural factors conditioning women's "confidence gap" or confidence loss, they essentially focus on the individual and how she can self-transform into an assertive and confident worker.

The 2014 best-selling self-help/advice book *The Confidence Code* is another important reference point in the turn to confidence in the work domain.[21] Like *Lean In*, it presents women's development of self-confidence and obligation to change their psyches and behavior as crucial for individual self-achievement and career success and for facilitating the greater "revolutionary" goals of social equality and diversity. The book's premise is that there is a "crisis" that is peculiar to women, the product of self-doubt and perfectionism, which is holding them back in public life. It is understood in both *The Confidence Code* and *Lean In* as referring almost exclusively to women's failure to achieve senior positions in the corporate world of work—an exclusion reflected also by the visual narrative of female empowerment on the "Lean In Collection."[22]

The Confidence Code's starting point is that "the reality looks foreboding."[23] It offers a "pragmatic" and fatalist view that masculine domination and gender inequality are virtually impossible to challenge at the structural level, and thus, the only way to challenge them effectively is for women to internalize both responsibility for the problem and the program of action required to resolve it. The authors use the metaphor of women's "internal shortage" of confidence to suggest that, like any other consumer commodity which one might be short of, it can be purchased. "It may be unevenly and unfairly distributed, but it's straightforward to acquire," the authors write.[24] The interest is not in why this "commodity" is unequally and unjustly distributed—let alone what can be done to redress its distribution. Rather, it is the "quick fixes" that will enable its "straightforward" acquisition, for example, practicing "power positions" such as sitting up straight, getting a good night's sleep, exercising, meditating, and expressing gratitude.[25] Six years after its publication, *The Confidence Code* gained renewed popularity during the COVID-19 pandemic and the aftermath of the killing of George Floyd, evidenced by the launch in October 2020 of an online course for women that draws on the best-selling book. "Checking in with yourself and maintaining morale is vital any year, but can feel like a herculean task in 2020," explains a promotional article for the course.[26] "Your Confidence Code" includes thirteen video lessons, eleven video exercises, personal interviews, and action steps built for "embracing ourself and casting out insecurities." As in body confidence messages discussed in chapter 1, here, too, the response to social injustice is to work on the self (enabled by purchasing a $149 online course) rather than working on challenging the injustice—for example, governments', workplaces', and societal policies' failure to protect and support women during the pandemic.

A similar construction of women as confidence-lacking subjects who can and should adopt prescribed strategies and exercises to overcome this flaw can be found in various workplace communications. For example, on the website of the global leading specialist recruitment consultancy and outsourcing provider Robert Walters, which prides itself on "empowering women in the workplace," women are offered "top tips for career confidence" and advised to "build your image to yourself and to others as someone who is prepared to take risks and wants to develop new skills."[27] Similarly, the Human Resources website HR Daily Advisor exhorts women to "remove qualifiers from your speech," "own and defend your point of view," "stop waiting for the perfect moment," and "articulate your differentiations" in order to build their confidence in the workplace.[28]

We see these types of solutions being recited in a variety of other media and genres. Newspapers and women's magazines frequently publish tips for women on how to boost their confidence at work and offer confidence-assessment quizzes.[29] Apps such as *Clementine* and *Sanity & Self*, which target women, offer sets of tools, exercises, and daily reminders aimed at helping them to achieve positive self-regard and self-belief.[30] In her highly popular TED talk *Your Body Language Shapes Who You Are*, Harvard Business School social psychologist Amy Cuddy uses the image of none other than Wonder Woman, recommending the famous pose—arms akimbo, feet wide apart, and staring confidently forward. She explains: "Before you go into the next stressful evaluative situation, for two minutes, try doing this [practicing power poses], in the elevator, in a bathroom stall, at your desk behind closed doors. That's what you want to do. Configure your brain to cope the best in that situation. Get your testosterone up. Get your cortisol down. Don't leave that situation feeling like 'oh, I didn't show them who I am.' Leave that situation feeling like, 'I really feel like I got to say who I am and show who I am.'"[31]

What emerges clearly from all these examples is that there is a paradox: for women to gain confidence they need to work continuously on its manufacture through self-governance and self-improvement. Thus, their confidence is contingent always on their conscious and intense labor, what Micki McGee describes as "a cycle where the self is not improved but endlessly belaboured."[32] This labor-intensive manufactured confidence is contrasted to what *Lean In* and *The Confidence Code* authors describe as their male counterparts' "effortless" and "honest" confidence.[33] "Despite being high achievers, even experts in the field, women can't seem to shake the sense that it is only a matter of time until they are found out for who they really are—impostors with limited skills or abilities," Sandberg writes in *Lean In*.[34] Thus, even women in positions of power such as former International Monetary Fund (IMF) managing director Christine Lagarde, whom Kay and Shipman interviewed for their book, or celebrities like Emma Watson and Kate Winslet, who confessed to having dealt with "impostor syndrome" and successfully acquired confidence, must carry on self-managing and governing themselves or risk "running out" of its supply.[35]

While these and similar texts are cast as empathetic "feminist" endeavors by women to help other women, they problematically, if inadvertently, locate the blame for gender inequality in the workplace in women's psyches. Echoing the tendency to blame women for "bullying" themselves in body confidence messages (discussed in chapter 1), in *The Confidence Code* Kay and Shipman go to some length to discuss what they call women's "self-inflicted confidence wounds."[36] These include women's defective desire to be liked and to please others, their "horror of being criticized," and their excessive rumination and self-beratement.[37] For a book purporting to boost women's self-confidence, *The Confidence Code* is full of quite harsh observations, which infantilize and belittle women and reiterate the message that women have only themselves to blame. For example, the authors write, "Part of the problem is we [women] can't make sense of the rules," "all too often, women don't see, can't even envision, what's possible," "our own obsession with our physical appearance drains our confidence," and "a woman's brain is not her friend when it comes to confidence."[38] A cursory look at current popular discussions about women and work, for example on LinkedIn, websites related to mothers and work, and women's magazines, reveals how these ideas have achieved the status of common sense in this domain.[39]

Girl, Stop Apologizing: Stepping Up the Confidence Cult at Work

A search of Amazon.com's Best Sellers list in the category Women and Business shows that alongside *Lean In*, which continues to be in the top-ten list, there are strikingly similar titles that reiterate and perpetuate the idea that women suffer from a confidence-related crisis whose solution is individualized and psychologized. Among these titles are *Brave, Not Perfect*, a book marketed as the "new Lean In" by the founder and CEO of the American nonprofit Girls Who Code, Reshma Saujani; *Do It Scared: Finding the Courage to Face Your Fears, Overcome Adversity, and Create a Life You Love* by Ruth Soukup; and *Get Over Your Damn Self: The No-BS Blueprint to Building a Life-Changing Business* by Romi Neustadt.[40]

Topping this list (number one, two, and three for the Audible, hardcover, and Kindle editions respectively) is *Girl, Stop Apologizing*, by American blogger, entrepreneur, motivational speaker, and self-confessed "proud feminist" Rachel Hollis.[41] As implied by its title and like other titles in the genre, the book calls on women to turn inward to overcome their apologetic self and build their self-confidence, and it centers this project on working on the self by self-monitoring, constant calculation, and cultivation of an entrepreneurial spirit. However, the 2019 Women and Business Amazon number 1 best seller also lays bare three additional significant aspects of confident exhortations to women in the context of work, which resonate with the confidence culture more broadly: (1) positive affect and the prohibition of negative feelings; (2) normalizing struggle; and (3) obligatory vulnerability. In what follows, we look at each of these aspects as manifest in Hollis's best seller and in wider contemporary discourses about women and work.

Positive Affect and the Prohibition of Negative Feelings

Girl, Stop Apologizing is marked by a particular emotional tone that is emblematic of the confidence cult more broadly. Peppered with inspirational and motivational aphorisms (e.g., "you are enough," "you are made to have the dreams you're afraid of having," "be the kind of woman who understands that she was made for more," and "be the kind of woman who never asks permission to be herself"), positive psychology, and cheerful anecdotes, the book emphasizes positivity (the title of one of its chapters), optimism, gratitude, happiness, feeling good, and doing what you love.[42] The reader's goal, Hollis states from the outset, should be to "cultivate new positive characteristics in yourself."[43] Crucially, this emotionalism and inspirational discourse involve systematically regulating and denouncing "negative" feelings such as hurt, grudge, bitterness, sadness, despair, and (political) anger. "I am one of the happiest gals you know because I choose it every single day," Hollis writes in her chapter on positivity; "I regulate my thoughts because thoughts control feelings."[44] For example, Hollis tells her readers how she knowingly censored herself from writing on her blog about topics she knew would make people angry, replacing them instead with "what people loved."[45] She encourages the reader to embrace the idea that she can want things for herself and need not justify her dreams to anyone. However, there is a profound caveat to this incitement: "I don't mean that you go around middle fingers up, like a Beyoncé song. I don't mean that you turn bitter and rude and shove your goals into other people's faces to prove a point."[46] Thus, Hollis explicitly exhorts women to self-police and censor their negative feelings. Against Beyoncé's putative bitterness and rudeness—a textbook iteration of the pathologized "angry Black woman"—Hollis establishes the desirable femininity as *not* angry, *not* rude, *not* bitter, and, implicitly, *not* Black. This chimes closely with Lisa Blackman's observation in relation to self-help media culture: Hollis appears as the postfeminist woman who relentlessly works on her self-confidence and achievements in her relationships and the workplace, while the stories of her "sisters"—"bitter" and "rude" women of color like Beyoncé—"who cannot or who are unable to achieve such success stand as cautionary tales, marked out as pathological and seen to lack the psychological and emotional capacities to effect their own self-transformation."[47]

On the other side of the Atlantic, the highly successful UK business executive and mother of nine Helena Morrissey promotes a very similar message in her best-selling 2018 book, *A Good Time to Be a Girl*.[48] While the book's subtitle, "Don't Lean In, Change the System," positions it explicitly as a critique of Sandberg's individualized focus and lack of attention to the structural, and while it does indeed to some extent acknowledge the structural sources of gender inequality in the business world and the need to tackle them, in most other respects it fails to break out of the confidence culture paradigm. Dispositions such as resilience, boldness, and confidence are presented as essential for success in the workplace and for achieving the greater good of gender diversity (rather than equality) in business, and Morrissey recites familiar mantras such as being "comfortable in being fully myself," letting go of perfectionism, and "not let[ting] any preconceptions put you off from doing what you really want to do, or in any way dent your ambitions and expectations."[49] Also, like other confidence cult authors such as Rachel Hollis, Morrissey cajoles women to speak up and be bold but "not belligerently or militantly."[50] Rather, she stresses the importance of eschewing negative thoughts, practicing positive thinking, and feeling happy, optimistic, and confident.[51]

Hence, it transpires that for Morrissey, "changing the system" (according to the book's subtitle) and "redefining power" ultimately are about women changing their leadership styles and attitudes by "tap[ping] into their own, feminine brand of power."[52] She recognizes that she could be accused of gender essentialism but nevertheless advocates that to achieve a "broader definition of power," women should capitalize on their uniquely feminine qualities of "empathy, social sensitivity, collaboration and gentleness."[53]

The calls from successful and powerful women like Hollis and Morrissey for women in the workplace to embrace positivity and denounce negative feelings and thoughts have gained significant support from cognitive science studies. For example, writing in the *Financial Times*, American cognitive scientist and the president of Barnard College Sian Leah Beilock encourages women to work to overcome their insecurities by "lift[ing] ourselves up and remind[ing] ourselves in very specific terms of what we have accomplished," "spend[ing] a few minutes jotting down your thoughts before a high-pressure situation," "keeping a running list of achievements and the positive feedback you receive," turning "a negative ('I'm so worried about this project') into a positive ('I am so excited to ace this project')," and "keeping a sense of humour and a positive outlook even in the most stressful or frustrating situations."[54]

In this way, cognitive science, positive psychology, and emotionalism mutually reinforce the encouragement to women to constantly regulate their negative thoughts and feelings and replace them with positive ones. Constant self-regulation of one's thoughts and feelings is enshrined explicitly as a positive choice and a desirable practice to adopt, deriving its authority from the "psychological complex" and the consolidation of regimes of mental measurement, classifying, calculating, and making intelligible one's traits, desires, anxieties, and feelings.[55]

Normalizing Struggle

Lean In has been attacked for failing to criticize the long-hours corporate culture and for encouraging women to find better ways of adjusting to, rather than changing, the corporate game.[56] This critique applies to the confidence culture more broadly, which, as we have argued, proposes ways in which women can positively and constructively develop strategies to change themselves *within* the existing capitalist and corporate realities they face rather than disrupting and seeking to change those very realities. However, in *Girl,*

Chapter Two

Stop Apologizing and wider contemporary discussions about women and work we see a further alarming step in this direction. In Hollis's book we note not only absence of any criticism of the always-on work culture but also its downright glorification. To realize her dream, Hollis tells her readers that she gave up watching evening television during the week with her new husband, worked through every weekend, and, to add to her already-inflated working hours, did several other jobs for free. "Do you think it wasn't discouraging to be treated badly when I was working for free? Of course it was. But, dude, look where it got me!" she declares self-congratulatorily. "I'm editing this chapter on the stairs of an overcrowded gate at the Toronto airport," Hollis writes. "I'm choosing to sacrifice some rest time in order to make this [her book] happen."[57] For Hollis, these long hours are temporary, self-chosen, goal-oriented, and have a tangible result. For the vast majority of other women caught up in long-hours cultures at work, overwork and its attendant exhaustion are simply a routine feature of their lives—and there is not a best-selling book at the end of it to help sweeten the pill.

This "new normal" of working life is perpetuated in wider discourses and representations of women, work, and confidence.[58] In the popular television series *The Good Wife*, for example, the construction of the lead female character, Alicia Florrick (Julianna Margulies), as a confident, assertive professional woman who "kicks ass" is inseparable from the valorization of her competitive, long-hours, and highly demanding job.[59] On LinkedIn, users (especially millennial women) frequently boast about working almost around the clock without a break; "I developed a workaholic habit . . . 17 hours a day, most days, but I had the MOST rewarding years of my entire life" is a typical comment. Less celebratory accounts are found in proliferating posts by women academics, doctors, and others detailing the health and emotional costs of punishing work schedules and an always-on work culture.[60]

Sometimes this "new normal" is framed in generational terms. On the one hand, we frequently hear about how millennials push for work-life balance and are not willing to put up with the always-on taxing work cultures that previous generations supposedly accepted and propelled. On the other hand, there is a wealth of representations and self-representations, like the LinkedIn posts, that glorify working around the clock as part of a contemporary ideal of the millennial professional woman. An ad by the online freelance marketplace Fiverr prominently displayed in 2017 on New York City subway cars shows a young and beautiful woman staring straight at the camera, and below her chin the text reads: "You eat a coffee for lunch. You follow through on your follow through. Sleep deprivation is your drug of choice. You might be a doer." The ad is part of Fiverr's campaign In Doers We Trust, which enshrines always-on "doers," many of whom are signified as women, and, as Jia Tolentino poignantly observes, dresses up the cannibalistic nature of the gig economy (and contemporary work culture more generally) as aesthetic.[61] Still a further manifestation of this new ideal was seen in 2021, when in the midst of a devastating pandemic and global recession that have disproportionately affected women and people of color, the Super Bowl commercial for the website builder Squarespace exhorted women to work on a "side hustle" at the end of the traditional working day. "Working 5 to 9 . . . A whole new way to make a livin' . . . 5 to 9 / You keep working working working," Dolly Parton's singing accompanies this commercial, in a bitter twist on her original "9-to-5" hit and the 1978 film comedy of the same name.[62]

In Sheryl Sandberg's second best seller, *Option B: Facing Adversity, Building Resilience, and Finding Joy*, which she coauthored with motivational psychologist Adam Grant, the authors describe the approach of harnessing this "new normal" as "normalizing struggle."[63] It is a method to tolerate or indeed embrace a landscape that is unequal and insecure by design, through the systematic individualized favoring of "positive" feelings and outlawing of "negative" feelings and affect.[64] Instead of questioning the neoliberal order that created the struggle and pain borne by its subjects—having to work seventeen hours a day, being in precarious employment, being constantly sleep deprived, et cetera—this mode of apprehending and being in the world encourages acceptance of the existing order as the only possible order, or the best of all possible orders, and harnesses individual resources to survive in neoliberalism with resilience and "courage" (the latter term being popularized by Brené Brown, whose ideas we discuss in the next section). At a time of rising precarity and inequality, when women are being disproportionately affected and injured by recession and financial insecurity, and amid evidence of increasing stress levels in the workplace and the detrimental effects of the always-on work culture on workers, especially women, such contemporary representations of women and work are teaching women that insecurity, exploitation, and being "always on" are normal and inevitable.[65]

Many have raised hopes that COVID-19, which forced millions of workers to work from home, will propel a major shift away from the toxic always-on work culture. At the same time, mounting evidence shows that the "new normal" of COVID-19 has been particularly punitive for women and especially mothers. School closures, overburdened health-care systems, and social distancing measures have increased many women's unpaid care and domestic load at home, which, in turn, has made them less able to balance these responsibilities with paid work. More caring work at home has also meant that more women have been forced to scale back, leave, or seriously consider leaving the workforce. Simultaneously, women, and particularly women of color, have been fired or furloughed at a higher rate than men during the pandemic, stalling their careers and jeopardizing their financial security.[66] In addition, Black women—who already faced more barriers to advancement than most other employees—are now coping with the disproportionate impact of the pandemic and racial violence on the Black, Asian, and minority ethnic community. On the one hand, the convergence of the pandemic and the resurgence of Black Lives Matter and other racial protests in 2020 has contributed to challenging the existing order. We hear more and more calls to refuse racial and patriarchal capitalism and to harness "negative" feelings such as anger. Yet, as noted earlier, the extraordinary events of 2020 have provided a fertile ground for the fortification and expansion of the confidence culture and its mantras. An example of this can be seen in a *Boston Globe* article discussing the implications of the "she-cession" following the COVID-19 pandemic. "To the women who are dropping out: No apologies and no regrets," the article states. It goes on: "Consider this an invitation to the COVID-19 No Apologies Tour. Women who leave the workforce or reduce their hours because of the pandemic should not feel guilty about hitting the pause button. They need to do what's best for them and for their families. And when these women are ready to return to work, they should come back with confidence."[67] A profound crisis caused by government failure, which sees mothers leaving the workforce and scaling back in droves, is cast as an opportunity to press the "pause button," which women ought to embrace unapologetically and from which they will emerge "with confidence."

Obligatory Vulnerability

The implicit but consistent message in all the examples discussed so far is that insecurity is abhorrent and thus must be covered up by manufacturing confidence. However, alongside these incitements a seemingly reverse move has emerged in recent years, and markedly in the context of the difficult events of 2020, toward embracing vulnerability and foregrounding insecurity and pain. Paradoxically, in workplace-related discussions vulnerability is seen increasingly as advantageous and even mandatory to enable confident and successful performance, especially (although not exclusively) for women. Business leaders such as David Solomon, CEO and chairman of the investment bank Goldman Sachs, and Apple's CEO Tim Cook have encouraged their leaders to "be more vulnerable," to share their personal lives and "put themselves out there a lot more than they probably are comfortable doing."[68] Being what leadership coach Patrick Williams calls "courageously vulnerable at work" is now regarded as crucial for companies' health and productivity— a view supported by a stream of management and business studies.[69] "Today's most successful companies," writes Williams, "know there must be an outlet for emotional vulnerability in the workplace."[70]

While male business leaders like David Solomon and Tim Cook have been vocal in their calls to business leaders and employees to embrace vulnerability, it is powerful women who seem most ready to demonstrate this publicly. As Catherine Bennett observes, it has now become public ritual for a successful woman to admit to her inner insecurity and confess her self-doubt.[71] Bennett notes that the public self-abasing accounts from powerful women such as Michelle Obama, Arianna Huffington, Lena Dunham, Tina Fey, Maya Angelou, Lady Gaga, and Emma Watson have found a more receptive than critical audience. For example, in promoting her *New York Times* best seller *The Moment of Lift*, which focuses on women's empowerment, Melinda Gates, co-chair of the Bill and Melinda Gates Foundation, shares stories of her "crises of confidence, imposter syndrome, sweaty palms" on multiple platforms.[72] In a *Teen Vogue* op-ed, for instance, Gates recounts how because of her severe impostor syndrome, she once asked her husband, Microsoft founder Bill Gates, to leave the room before she gave her lecture.[73] Similarly, in a meeting of executives of the multinational professional services network Pricewaterhouse-Coopers (PwC) discussing diversity and inclusion in the workplace, partner Lisa Feigen Dugal and senior manager Kyla-Gaye Barrett talked about the crucial role of making oneself vulnerable in order to be a good manager. To demonstrate this, they shared personal details about their respective identities as a Jewish American woman and an immigrant from Jamaica, confessing to their difficulty in exposing these personal aspects before.[74]

Similar confessions of confidence crises and vulnerability can be found in the plethora of women and work advice books and memoirs. In *Girl, Stop Apologizing*, for example, Hollis goes to some lengths to retell early life traumas from being bullied, feeling ugly and unworthy, and giving birth. She invites the reader to check her Instagram account for photos of her "preconfident" vulnerable self and recounts in detail the story of her 52-hour agonizing labor.[75] In *Lean In*, Sandberg alludes to suffering some insecurities earlier in her career, while in her later best seller, *Option B*, which is grounded in Sandberg's experience of grief, she discloses this vulnerability in a highly confessional fashion. Thus, if only a few years ago we wrote, "If confidence is the new sexy, then insecurity (in women) is undoubtedly the new ugly," we seem now to be witnessing another turn where confidence *is* the new sexy while vulnerability simultaneously is the new beautiful and allows for confident women to be "relatable."[76]

There appears to be a curious turn from the "self-made woman" of the late 1990s and early 2000s and the millennial Wonder Woman (Amy Cuddy), who was encouraged to airbrush her insecurities and reframe them as confidence and resilience, to celebrating a female subject who foregrounds her pain and vulnerability as a vital asset for success at work.[77] Interestingly, users on the professional and employment-oriented platform LinkedIn in the past tended to publish posts presenting their polished, confident selves. Now more and more individuals are publishing accounts highlighting their vulnerabilities— a trend that achieved even greater prominence in the wake of COVID-19 and the aftermath of the killing of George Floyd. For instance, it has become quite common for LinkedIn users to publicize accounts of the personal hurt and difficulties experienced in their workplace, including mental health problems and traumatic experiences related to racism, abuse, depression, and burnout. These posts often conclude with empowering lessons the poster gained from her difficult experiences and are sometimes accompanied by an inspirational quote or a photo of the poster in a confident "power pose" of the kind taught by Amy Cuddy. Rather than being contradictory, confidence and vulnerability seem to have become complementary and mutually reinforcing of the ideal feminine professional self.

Notably in these and many other contemporary accounts, specifically those related to women in corporate and entrepreneurial careers, vulnerability and trauma act to authenticate and authorize the speaker and her achievements. This is illustrated vividly in the following extract from *Girl, Stop Apologizing*, in which Hollis addresses her reader as a friend: "I am your friend, Rachel, and I am telling you that I walked through trauma and I walked through pain and I have been bullied and I have felt ugly and unworthy and not enough in a hundred different ways. And I have decided to reclaim my life. I have reclaimed it and fought back against the lies and the limiting beliefs over and over and over again. I have built on that strength by looking at what is true, not what is opinion. And you can too."[78] Hollis's book contains many such clichéd motivational statements ("reclaim your life," "fight back against limiting beliefs," etc.), yet it is Hollis's experience of vulnerability that seems to validate them and endow them with authenticity and authority. The same process of validation seems to be at work in public appearances of successful women such as Sheryl Sandberg and Melinda Gates, whose revelations of painful or difficult experiences grant them validity and justify their generic inspirational and motivational injunctions.

One of the most influential speakers and writers about vulnerability in the context of the workplace and more generally is Brené Brown—social work professor, best-selling author, and star of a highly popular TED talk and the 2019 Netflix program *The Call to Courage*. Brown promotes vulnerability as "the birthplace of innovation, creativity, and change" and calls on people to attend to their uncomfortable and difficult feelings and to cultivate a willingness to be seen by others in the face of uncertain outcomes.[79] For instance, about good leadership, Brown writes:

> We all come from hard stuff and have to wade through more of it during our entire lives. When we own these difficult stories and experiences, rumble with them, and address them, we can write a new ending—an ending that includes how we're going to use what we've survived to be more compassionate and empathic leaders.
>
> When we deny our stories of struggle—when we pretend everything is ok when we're really in deep struggle—the hard stories own us. They own us, and they drive our behavior, emotions, thinking, and leading.[80]

Brown's ideas have been adopted widely and have popularized the notion that work cultures and leaders need to nourish vulnerability in themselves and their employees. This includes, for example, encouraging difficult, uncomfortable conversations with colleagues or when recruiting, choosing candidates who exhibit a willingness to be vulnerable by confessing to mistakes in their interviews, admitting to potentially embarrassing hobbies, taking risks, and embracing hard conversations. Her emphases on "having difficult conversations" and embracing courage, shame, and vulnerability have been frequently appropriated in discussions (including in her own media, e.g., her podcasts) about racism in the workplace and society more widely, following the George Floyd killing and the reinvigoration of Black Lives Matter in 2020.[81]

On the one hand, the turn to vulnerability appears to challenge the confidence cult. As implied by the title of one of Brown's best sellers, *The Gifts of Imperfection*, vulnerability is a response to the unviability and the tyranny of the perfect.[82] Brown's "list of core emotions," which she cajoles people to "wade through," includes many of the "negative" feelings that the confidence cult disavows, such as anger, anxiety, blame, disappointment, disgust, guilt, humiliation, regret, sadness, shame, and vulnerability.[83] Indeed, the incitement to present oneself as vulnerable, "to show up and be seen when we have no control over the outcome" as Brown defines it in her TED talk, seems to refute the injunction to present oneself as confident and perfect. If the earlier iteration of the confident woman treats failure as "a temporary obstacle to be overcome," by contrast, the contemporary modern confident woman is encouraged to embrace failure as her "most powerful path to learning if [she is] willing to choose courage over comfort."[84] While the imperative to be confident is predicated on self-responsibilization, self-governance, and repudiation of dependence, the invitation to be vulnerable ostensibly is an invitation to be dependent and to rely on others in the face of failure, discomfort, and difficulty.

On the other hand, this new normative ideal of vulnerability seems to be deeply implicated in and to bolster the confidence cult. First, the call to embrace vulnerability furthers the imperative to look inward and work on the self. The focus is largely on how individuals in (and outside) the workplace ought to deal with failure, adversity, and problems, by relying on individualized and psychological techniques. By and large, the incitement to be seen in one's vulnerability is not accompanied by a parallel call to rely on others and invest in developing a community, nor by discussion of and investment in structures that support and protect employees. Second, there is very limited if any discussion of the structural sources of vulnerability, crucially poverty, ill health, racism, and sexism, or of the collective and structural solutions needed to address them. Rather, the focus is almost exclusively on how high-powered individuals and particularly leaders (e.g., Brown's most recent study focuses on C-suite executives) can change their emotional and behavioral conduct, and not on how they can change the work structures they have designed and which they manage. Third, as Brown puts it, embracing vulnerability is about *being seen*. In other words, it is a performance. However, rather than demonstrating uninhibited vulnerability, good employees and leaders need to embrace a strategic and *controlled* performance of vulnerability. This point is vividly illustrated by the film *Late Night*, discussed earlier: Several times throughout the film we see Molly hurt, humiliated, and dispirited by her treatment at work. We see her breaking down in tears but receiving no support and having to hide her pain. Becoming the ideal professional woman means using her vulnerability strategically and in a willing and controlled fashion (Annalise Keating in the television drama *How to Get Away with Murder* is another example of a professional woman who uses vulnerability skillfully). Fourth, vulnerability is instrumentalized into "lessons" that are decontextualized from concrete contexts and is translated into inspirational "magic'" solutions. Indicatively, Brown's popular website displays downloadable printouts, quote cards, and flashcard definitions with inspirational and motivational adages. Fifth, although "negative" feelings are allowed, the injunction is to "wade into" them in order to overcome them, use them as an "opportunity for growth," and produce alternative "positive" feelings.[85] For instance, alongside Brown's list of core emotions, which consists predominantly of "negative" feelings, her weekly newsletter entitled "TGIF" (an acronym for Trust, Gratitude, Inspiration, and Fun) is aimed at helping people cultivate these positive emotions in their everyday lives, in very similar ways to those techniques promoted by the confidence culture and the happiness industry. This is demonstrated in Brown's contribution to the September 2019 *Vogue* special issue "Forces for Change"—a confidence-cult textbook par excellence, which was edited by Meghan Markle. In it, Brown confesses the hurt and shame she has experienced from the social media vitriol. She uses her confession, which is accompanied by two photos in which she appears happy and confident, to reiterate her self-confidence mantra: "Owning our story, owning what we believe, and loving ourselves is the bravest thing we'll ever do. Do the world a favour: speak your truth. Follow your wild heart."[86] Similarly, Melinda Gates uses her vulnerability confessions to urge her young readers to "use fear as fuel. Embrace that jittery feeling and reframe it for yourself as the incredible, empowering feeling of pushing yourself to grow."[87]

Finally, the commandment to harness vulnerability and its endorsement are profoundly gendered, just like the confidence culture. As we noted earlier, in discourses about the workplace it is women who seem to be both the prime addressees *and* enthusiastic recipients of the call to embrace vulnerability. Moreover, the meaning and valence of vulnerability change depending upon who is expressing it. As Sarah Banet-Weiser observes, in the current cultural and political moment, women's public accounts of their vulnerability (of sexual abuse, but not only) are situated and authorized differently from statements of powerful white men confessing their vulnerability and victimhood.[88] Expressions of vulnerability by women can be readily dismissed as subscribing to narratives of "victimhood," while similar accounts by men may betoken a highly valued "sensitivity." Recent research shows how performances of vulnerability by young men may be used to display "hipster" credentials of sophistication, "wokeness," and anti-sexism while working to distance individuals from more disparaged or even "toxic" versions of masculinity.[89]

Conclusion

The focus on confidence has been central to putting workplace gender inequality on the agenda and has inspired and empowered many women in their professional lives. At the same time, as we have demonstrated in this chapter, this emphasis turns systematically away from critiques of contemporary work and the broader neoliberal cultures and structures that produce women's self-doubt and obstacles to their progress and success. Furthermore, while these discussions seemingly address all women in the workplace, they are marked by a white, middle-class, and corporate bias and are implicated in the rise of what Dawn Foster calls a corporate "1% feminism."[90] Indeed, even the turn away from the tyranny of the perfect and the confident Wonder Woman toward the embrace of vulnerability and imperfection seems to be a site of privilege. After all, in times of such sharp and divisive inequalities, insecurity, and precarity, very few individuals can afford to be seen to be weak, vulnerable, and lacking control and to deliberately refuse the confidence imperative.

Even those women who can afford to be seen in their vulnerability are quick to contain, police, mute, and outlaw these "negative" feelings. Brené Brown's immensely popular incitements to embrace vulnerability at work and their many iterations, for example in advice literature and the mediated appearances of successful women in the domain of work confessing to their impostor syndrome and vulnerabilities, teach us that insecurity, inequality, and struggle are the "new normal" and that the best way to cope is by reframing them as an opportunity for growth. Thus, in a similar way to how women's anger is represented in popular culture and the media, even when unleashed, female vulnerability continues to be regulated carefully so as not to exceed the allowed "safe" level and ultimately to reinforce the confidence cult.[91]

We return to these critiques in the book's conclusion, where we show how some of the blind spots and weaknesses examined in this and other chapters in this book are addressed by contemporary cultural texts; how they open a space to think and act beyond the confines of the confidence cult, while at the same time even they continue to perpetuate some of its pitfalls.

confident relating

"WE WILL HELP YOU KICK UP YOUR CONFIDENCE," declares *Cosmopolitan*, promising to show us "How to fix your low sex drive: it's all about confidence."[1] *Glamour* offers to share "the art of perfecting sexual confidence and body positivity in the bedroom," while *EnFemenino*, a popular Spanish magazine, tells readers, "Be confident in yourself. Men love it! You cannot imagine how much it turns a guy on seeing that you manage confidently in bed . . . even if it's not true."[2]

Messages like this are ubiquitous today, particularly in media targeted at women, such as magazines, self-help books, blogs, and certain apps. In content focused on dating and intimate relationships, confidence has become a "commandment" and lack of it one of the chief obstacles that women are said to face in forming happy and successful relationships.[3] While magazines like *Cosmopolitan* were once well known for their frank sexual advice and tips on positions, toys, and "spicing up" your love life, in the contemporary mediascape this is joined by a focus on attitudes, feelings, and dispositions. "You know it on Insta as PMA (Positive Mental Attitude)," say typical articles, offering instruction on positive thinking, self-esteem, and feeling more confident.[4]

In the previous two chapters we examined how the confidence cult(ure) materializes in the domains of body image and work. Here we turn our critical gaze to the sphere of relationships: one's relationship to others *and* to oneself. In the first part of this chapter we examine how the confidence cult is transforming sex and relationship advice, looking at examples from digital magazines like Cosmopolitan.com and Glamour.com to show how confidence is increasingly represented to women as a vital disposition for having an adventurous and pleasurable sex life and as an essential attribute of attractiveness, which it is women's responsibility to nurture and maintain. Although magazines are said to be dying out in their printed forms, their digital incarnations attract millions more readers to similar content and are mirrored by a huge array of similar "lifestyle" content across all forms of media.[5] An indication of the volume of confidence messages can be seen in the fact that a search on the term "confident dating" in November 2020 generated *85 million* results on Google, centered on the importance of developing, or at least displaying, confidence in order to form and maintain successful relationships. We will examine the nature of these messages, locating them in a wider context of feminism, postfeminism, and neoliberalism and connecting them to the domains discussed in previous chapters.

In the second part of the chapter we look at a different form of intimate relationship—one's relationship to one's own self—a relationship on which many forms of media are more and more focused. When addressing women's relationships with their selves, advice increasingly comes in the form of questions like these: "Are you meeting your core needs for connection and fun?"[6] "It is important to look inside yourself and make sure that you are not vulnerable to 'over-bonding.' . . . Do you feel secure about yourself?" HuffPost offers us "11 ways to improve your relationship with yourself," while *Psychology Today* suggests "12 keys to a great self-relationship, starting now," declaring, "Your relationship with yourself is arguably the most important relationship in your life."[7] Such ideas have been popularized by the focus on self-love and self-care, as well as by trends such as self-marriage, in which individuals, mostly women, choose to marry or partner themselves, with Emma Watson, for example, describing herself, in an interview in *Vogue* to mark her thirtieth birthday, as "happily self-partnered."[8]

In 2018 Apple described "self-care" as its "app trend of the year," highlighting the extraordinary proliferation of psychologically oriented apps designed to help individuals feel calmer and happier and lead healthier and more mindful lives. The visibility and prominence of these apps have further increased dramatically during the COVID-19 crisis, as we discuss later in the chapter. A significant number of these apps center on the cultivation of confidence and resilience and offer themselves as "a personal therapist in your handbag" that will help to bring forth a "more confident you." We will examine some of the most popular apps, looking at how they construct the idea of a self that is struggling and needs to be supported through positive messages, affirmations, practices of gratitude, and exercises to inculcate a happier self.

Finally, in this hyper-reflexive moment no trend is seemingly complete without its countertrend—in this case a growing genre of anti-self-help, which includes best-selling titles such as *The Subtle Art of Not Giving a F*ck*, *The Little Book of Bad Moods*, and *How to Fail*.[9] Although these texts—and many others—position themselves explicitly as a rejection of and antidote to traditional self-help media, to what extent do they break with contemporary messages about self-love, self-care, and self-transformation? In the third part of the chapter we examine this growing oeuvre and how it is situated in relation to current injunctions to confidence. But first we turn to the confidence cult as manifest in contemporary sex and relationship advice targeted at women.

Sex, Love, and Relationship Confidence

A growing body of scholarship documents the way that discourses of work, management, and entrepreneurialism increasingly shape our ways of thinking, feeling, and talking about our most intimate relationships. We "invest" time with friends, "work" at marriages, "upskill" with new sexual techniques, "manage" different levels of desire, and "strategize" about our long-term relationships. While notions of a coup de foudre and falling in love are still evident, if contemporary advice media are reflecting and shaping current preoccupations, people today are enterprising subjects who seek out vast amounts of instruction about everything from creating a dating profile to how to kiss or perform oral sex. As Melissa Tyler argued in relation to our intimate life, it is "no longer enough to be 'doing it,' we should be 'managing it,' 'working at it,' 'improving it'"—all the time and in constantly new ways.[10]

Research has shown that the labor involved in this project is highly uneven. There is a dramatic gender asymmetry in which, in heterosexual relationships, women are responsible for vastly more relationship work.[11] A growing literature in this field shows how women are enjoined to become "sexual entrepreneurs": compulsorily sexy and always "up for it," "interpellated through discourses in which sex is work that requires constant labour and reskilling" (as well as big budgets for the outfits, cosmetics, lingerie, and sex toys required).[12] Women are also urged to be excellent communicators, capable of asking for what they want, while simultaneously looking after their partner's ego and displaying sophisticated emotional sensitivity. In recent years, this emotional work has further extended to include the psychic labor of "confidence." Among the central concerns of contemporary sex and relationship advice are the imperatives to "love your body," "be confident," "transform your feelings about sex," and "become a sexual adventurer."[13] What unites these themes is a concern with transforming the self and making over one's interior life as a happy, positive, and confident subject.

Confidence Is the New Sexy

Magazines aimed at heterosexual women are one locus among many of sex and relationship advice that has the development of confidence at its core. In 2015 *Elle* magazine launched its first "Confidence Issue: A Smart Woman's Guide to Self-Belief," followed quickly by *Cosmopolitan* instigating a monthly "confidence revolution" column, with its structuring ideas of "love your self, love your body, love your man." The theme resonated with other content such as an ad for Head and Shoulders that featured a "date night confidence coach."[14] Across such content confidence is presented as an unexamined good and something that can and should be cultivated to make yourself more attractive and more appealing. Women are repeatedly told that if they want to attract love, "what really works is looking at the inner you and doing the inner work necessary."[15] To become lovable one needs a "mental makeover," *Cosmo* tells women. Confidence appears to be increasingly promoted as the "wonderstuff" of intimate relationships, built around the idea that self-love is a prerequisite to being loved. "Love your body and he'll love it too" is a typical "commandment" and the subtext to plenty of these guidelines.

Much of this advice assumes a heterosexual readership and has a deeply regressive character based on "pleasing your man" and keeping him from "straying." Self-confidence is mobilized as part of an array of strategies designed for these purposes—adding to the work on the body (to keep yourself young, slim, sexy) and construction of sexual expertise expected of women. "Sex appeal is all about self-confidence," asserts one typical article.[16] "Insecurity isn't sexy!" declares another article, entitled "30 Things Men Wish Women Knew," while yet another on "What Men REALLY Think When You're Giving Him a Blow Job" advises: "Men are visual. If you're shy and hiding, that won't make a blow job better. On the contrary, you risk him thinking about that other chick or some porn star instead of seeing you. Confidence is key. Fake it if you must."[17]

The injunctions to confidence are not limited to general articles on sex and relationships but are also to be found in responses by relationship therapists to individual problems, as discussed in research by Laura Favaro.[18] In one such case a woman writes of her hurt that her husband "ogles other women." The agony aunt responds, "Men are drawn to confidence and if you are feeling a little low about yourself atm [at the moment] then this may be why he is looking at the maid that is more forward and comfortable in her own skin. Remind him why he married you and bring out your best side again."[19] As Favaro comments in her perceptive reading of this advice, not only does this offer no reassurance, but it *blames* the woman who is suffering for having brought this upon herself through her lack of confidence, and she is called on to undertake yet more work on herself to keep her husband's attention.[20]

The "work" of feeling confident in a relationship is women's alone. "The problem is YOU," says one article (lest there be any doubt) and you need to "do the work": "Only you can help you. Want the truth? You have to stop blaming others for your low self-esteem and accept some responsibility. Sure, sometimes life is tough, and some of us are dealt a rough hand every now and then, but only you can take the initiative to address your confidence issues. Make an effort to notice what you're doing to bring yourself down; recognising where you're going wrong is the first step to improving your confidence. . . . Positive mental attitude!"[21]

The work required is intense psychological labor: identify the problem, pay attention to your thoughts and feelings throughout the day, notice triggers, practice gratitude, exercise your "confidence muscle," love yourself "on the inside," and, in the meantime, "fake it till you make it." This work is to be enacted in relationships on top of the other labors already demanded: self-maintenance ("don't forget to wax"), dressing for "sex-cess," buying and wearing sexy lingerie (such as the aptly named Ego Boost Bra), donning killer heels, and making sure that you don't get stuck "in a rut" and always have something new, sexy, and special for "him"—whether a new sex toy or a sexy striptease.[22] "Positivity works wonders, but that doesn't mean you can skip products," says *Cosmopolitan*—or the work, we might add![23]

Chapter Three

Interestingly, during the time we were writing this book a change seemed to be underway. Confidence is still promoted as a compulsory project for women in relationship advice, but, perhaps in response to feminist critiques of the kind of advice discussed above, there has been a shift in tone across *some* magazines—even those targeted at a heterosexual readership—to adopt a more individualistic "Do this for yourself!" vibe rather than one tethered to pleasing a man or men.

This shift is allied to several developments. First, a welcome shift in sex and relationship guidance offers greater recognition that not all readers of women's magazines are heterosexual, as well as opening up gender diversity alongside a new focus on women's sexual pleasure. For example, in February 2020, *Cosmopolitan* (UK) subtitled its "Love" section with "Help and tips for your sex life, relationships and love life *whatever your sexuality, sexual orientation, gender identity, and star sign.*"[24] Articles included a focus on bisexuality, trans, consent, sex after childbirth, casual hookups—as well as an enormous number of pieces about the love and sex styles of different astrological signs! Similarly, Glamour.com gives us "8 ways to orgasm on your own that you may not have thought of . . . because #self-care: Welcome to your pleasure plan."[25]

Second, the change is also connected to the new visibility of feminism in popular culture since the mid-2010s and especially in the wake of #MeToo. Many women's magazines have embraced the new "popular feminism," with feminism special issues and content focusing on feminist "topics" such as sexual violence, abortion, sexual harassment, and the gender pay gap—particularly those publications that target a middle- and upper-class demographic.[26] The new feminism seems to be underpinned by an increasingly stable set of ideas about (body) positivity, the embrace of imperfection, and a stress on not comparing oneself to others and refusing judgment. The emphasis is on running upbeat pieces that inculcate this new ethos; for example, *Cosmopolitan*'s website offers pictures of "women who show us numbers and sizes mean nothing."[27] Female friendship is also given greater prominence, such as in *Marie Claire*'s advice on "how to have a good date": "Treat every date like an opportunity. . . . Dating should be empowering. . . . Don't mope. . . . Don't go out if you are feeling low—you are unlikely to shine. . . . You need to be in a much more confident place so meet up with some girlfriends to remember how awesome you are."[28]

Here, importantly, friends are a source of support rather than rivalry or competition. The "feminist feeling" is also supported by magazines' language, which offers a kind of feminist vernacular or demotic organized around woman-to-woman praise, strength, capacity, and solidarity: "You go, girl!" "We got this!" "Let's kick ass!" "You rock!" and so on.[29]

Third, this shift is closely related to the growing focus on happiness, wellness, self-care, mindfulness, affirmations, defiance, gratitude, and inspiration. These are considered in more detail further on in this chapter, but here it is important to note how in magazines these dispositions index a partial move away from body-shaming, redolent of the LYB ads we discussed in chapter 1 (though shaming for having the wrong—i.e., negative—attitude is still prevalent), toward a language that emphasizes possibility and "positive mental attitude." Women are exhorted to love themselves, and there are frequent reminders also to be positive about others. "Pump up the positivity," "think yourself positive," "eradicate the word 'can't' from your vocabulary," "rewire your thinking," and "don't say 'problem' say 'challenge,'" advises a typical article on fourteen positive life hacks that will "turn your frown upside down."[30]

Strikingly, then, the prominence accorded to confidence has not diminished as a result of these new trends and may indeed have become *more* significant—nor indeed has the labor required to achieve this lessened. Rather, developing confidence is newly presented as something that you should do *for yourself*. Cosmopolitan.com offers "7 happiness hacks from a seriously positive person" and "6 lessons about conquering your insecurities." It explains that "confidence isn't about being perfect, it's about seeing perfection in imperfection." Another article advises "how to fall in love with yourself," noting that you need to step back and "become your own best friend." This shift is part of creating a new, upgraded—possibly even "woke"—subjectivity, something that you owe to yourself (and perhaps to other women), something that connects aspiration, authenticity, and personal branding, focused around being your best self and living your best life. This self-love mantra is seen beyond magazines and self-help, including in music and celebrity culture. For example, in the popular song "Simply Complicated," Demi Lovato tells us, "When I'm comfortable in my skin I feel confident, and when I'm confident I feel sexy, and when I feel sexy, watch out!"[31]

The incitement to confidence in intimate relationships is largely seen in sex and relationship advice targeted to heterosexual women, but increasingly it seems to be part of a more general strategy linking attractiveness and desirability to self-belief. In 2019, *Diva* magazine, targeted at lesbian and bisexual women, partnered with Ella International Lesbian Festival with their brand message to "feel the Ella spirit and do it for yourself." While the exhortations to be "fearless," "courageous," and "present" may have a different meaning in relation to queer visibility and pride, the words and phrases are strikingly similar to those that have become mainstreamed through LYB discourses in campaigns from Dove, Nike, and others (discussed in chapter 1). This is underscored by a focus on work and spending on the body—reframed as an act of "self-care." An article titled "On Body Confidence in the Bedroom" does, however, frame this in terms of a broader homophobic context, noting that "with female-female sex so highly sexualised by the wider community, it's no wonder that women loving women can struggle with confidence."[32] The advice offered in *Diva* is significantly less likely to be about bodily discipline than advice directed at heterosexual women, but in general the confidence-wellness mantras of "accept your flaws," "work on loving yourself as you are," "embrace imperfection," and "loving yourself sets expectations on how you want to be loved by others" differ little from other sex and relationship advice.[33]

As we have noted, it is rare to see articles that locate difficulties with relationships in a wider context of inequality or power imbalance, relating to, say, appearance norms, expectations, sexual double standards, overwork, or debt. When such acknowledgments do appear, they are quickly glossed over, relegated to peripheral importance relative to women's own culpability. "Understand that it is we ourselves who construct our destiny and that satisfactions and joys depend on our own work," says one article.[34] *Cosmopolitan* Spain offers similar insights: "Everybody has problems . . . but don't go and self-victimize. Confront problems in an energetic and positive manner."[35] This advice serves to let magazines off the hook—sometimes explicitly so, as in the following quote: "Fatphobia is everywhere in the media. . . . Negative thinking will damage you more than fashion mags."[36] It places the responsibility back onto women's own putatively negative, insecure, and damaging thought patterns and, following a neoliberal logic, locates a lack of confidence about sex, dating, or intimacy as women's own fault, the result of "self-pity, insufficient personal drive and a lack of personal responsibility for one's life."[37]

Self-Care and the Confidence Cult

It is not just in our intimate relations with others where messages about confidence, resilience, and positivity are proliferating. Increasingly, as the last section hinted, our *relationships with ourselves* take center stage across media and popular culture. Upbeat messages and inspirational slogans are everywhere in affluent Western societies—they wink down from posters, they cover Facebook walls and drive Instagram feeds, and they have transformed the greeting card industry in the last decade, which pushes millions of mugs, T-shirts, trinkets, and postcards every day, instructing us to "Live Love Laugh," "Note to self: Relax," or "Go confidently in the direction of your dreams." The sheer volume of self-care commandments that has characterized the period of the global pandemic—as well as their contradictory nature—is also worthy of comment. Like the "carewashing" and "wokewashing" messages considered in chapter 1, exhortations to individual well-being have become ubiquitous, from retail giants to workplaces, health insurers to governments, even as the resources to actualize care of the self continue to be radically unequal. Celebrity culture, too, is increasingly animated by self-care messages and accounts of psychological transformation, regaling us with stories of how a particular pop star or actress has turned her pain into music or channeled it into a charitable enterprise supporting mental health or a range of products that will help others feel better. Only rarely do these go beyond individualized interventions, as was the case in the UK when Manchester United soccer player Marcus Rashford campaigned around the scandal of poverty and children going hungry.

Popular television is also changing rapidly, with shows like *Queer Eye* (Netflix) or *Shrill* (Hulu) emphasizing confidence and self-worth above weight loss or surgical transformation. These shifts have a long history going back to the 1960s (see the book's introduction), but they have dramatically intensified in recent years to go significantly beyond what Christopher Lasch called the "culture of narcissism" or a mere focus on assertiveness and personal growth.[38] Messages about self-love and self-care have today taken center stage in a moment that is characterized by increasing economic and social precarity, overload (as people work long hours or multiple jobs), and worsening mental health.[39] Against this backdrop, the dramatic rise in attention to self-love might be seen as a benign and positive development, advocating kindness, caretaking, and a different framework for valuing oneself and others. Indeed, the number of messages that simply remind one to "breathe" or to "take five minutes" for oneself testify to the levels of distress, tension, and time-famine being experienced by many.

One site (among many) where these messages are prominent is smartphone apps developed to help people live happier and more mindful lives—to feel calmer, sleep better, have greater self-esteem. There are now thousands of these developed for different phone platforms. Indeed, in 2018 alone, more than three thousand new self-care apps were launched, primarily driven by a female and millennial market.[40] In 2020, one of the biggest health and consumer trends was the drive to self-care apps; according to a McKinsey report, these apps grew downloads and new sign-ups between 80 percent and 250 percent by the end of April 2020 alone.[41] They range from material developed by professional psychologists, such as the increasingly popular electronic/digital forms of cognitive behavioral therapy (CBT), to numerous commercially produced apps such as Confidence Coach, Happier, Resilient, Build Confidence, SuperBetter, I Am, Happiness Wizard, and Shine. The apps vary significantly in the amount and sophistication of content, but they share similar design, with most offering considerable free content with the opportunity to unlock extras such as guided meditations or short courses (e.g., "10 days to a more confident you") by signing up for a premium subscription.

"Wellness," "health and fitness," and "self-care" are contested commercial categories that include a variety of different apps—including market leaders Headspace and Calm, which focus on mindfulness and meditation, yoga courses such as Yoga Studio, and diet or workout apps like Lose It (designed by FitNow) or Sweat (by Instagram influencer Kayla Itsines).[42] In what follows we focus on commercial psychological self-care apps that are centered on mental health and well-being.[43] We look here at apps organized around *everyday* mental health and feeling better for people without diagnosed mental health problems, including Shine, Resilient, My Confidence Coach, and SuperBetter.

The Gendered World of Confidence Apps

As smartphone apps proliferate, a growing body of academic research examines them. Much of this is focused on examining the trend toward self-tracking and self-monitoring that has been understood as giving rise to a "quantified self" (QS).[44] For Deborah Lupton the QS is best conceptualized as a "self-tracking" or "reflexive monitoring" self who uses the affordances of digital technology to collect, monitor, record, and share information—quantified and non-quantifiable—about oneself while engaging in "the process of making sense of this information as part of the ethical project of selfhood."[45] Some of the apps that have received the most attention are those which track exercise, diet, and sleep patterns, as well as a variety of different health measures including blood pressure, heart rate, and glucose/insulin levels. As in health monitoring more broadly, women are positioned as key actors, called on to monitor their own health but also that of their families. The rapid growth in apps relating to menstrual cycle, pregnancy, and childcare offer a further sign of the way in which this medium is strongly gendered.[46] Similarly, evidence from the COVID-19 crisis shows how self-care apps were particularly targeted at women, and disproportionately women of color, through their roles as teachers, nurses, carers, and retail staff. For example, the major UK high street retailer Tesco gave its 420,000 (majority-female) employees free access to the meditation app Headspace and the mental health platform SilverCloud.[47] Headspace Premium was also offered free of charge from March 2020 onward to millions of key or essential workers, including teachers and support staff in the US, the UK, Canada, and Australia and to all health staff in the US and UK.[48]

The psychological apps focused on confidence and resilience are no less gendered, with most targeted at an imagined female user, even when they are ostensibly gender neutral. Formal neutrality is often undercut by other signifiers of gender—such as color coding, language, and assumptions. My Confidence Coach, for example, is entirely designed in hot pink and refers to potential users as "ladies, leaders and little girls." Its age categories are striking, highlighting the focus on a millennial (and younger) audience ranging from "under 12" to "over 25." There are three age-differentiated categories for those under twenty-five years old, but anyone older is simply "25 or over"! The gendered visuals of apps in general are reinforced by a similarly binary and essentialist language: typically, men are exhorted to "mind max," "power up," and "build strength and stamina," aided by targets and "hero quotes." Women, by contrast, are guided to "empower from within," "build self-esteem," and "stay positive" with inspirational aphorisms, affirmations, and gratitude.

An example that breaks this mold is SuperBetter, designed to "build resilience—the ability to stay strong, motivated and optimistic even in the face of change and difficult challenges." The app design uses rainbow-colored bubble writing and the slogan "Everyone has heroic potential." Designed by Jane McGonigal, it is based on research which shows that "we are better in games than in real life," as we are more determined, less likely to give up when we fail, and more likely to collaborate and cooperate, to behave more resourcefully, and to be happily productive.[49] In the app and her book of the same name McGonigal uses these insights to develop a psychological app based on "living gamefully." Using a language familiar from gaming, users are invited to "power up" (even a simple stretch counts) and are given "bad guys to battle" (e.g., anxiety) and "quests" to complete.

As well as age and gender assumptions, many apps are implicitly coded as classed and racialized texts through, for example, common images of white women gazing serenely at sunsets on beaches or at light dappling through trees. The stock images of raindrops on a leaf or of ferns unfurling are recognizable as part of a corporate visual habitat associated with the middleclass, white, and feminized world of spa hotels, beauty clinics, and upmarket cosmetics/cosmeceuticals. As Raka Shome has argued of the Western "wellness" industry more generally, it "recycle[s] earlier colonial logics of representing white women, where, in the pursuit of wellness, white women fuse with the spirit of nature."[50] The colonial logics at work include the appropriation and commodification of non-Western religious and cultural practices as "soul treatments" for feminized and racialized Western middle-class consumers.[51] Nature, repeatedly presented in hyperreal and "inspirational" form in these apps, is deeply implicated in this process, connected to what Shome suggests may be a promise of transcending corporeality.

Shine, Believe, Be Thankful, Reset

The architecture, content, and messages of different confidence, resilience, and self-care apps addressed to women are very similar. Indeed, the design and layout of the apps so resembles other apps that sometimes even the headings are the same, as with Here and Now, Gratitude, My Time, and Confidence Quotes. The content of the apps is also strikingly similar: articles ("challenge your negative thinking," "let go of perfect"), quizzes ("what's your self-care style?"), affirmations ("I deserve to be loved for who I am," "I fix what I can and accept what I cannot"), gratitude journals, podcasts, challenges, check-ins for mood, and premium content for more focused work (e.g., Resilient offers a thirty-day "negativity detox," while Shine has multiple invitations such as "Grow your confidence in 10 days").[52]

The semantic or thematic heart of messages across apps is also very similar—differing mainly in tone and branding rather than in the core ideas and values articulated.[53] Resetting your mindset is an overall goal for many: "We will message you with a fresh take each weekday," promises Shine. "It takes about 5 minutes a day and is proven to improve your mindset." My Confidence Coach explains that "confidence is like a muscle, we have to work it"—itself, of course, a metaphor from the fitness repertoire. An emphasis upon reframing negative experiences in more positive terms is a salient characteristic, as is rendering injuries as opportunities for learning or growth (as we saw in chapter 2). For example, Shine advises, "Next time you feel lonely try leaning in to positive solitude" (see chapter 1). The apps ask their users questions like "How many negative thoughts have been endlessly repeating in your mind?" and offer to help us "release those negative beliefs we hold about ourselves and move forward" (Shine). My Confidence Coach asks users, "Could you actually be the one blocking your own shine?" In ways redolent of our analysis in other chapters, women are presented as blocking their own potential, being their own worst enemies (for example, through perfectionism), and needing coaching on how to reset their ways of thinking, feeling, and relating.

A focus on physical and mental well-being is central to this, with instructions on breathing as part of "practicing positivity": "Use your breath to remind you of your power and increase your endorphins."[54] Meditations and mindful practices are at the heart of these apps, which promote relaxation and slowing down and being in the moment. Cutting down on alcohol, exercising, quitting smoking, and drinking more water are also encouraged. But mostly the work required is intense psychic labor to make over your internal life—working with your own resources ("your internal motivation is gold—here's how to unlock it") to move from negativity to positivity ("how to kickstart your own upward spiral," offers Shine). "My body achieves what my mind believes" has become a characteristic statement—articulated in these words by Olympian Tom Daley in another location—his affirmations podcast, sponsored by L'Oréal.[55]

Affirmations are central to this labor of self-care and self-transformation; they are positive statements about oneself that are part of the resetting process. They turn the negative voices inside our heads into positive statements such as "I'm worth it," "I'm enough," "my future is what I make it," "my best time is now," "I choose to succeed," "I am the CEO of my own life," and so on. The apps feed these ideas, while also turning them into second-person statements such as "you are perfect the way you are" or "you got this." Like the friendly tone of women's magazines (explored earlier in this chapter) or the motivational language in advice books (examined in chapter 2), the apps infuse a tone of warmth, possibility, and defiance of expectations—apart from the expectation to be positive, confident, and resilient. The famous phrase "Because You're Worth It" was introduced by L'Oréal in 1973, and similar slogans have been circulating since.[56] However, one of the distinct aspects of their current iterations is how they become, through the individualized and personally customized technological affordances of apps, intimate companions that govern the self, as if to take over and become the user's own voice or psyche. Users commonly receive these affirmations via their headphones, an auditory experience that reinforces a sense of these affirmative commandments becoming an extension of oneself (or, the extension of woman, to recall McLuhan's famous metaphor).

Gratitude is a central affect in these apps, and gratitude journals have become a cornerstone of the corporate self-care movement, almost ubiquitous in apps targeted at women (less so those at men). Shine's content is exemplary, with articles that explain the importance of being thankful and outline multiple moments in which gratitude can be practiced—while waiting for apps or web pages to load, or undertaking daily rituals such as cleaning your teeth, or indeed by deliberately setting an alarm to record thanks. The app offers multiple opportunities to "check in" with your current mood or to record something you feel grateful for. A regular writer for the app, Thalia, explains that her mission is "all the feels"—that is, to change our way of relating to ourselves.[57] As we have argued in chapters 1 and 2, gratitude, an affect historically associated with femininity, encourages the restraint that for decades women, and perhaps especially minority women, have been demanded to exercise over their angry thoughts, feelings, and speech. Gratitude may work to secure the erasure of critique, doubt, and anger in favor of accepting and endorsing the status quo—being grateful for *what there is*. It is one of the central moral virtues of the entrepreneurial, responsible, individualized selfhood demanded by neoliberal capitalism.[58]

Inspiring Confidence

The final "staple" of self-care apps is to be found in their "inspirational" content. For example, My Confidence Coach offers hundreds of inspirational messages, all purportedly written by the site's founder, Dr. Nicole Steele (some of which are available to buy in its merchandising): "The most beautiful thing a girl can wear is Confidence" and "Believe in yourself so strongly that the world can't help but believe in you too." Resilient in turn offers us "18 Important Quotes About Life Lessons," "19 Beautiful Quotes About Light," "18 Quotes About Staying Positive," and so on and on. These eclectic lists and pages bring together pithy aphorisms from a variety of sources: a quote from Napoleon here, one from the Dalai Lama there. None are longer than a sentence or two, and all have an already familiar quality centered on building positivity: "It is not the mountain we conquer but ourselves" (Edmund Hillary), "Life shrinks or expands in proportion to one's courage" (Anaïs Nin), and "Life isn't about finding yourself. It is about creating yourself" (George Bernard Shaw). As we have argued elsewhere, in these apps, quotes are used in a manner that Fredric Jameson has called the "random cannibalization" of ideas and bell hooks describes as "eating the Other."[59] In this way, a line from the thirteenth-century Sufi poet Rumi may be juxtaposed with a quote from Gandhi's resistance against British imperialism, and both in turn placed next to a motivational slogan from US basketball player Michael Jordan or a pithy maxim from Apple creator Steve Jobs. This might properly be expected to produce a sense of radical disjuncture, but the quotes are so decontextualized and dislocated that barely any sense of jarring is produced. It works to effect a kind of "spiritual neoliberalism," in which Western women are incited to achieve enlightenment or resilience through consuming the histories, struggles, and religions of Others, stripped of any history or context.[60] These inspirational reminders are like "feeds" designed to inculcate a confident self. Confidence here is constructed as positive mental attitude and self-belief, in which women are enjoined to see themselves as survivors, not victims, and in which an affirmative tone eviscerates doubt, pain, or ambivalence.

The emphasis on "inspiration" as a route to confident subjectivity is perhaps most pronounced in apps but characteristic of the confidence cult(ure) more broadly. This emphasis is both political and aesthetic and is deeply gendered, classed, and racialized. In many but not all apps, inspiration becomes a kind of "magical thinking" that is "lifted out" of everyday life, offered up as a series of timeless and universal psychological truths. This is underscored by the visual motifs of majestic landscapes seen in confidence apps—mountains, waterfalls, sunsets—and the striking absence of anything resembling the urban spaces in which arguably most of these apps' consumers live, almost as if the inspirational quote would lose its power if set against a photograph of a housing estate, busy road, or hospital ward. Shine is different in this respect and locates itself within a more recognizable everyday—pastel shades and graphics, audio content and no photos. It also adopts a familiar millennial vernacular that helps to ground its content in feelings and situations that are more "relatable." For example, Shine's new year email greeting to one of us empathized with the pressure "to be your best self all the time, Rosalind," and on how easy it is to make unrealistic resolutions: "Oh and next year, I've really got to hit the gym." Yet paradoxically it is this very relatability that intensifies its potential force as a confidence technology—it is there all the time, it engages constantly on topics big and small, and its writers and producers work relentlessly to interact with you, to understand you, to tell you how grateful they are that you "showed up," and to tailor their content to creating a Shine-ier version of you.

Work and Interactivity: The Coach in Your Pocket

The interactivity offered by smartphone apps marks a significant amplification and intensification of the work and self-surveillance demanded by the confidence cult(ure). The apps offer themselves as coaches, friends, or therapists on your phone and, even in the most basic settings, they are "in touch with you" at least once a day—often multiple times. Shine will send you a daily text, with a podcast every morning on topics such as "putting your best you forward," "reflecting on your week," "calling out your worries," or "making progress over perfection." The app also encourages you to "check in with yourself" via the app *at least three times a day*. Its "morning mindset" check-in at the time of writing says, "Wake up feeling refreshed! Research shows that a morning routine helps you feel more energized throughout the day. Let Esosa E guide you through a morning practice that includes stretching, breathing and setting an intention for your day." The app's midday check-in worries about a slump in your mood and offers yet more inspiration to energize. Meanwhile, "evening vibes" checks in with you to help clear away clutter and anxiety, to calm and de-stress before bedtime. Watching/listening to only the four "basic" daily videos takes a full twenty-five minutes a day (even without a premium subscription) but still only represents a fraction of the engagement and interactivity that is possible with the app—quizzes, free writing, and a gratitude journal are others—and the app also encourages you to record your feelings in real time, offering three options with emojis: "meh," "ok," or "great." The app then responds with an appropriate gif—checking "great" produces huge applause, for example. A less positive response brings offers to "talk it out," listen to a meditation, read up on advice, or do some free writing.

While Shine stands out for the quality of its content (a point we return to in our concluding chapter), many other self-care apps also involve significant levels of interactivity and incitements to work and to record progress—whether that is noting in-app when you have drunk a glass of water or recording when you have turned a negative to a positive thought. Often this operates in gamified ways so that recording progress or doing the work set by the app—stretches, expressions of gratitude, affirmations of your own capacity (e.g., "I can do this")—is necessary in order to move on within the app, for example, to gain access to more content or to get "scores" or feedback for the day. Smartphone applications will also send notifications, reminders, and messages of encouragement/discipline at regular intervals, which makes the experience quite different from engaging with a fixed text such as a book, magazine, or TV show. While there is always an option to "skip this," the apps work to shape behavior and psychic life more forcefully (both intensively and extensively) and more intimately than other media. Apps incite extraordinary levels of intimate (self-)surveillance across multiple areas of life—from checking that you are eating the "right" things and for the "right" reasons (e.g., no "comfort eating" or "bingeing"), to stopping comparing yourself to others, to "cleansing" from social media in a kind of digital detox. What is striking then is the way that they break down the labor of becoming confident into a minutiae of itemized steps, inciting constant attention, time, and work. It is like a Taylorization of becoming confident—a McConfidence perhaps.

Anti-Self-Help

Against the proliferation of messages about self-care, self-love, and confidence in relationships, over the last few years there has been a rise of what seems to be an opposite trend: anti-self-help. If the messages we discussed so far emphasize the need to continuously work on oneself toward the betterment of our relationship with others and ourselves, then the texts and exhortations we examine in this final section (seemingly) reject the premise of self-improvement, self-love, and confidence in relating to others and ourselves. *Not That Kind of Girl*, Lena Dunham's autobiography, is a good example of a hybrid of genres that foregrounds failure.[61] Subtitled "A Young Woman Tells You What She's 'Learned,'" it immediately distinguishes itself from other postfeminist memoirs or conduct manuals through its inversion of familiar narrative strategies that move from confusion to wisdom or loneliness to happy relationships, or which express a desire that others should learn from the author's experiences.[62] The chapter on dieting, for example, starts with Dunham's fear of being anorexic, moving on to her spell as "the world's least successful occasional bulimic," followed by several pages of itemized food consumption: "2 sips of ginger ale," "one quarter of a peach," etc., and ending abruptly with a one-line note saying: "I went totally nuts and ate all the things."[63] As noted elsewhere, "this is the antithesis of 'self-help' and successful 'makeover.'"[64] There is no growth, no self-improvement, and no metamorphosis into responsibilized neoliberal adulthood. Indeed, the book jacket tells us that Dunham is already anticipating her "future shame at thinking I had anything to offer you."

This emphasis on failure and vulnerability is also becoming more mainstream across celebrity texts of other kinds—from posts on Instagram to interviews. For instance, in an interview for *Vogue* in 2017, pop star Selena Gomez talked about her struggles with mental health, declaring: "We girls, we're taught to be almost too resilient, to be strong and sexy and cool and laid-back, the girl who's down. We also need to feel allowed to fall apart."[65] A sidebar on the digital platform allows readers to click through from Gomez's disclosures to a surreal list of five other links: in top position, a list of Selena Gomez makeup products, followed in descending order by a mental health "quiz," a mental health "assessment," a mental health "care plan," and "the top 3 symptoms of bipolar syndrome." A subsequent article in *Vogue*, published during the 2020 COVID-19 pandemic, celebrates the launch of Gomez's makeup line.[66] Continuing the vulnerability-confidence theme, she describes how she was "heavily involved in the whole process" (of designing the products) "because I care so much about mental health and I believe it's a part of your self-esteem." Here makeup products become figured as self-help tools that will generate self-love, self-expression, and improved mental health.

More recently, in the anti-self-help genre, Sophie Hannah has given us *How to Hold a Grudge*, Haemin Sunim offered *Love for Imperfect Things*, whereas Karen Rinaldi twists mainstream self-help with *It's Great to Suck at Something*.[67] Meanwhile, an entire subgenre of "activity books" is being published that defy the compulsory gratitude trend—an early example is Keri Smith's *Wreck This Journal*, in which she encourages readers to "poke holes through pages, crack the spine, paint with coffee, rip pages out, ball them up, and throw them off the top of a tall building."[68] Bloomsbury has also published *The Little Book of Bad Moods*, an antidote to "creative coloring books," which offers the chance for readers to detail their every frustration, draw the emojis they hate the most and "that need to be punched in the face," and keep lists of (for example) everything that is wrong with your partner.[69] The book also features an "ingratitude diary."

Often these new anti-self-help titles project an air of challenging received wisdom, of gamely—and somewhat bravely—telling it how it is. Oliver Burkeman, for example, called his book *The Antidote* and promised it would be a book for "people who can't stand positive thinking."[70] The "alternative path to happiness," it turns out, "involves embracing failure, pessimism, insecurity and uncertainty" (so says the marketing blurb on the book cover). The tendency is underscored in an entire subgenre that some commentators identify as "sweary self-help."[71] It includes titles such as *Unf*ck Yourself*, *F**k Anxiety*, *You Are a Badass*, and *How to Make Sh*t Happen*. The idea here is that the authors will "cut through the crap" and "call bullshit" on self-help orthodoxy.

But how new are the ideas in such books? To what extent do they really live up to their promises to overturn everything we thought we knew? In particular, how and to what extent does the anti-self-help trend challenge the confidence culture's mantras of self-love, self-care, and self-transformation?

Perhaps the most successful in the trend is Mark Manson's *The Subtle Art of Not Giving a F*ck*. Describing himself as a professional blogger and entrepreneur, Manson offers readers a quick tour through Western philosophy, laced with personal anecdotes, profane humor, and a brutal tone that often falls into casual sexism—as, for example, in the way in which he uses women's bodies in general as "trophies" or trinkets of success. For instance, in one of his many "tough love" lessons he tells us to get over the fact that life isn't going to be perfect and we need to cultivate self-acceptance: "We're never going to cure cancer or go to the moon or feel Jennifer Aniston's tits. And that's okay."[72] In turn, an analysis of false memory syndrome falls into downright misogyny, betraying both homophobia and hatred of feminists.[73] Yet, stripped back, the book hardly seems as "counterintuitive" as its subtitle suggests. On the contrary, its core messages seem to be wholly in tune with the confidence culture and the vulnerability turn that we noted in previous chapters: be honest, embrace your faults, it's OK to fail, give up on being perfect, choose what really matters, don't sweat the small stuff, cultivate self-worth. Indeed, as Micki McGee observes, Manson's advice clearly resonates with the cruelty of contemporary culture, advocating being extremely conscious and strategic about what one cares about.[74]

How to Fail

Manson's advice is not focused on relationships, but another book that is, and exemplifies the anti-self-help trend du jour, is *How to Fail* by British journalist, novelist, and blogger Elizabeth Day. In *How to Fail* Day narrates how she funded the podcast of the same name by selling her wedding dress on eBay—the failure of her marriage representing part of the impetus, as well as the vehicle, for her spectacular success at failing. The podcast was downloaded thousands of times within hours of being posted, topping the iTunes charts along with shows like *Serial*. Day was offered a book contract within a week of the podcast going live.

The resulting book is well written and engaging, funny in parts, moving in others. Part memoir, part anti-self-help book, the "how to" device is only partly ironic. There are set pieces with easy targets—such as "How to Fail at Being Gwyneth Paltrow," which allows for much jocular sending up of the

Goop founder and her obscure and expensive "treatments." But there are also significant chapters, most of which are focused on intimate relationships: "How to Fail at Dating," "How to Fail at Friendship," and "How to Fail at Families" are among these. Drawing on her own and others' stories—mostly those she has interviewed for her podcast—Day pulls together a narrative that has a clear, strong center: self-belief and self-acceptance, she tells us, are key to how we live. The importance of confidence pulses through the book like a heartbeat: if she had been more confident, she would not have repeatedly accepted the journalistic assignments that no one else wanted; she might have asked for a pay rise; she would have avoided all those dates with unsuitable men. Greater belief in herself would have helped her to listen to and tune in to her inner voices, to determine what she wanted, and to prevent her building her life around pleasing others. She describes how online dating caused her to try to fashion herself into the image of someone she thought would be lovable—instead of being herself, she became what others have called a "manic pixie dream girl," what she dubs as "the winking emoji face made human," as she tried so hard for banter and sexual knowingness.[75]

The book shows vividly how painful this was. Instead of taking "the time to work out what I wanted from a relationship . . . I had allowed myself to be shaped by the stronger wishes of other people—both boyfriends and male bosses."[76] Day looks back on her younger self, noting how the *outward* impression she gave was of someone confident who knew what she wanted. In reality she was "lost and scared" because it was not a true confidence that comes from "faith in herself" and finding "herself worthy of her own respect," but instead it was the *performance* of someone craving male approval and affirmation.[77] Even when she was hurt during the breakup of a significant relationship, she didn't allow herself to show her feelings, instead performing like the (fake) "cool girl" in Gillian Flynn's novel *Gone Girl*. "Instead of looking inward for confidence," Day reveals, "I latched onto partners either to rescue or complete me."[78]

To get to a place of self-belief and self-love, failing—and allowing herself to be vulnerable—were essential. She writes, "Relinquishing control and making yourself vulnerable—these are terrifying things to do, and yet, if my dating stint taught me anything, it was that you had to be willing to expose yourself. . . . I would argue that failing in dating is a necessary precursor to working out what you want and finding someone nice."[79] To get to this, though, you have to "be brave enough to take the leap" to being real, open, honest with yourself and others, and vulnerable.[80] "It will panic you and make you scared, but once you allow those feelings to subside and once the vortex calms, you will rediscover yourself."[81]

None of this advice seems controversial, but neither does it seem new. Rather, what is striking is the way in which this emblematic anti-self-help text focused on failure instead of success articulates many of the themes that characterize contemporary mainstream self-help across media, from books to magazines to apps. Once again, self-knowledge, self-belief, and compassion are core, with good relationships with others presented as the outcome of work to know and love yourself, resulting in self-acceptance that is the well-spring of being able to be vulnerable and to truly be open to love. Perfection is disparaged and the outward markers of success are treated with suspicion. *How to Fail*, rather than challenging the orthodoxy, seems entirely to express it. Confidence emerges from this once more as a central disposition to be fostered and cultivated. Failure is allowed, but only under the condition that it has been overcome. Indeed, the "fashion for failure" is premised on the author's post-failure status;[82] one can advocate for failure and teach how to fail only when she is already on the other side, when failure can be referred to as something that happened and is safely sealed in the past.

It is worth turning a critical eye on this warm, tender book—if only because it so perfectly expresses the way the confidence cult(ure) operates in and through contemporary relationship advice. It is an intimate and personal book, and also one that is explicitly feminist and in which the topics of body image, internet porn, and sexual harassment are mentioned. Yet it is not a book in which "the personal is political"; indeed, the sphere of political writing is at times caricatured through repeated contrasts with the (anonymous) figure of a leather-jacketed hipster who writes stories on a big canvas. It is not so much that the force of economic, political, and social life is *repudiated* in *How to Fail*; it is more that it seems not to exist at all—it doesn't even make it to the status of something that has to be discounted!

Despite the intimate personal style of the book and the way it so thoroughly furnishes details of a particular upper-middle-class London milieu, the story told is curiously decontextualized. As we have seen in other domains of the confidence cult(ure), the world with its hierarchies, inequalities, and injustices seems to recede so that self-belief comes to seem entirely dislocated, a wonderstuff that has to be personally manufactured by the individual—like a self-belief hormone perhaps. Mostly this is about working on yourself—perhaps, as Day recounts, coming to such a low point that everything has to be reevaluated, that you have to stop and cultivate a different set of values. But it at the same time develops through a familiar progress narrative in which, as time passes, things just "get better." This has, of course, been widely critiqued in relation to LGBTQ+ narratives designed to offer comfort to queer young people with a reassurance that things will improve or in relation to gender equality in the workplace, where women are repeatedly asked to exercise patience until things get better because "these things take time."[83] More generally, however, the narrative is problematic for its erasure of agency—no one, it seems, has to actually do anything, no struggle is needed; the passage of time will, in itself, make things better.

This comes across powerfully in a chapter in Day's book titled "How to Fail at Your Twenties," in which Day recounts how her own life—and her friends'/interviewees' lives—failed to live up to expectations (notwithstanding her degree from Cambridge University and securing a coveted staff job on a top newspaper). Her conclusion, though, is that this putative failure was valuable because "however much you might feel you are failing at your twenties when you are living through them, they are a necessary crucible. Your twenties are spices in a pestle and mortar that must be ground up by life in order to release your fullest flavour. By the end of them, you'll have more heart and more guts—and you'll know never to roast broccoli again."[84]

It is extraordinary that feelings of failure and lack of confidence are never related to a wider cultural context in *How to Fail*. The book contains no indictments of current social relations, offers not the merest hint that we are living in a world *designed* to ensure that some succeed and others fail. Despite what some would see as a routine "intersectionality disclaimer" early on in the book, Day's own immense privilege as a white, cisgender, non-disabled, healthy, beautiful, privately educated, and phenomenally successful writer is "checked" but never operationalized. In a similar way to Helena Morrissey's best seller *A Good Time to Be a Girl* (see chapter 2), which overlooks the huge impact her privileged background has made on her successful career, in *How to Fail* Day's privilege is never revealed to have made any difference whatsoever to her life. We note this not to make a cheap point—indeed, we are well aware that external privilege does not automatically translate into feelings of self-worth—but rather to underscore the extent to which the entire force of social relations is erased, as this project centers itself on the individual as entrepreneur of the self, the need to "create my own opportunities."[85] The solutions proposed are to be bold, enterprising, and brave and to take risks, "because when you take a massive gamble on yourself, you have to be the one who believes in your own value . . . and making brave decisions gets easier the more you flex the muscle of your emotional resilience."[86]

As we were copyediting this book, Elizabeth Day produced her second self-help volume, *Failosophy: A Handbook for When Things Go Wrong*, in which she distills everything she has learned about failure into seven key principles.

Coinciding with the second wave of COVID-19 in many parts of the world, the book was greeted as a "savior" and "survival guide" for the mental health crisis wrought by the pandemic, with Day's own positive diagnosis with coronavirus framed as yet another emblematic failure for our times.[87] An article in *Glamour* noted that Day's "subject matter has become accidentally pertinent in our tumultuous 2020, where it seems so many of us are failing at any number of things—from keeping our finances afloat in a pandemic, to maintaining our mental health in a year of fear and panic."[88] Perhaps even more than *How to Fail*, this second volume, with its attempt to produce general wisdoms, highlights the force of the confidence-vulnerability dynamic that we have traced here. It shows clearly that rather than being renegade knowledge that challenges self-help orthodoxies, anti-self-help texts like this are in fact the dominant discourses, albeit newly packaged as daring and defiant and in touch with their vulnerable side.

Conclusion

In this chapter we have looked at the way the confidence cult(ure) is materializing in the realm of relationships, shaping contemporary advice about intimate relationships with others and ourselves. Examining a range of media including women's magazines, smartphone self-help apps, and best-selling books, we have tracked the changing ways in which confidence is invoked as central to successful relationships. We note a significant shift away from confidence being required of heterosexual women because it is attractive to men, toward a more individualistic focus on pleasing, transforming, and developing the self. Often, though, the behaviors called forth remain the same—as when Elizabeth Day resignifies her labor on the body as an autonomous choice rather than something culturally demanded. This has the familiar postfeminist implication that "now that I'm enlightened I do this for myself, not to please a man."

Despite the documented trend for daring individuality, rebelling self-help, and exhortations to embrace failure, we demonstrated the clear contemporary investment in and cementing of self-belief and self-love—even as they sit alongside and become intimately entangled with authenticity, vulnerability, and anti-perfectionism. This entanglement became even more vivid during 2020, as self-help in all its forms proliferated during the pandemic, circulating ideas about the need for flexibility, acceptance, and gratitude. Exhortations to "accept the mess" (lack of control, anxiety, depression, loneliness, insomnia, etc.) sat alongside injunctions to repudiate perfection, to practice self-care and kindness, and to realize that "just getting through is an achievement." Meanwhile, women were subjected to endless calls to take care of everything, while also working to build their emotional resilience. The confidence cult(ure) is at the heart of these contradictory yet familiar injunctions.

confident mothering

FOLLOWING THE SUCCESS of their 2015 *New York Times* best seller, *The Confidence Code* (discussed in chapter 2), in 2018 journalists Katty Kay and Claire Shipman published a sequel, *The Confidence Code for Girls: Taking Risks, Messing Up, and Becoming Your Amazingly Imperfect, Totally Powerful Self*.[1] On the way to quickly becoming another *New York Times* best seller, this book was endorsed by Facebook COO Sheryl Sandberg and Olympic medalist Laurie Hernandez, with the latter describing it as "the book every girl needs to make her dreams come true."[2] *The Confidence Code for Girls* features a series of cartoon illustrations, quizzes, and exercises to help girls measure and increase their self-esteem, girls' inspirational quotes "meant to make you think or wonder or smile," and "confidence close-ups," which consist of stories about girls "in the midst of the ugly, scary process of confidence creation," who have overcome various obstacles and become confident. This popular guide is part of the exponential rise over the last two decades or so of what feminist scholar Sarah Banet-Weiser calls the "market for girls' empowerment": organizations, programs, products, and practices that market female empowerment to an imagined white, middle-class girl who is "in crisis" and is constructed as in need of becoming a confident entrepreneur and leader through a process of constant monitoring of and working on herself.[3]

In this chapter, we complement and expand the discussion on the market for girls' empowerment by examining the underlying market on which the market for girls' confidence depends, that is, these girls' *parents*. For the market for girls' empowerment and confidence to be economically viable requires parents ready to invest considerable time, money, and affective labor in resolving their daughters' "crises." Indeed, Kay and Shipman describe their guide for girls as a direct response to the pleas of the parents they met when touring the US to promote their first book: "We've discovered that the mothers and fathers we meet are desperate for help translating the Confidence Code into a formula that works for girls, so that their daughters can be empowered, from a young age, by the power and satisfaction of a confident life."[4]

Why is there such a seemingly ready market of parents willing to invest considerable time, money, and labor in finding the "formula" for their girls' empowerment and self-confidence? We start by situating the "pleas" of parents like those Kay and Shipman met within the broader context of insecurity and precarity of contemporary parenting and the intensification of regulation of parents by the state, the media, and, crucially, parents themselves. While both mothers and fathers are subject to these pressures, mothers are subjected to increasing regulation and policing and continue to be addressed as the parent primarily responsible for demonstrating confidence to *and* instilling confidence in their daughters. We then move to examine how confidence operates in the domain of parenting, highlighting its particular gendered character in the way it inculcates mothers and girls as its ideal subjects of crisis and consequent desirable transformation. First, we look at how contemporary popular discourses conjure women as subjects who can and should transform themselves from anxious, insecure, or simply confused individuals into confident mothers. Second, we show how confidence is constructed as a fundamental quality, which mothers are expected not only to possess themselves but also to cultivate in their children—especially their daughters—to ensure their development, happiness, and status.

The Market for Parents of To-Be-Empowered Girls

With the continued cutting back of the welfare safety nets, social security, and public infrastructures supporting nuclear family life, and the increasing privatization of state provision, parents individually are burdened with protecting their children and are first in line for blame if things go wrong.[5] In this context, "parental determinism" has become a dominant and, increasingly, unquestioned way of thinking.[6] It construes the everyday activities of parents as directly and causally associated with the failure or harming of their children and the wider society. As a wealth of research has argued, this deterministic and neoliberal rationale underpins, informs, and fuels the intensified regulation and policing of parents.[7]

Family and parenting are being positioned, more and more, as both the cause of national problems and key sites for intervention.[8] In the UK, the number of government-sponsored parenting interventions that reframe parenting as a "job requiring particular skills and expertise, which must be taught by formally qualified professionals," is growing fast.[9] The focus on "responsible" parenting emerged, most notably, during the Blair era. As Ruth Cain notes, the Blair government "emphasiz[ed] that the political burden on parents was now to police themselves effectively, as carers and producers of future citizens, with the state stepping in to provide re-education in the form of parenting classes and training and, in the more intractable cases, coercive measures such as Parenting Orders and Anti-Social Behaviour Orders targeted at both parents and children."[10] A potent example of the intensification of the state's policing of parents was the announcement in 2016, made by the then prime minister David Cameron, of his plan to stop family breakup by enrolling parents in state-backed parenting classes to learn how to raise their children properly.[11] This and similar interventions were aimed, almost exclusively, at parents from deprived backgrounds who consistently are constructed as needing to get parenting "right," and whose struggles are framed as "personal crises or accomplishments decoupled from economic and social circuits of accumulation and dispossession."[12] As Kim Allen and Anna Bull show in their investigation of how character education has come into being as thinkable and a "common-sense" policy agenda in the UK, a range of policy texts such as the Jubilee Centre publications present character "as a set of dispositions, required for success, that can be 'taught'" through parenting interventions targeted at working-class parents.[13]

The emphasis on the individual parents' responsibility for not just their own children but also the wider society is manifest vividly in the UK Department for Communities and Local Government's 2016 campaign for neighborhood planning, "Make a Plan, Make a Difference" (fig. 4.1). In one of the campaign's ads we are shown what appears to be a page from a children's pop-up book: on the left-hand side is a cluster of small houses, on a leafy street, signifying well-looked-after, owner-occupied homes. The right-hand side of the page shows a young, slim, white mother whose two young children stand,

Chapter Four

"I USED TO THINK THAT SOMEBODY SHOULD HELP MAKE SURE WE'VE GOT HOMES FOR YOUNG FAMILIES"

"UNTIL I REALISED I AM THE SOMEBODY"

Make a plan   Shape the future of your area
MAKE A DIFFERENCE   neighbourhoodplanning.org

Department for Communities and Local Government

4.1 Department for Communities and Local Government's campaign (UK)

one on each side of her, clutching her legs while she holds their heads protectively. Above the images are two captions, representing the mother's voice. Above the picture of attractive homes are the words "I used to think that SOMEBODY should help make sure we've got HOMES for YOUNG FAMILIES," while the caption on the right (assuming the viewer reads from left to right)— "UNTIL I REALISED I am the SOMEBODY"—signifies the "makeover" the mother has undergone. She used to locate responsibility for her family externally ("somebody"), but now she is rid of this undesirable belief. The government's ad exhorts young mothers to arrive at a similar realization, to internalize responsibility for governing themselves (signified by the normatively feminine and kempt look of the young mother in the ad), governing their children, and looking after their environment. Thus, being a "good parent" is firmly associated with the mother taking personal responsibility for social problems: "Make a plan, make a difference, shape the future of your area" implores the text below the image of the mother in the ad.

The father's or any other partner's absence is conspicuous: it is the mother, and she alone, who is constructed as responsible for her children and the neighborhood environment. Indeed, while both mothers and fathers are subject to manifold risks and pressures, regulation of parents by the state and the media is directed particularly at mothers.[14] In her study of today's American families, Marianne Cooper found that women are expected to manage increasing amounts of "security work" precisely at the historical moment when the state and public sectors withdraw their responsibilities for and resources to support families.[15] This has been brutally pronounced during the COVID-19 pandemic. As a result of school closures, overburdened health-care systems, social distancing measures, and entrenched gender norms, women's unpaid care at home, domestic load, and "security work" increased dramatically, resulting in many women being forced out of employment or forced to scale down. As a *New York Times* report puts it, the pandemic has thrown into sharp relief that women are the "shock absorbers" of society.[16]

Middle-class parents, especially mothers, frequently—albeit not always directly or explicitly—are positioned as role models whose "quality parenting" other parents should emulate. In both the UK and the US, the poor, disenfranchised "failing" mother is consistently vilified and denigrated compared to the white (upper-)middle-class mother, who is frequently idealized for her provision of "good mothering" and responsible action. In Britain, especially during the recent period of austerity, poor, working-class, and particularly poor single mothers have been demonized repeatedly in political discourse and in the press as contributing nothing to the economy, being incapable of governing themselves and their children in the "right" ways, and, thus, being responsible for making Britain a "broken society."[17] In the US, mother-blaming is directed most aggressively at Black, Latinx, and Native women, depicting them as lazy, sexually loose single mothers. The trope reaches back to the notorious 1965 Moynihan Report and was later reconceived in the Reagan era as the "welfare queen."[18] In the current moment in the United States, Jennifer Nash observes, Black motherhood is increasingly imagined as a space of crisis and a site of intense regulation.[19]

Idealization of middle-class mothers produces and is reliant on intense regulation—primarily by the media and, crucially, self-regulation: mothers policing each other and governing themselves. There is extensive research documenting the ever-expanding and intensifying scrutiny, policing, and pressure for mothers to be self-governing in the current mediated sphere.[20] Ellie Lee observes that public surveillance and monitoring of maternal decisions is fiercer than ever and has become connected to a growing set of claims about children's success or failure, for which mothers—often exclusively—are seen as responsible.[21] In particular, what the authors Julie A. Wilson and Emily Chivers Yochim call the digital "mamasphere"—a network of mommy blogs, corporate websites addressed to mothers, social media platforms, and mothering online communities—has become a key site and technology for mothers' self-governance and policing of their thinking, feeling, and behavior as they try to cope with the mounting insecurities that have enveloped their families and to secure their families' happiness and resilience.[22]

In this context, Susan Braedley and Meg Luxton note how neoliberalism encourages "investment parenting"—the investment by parents of substantial time, labor, and resources in their children to ensure a good market return.[23] However, in the current economic climate and in view of great uncertainty about the future of work, the idea of perpetual progress, of each generation being better off than their parents, is being fundamentally challenged.[24] The fact is, "younger generations today face less favourable mobility prospects than did their parents or their grandparents, and are more likely to experience downward mobility."[25] Furthermore, while education opportunities have expanded in recent decades, their benefit in terms of job outcomes has become more uncertain.[26] Thus, "investment parenting" and its associated middle-class practices of "intensive parenting" (and intensive mothering, in particular) are being complicated by new levels of insecurity and uncertainty since the investment is far from guaranteeing a commensurate market return, such as a place at a top university or a secure professional job.

Recent research highlights how a fundamental aspect of the regulation of mothers is its internalization by mothers themselves, through self-monitoring, policing, and governing.[27] These studies underscore the huge affective (as well as material) labor and money involved and the emotional cost of mothering in neoliberal times, which is invested in maximizing children's (and the family's) happiness. It is within this context of increased uncertainty, anxiety, and risk, and the concurrent intensification of regulation and policing of parents, that we situate the rise of confident mothering. In what follows we explore how the confidence cult(ure) works to inculcate and shape mothers' and girls' emotional lives, through messages, technologies, and programs that focus on constituting mothers as subjects that need to transform both themselves and their daughters from insecure subjects in crisis to confident and resilient women and girls.

The Cultural Landscape of Confident Mothering

In a guest post on the popular UK parenting website Mumsnet, the former UK women and equalities minister and cofounder of the Campaign for Body Confidence, Jo Swinson, observed how "astonishing" it was to see "how quickly confidence can evaporate on maternity leave" because of body image. Echoing tropes of the confidence cult and particularly LYB (discussed in chapter 1), the solution Swinson proposes is to "celebrate positive body image and challenge the negative attitudes and actions that lead to poor self-esteem." This can be achieved by following the "tailored guidance and activities" designed by the government, a link to which Swinson provides in her post. Swinson then moves seamlessly from imploring women to cultivate confidence in themselves as maternal subjects to positioning them as responsible for nurturing this same desirable disposition in their children: "It is absolutely vital," she writes, "that we support our children to develop resilience in the face of this pressure, to help them to avoid a lifetime of low body confidence and stop this cycle before it begins." While the post refers to "children," the image accompanying it is notably gendered, showing three girls and one boy looking in a mirror held by a young woman in a suit, with one of the girls holding a sign that reads, "reflect on positive body image."[28]

Swinson's post captures the "double whammy" of the confidence culture in the domain of mothering: women are exhorted not only to be confident themselves but also to instill in their children, especially daughters, confidence and resilience. As Wilson and Yochim note in their study of contemporary mothering and the digital sphere, mothers are caught up in "two unrelenting and entwined modes of affective labor," having to govern themselves *and* govern their children.[29]

So how does this intertwined imperative work? Below we examine how popular culture and media implore women to perform affective and aesthetic labor in the quest to become confident mothers who produce successfully confident children, what this address makes legible and visible, and what, in turn, it renders unintelligible.[30] We start by examining the address to mothers to become confident and authentic subjects before moving on to explore how they are constructed as the primary (if not exclusive) subjects responsible for transforming their daughters into similarly confident and resilient subjects.

Wear It like a Mum: Becoming a Confident Mother

Continuous with the confidence discourses, practices, and technologies identified in other domains (discussed in the preceding chapters), a plethora of self-help books, social media sites, advertisements, and programs are invested in urging and coaching women to overcome their supposed confidence crises and transform themselves into confident mothers. Maternal self-esteem and self-belief are central themes in a spate of "mommy blogs," mother websites, and self-help parenting books, such as *The Confident Mother*, *The Confi-*

dent Mom, *MomSense: A Common-Sense Guide to Confident Mothering, Swimming Upstream: Parenting Girls for Resilience in a Toxic Culture,* the UK best seller *Keep Calm: The New Mum's Manual,* and best-selling author of childcare books Gina Ford's *The Contented Mother's Guide.*

The trope of confident mothering is not entirely new, of course. In their influential book, *The Mommy Myth,* Susan Douglas and Meredith Michaels observe a *McCall's* magazine popular monthly column in the early 1990s entitled "The Confident Parent."[31] They argue that the column, written by therapist Ron Taffel, was an exceptional "breath of fresh air" in its attack on media messages that guilt-tripped working mothers and in its restoring of mothers' faith in their intuition.[32] However, today new meanings proliferate around confident mothering, appearing to be more complex than Douglas and Michaels described in relation to the 1990s. These meanings chime in with many of the features we have discussed so far in relation to the confidence cult(ure), including authenticity, positivity, heteronormative white femininity, and the expectation to continuously work on the self. In turn, as we discuss below, contemporary exhortations to confident mothering reinforce the wider confidence imperative and its notable gendered, racialized, and classed address.

Authenticity: Defying the "Mommy Myth"

Unlike earlier articulations, confident mothering is associated today with feminist language and goals. Specifically, becoming a confident mother is proposed as a reflexive and corrective response to the tyranny of perfect and the oppressive idealization of motherhood that held sway in previous eras;[33] it is constructed as (supposedly) refusing the diktat of "perfect mothering" and perfect femininity. For instance, the opening page of the Confident Mother website states, "You don't need to be the perfect mother. Simply focus on what's most important to you."[34] The confident mother is conjured up as unapologetically "authentic," rejecting the pressure to be perfect and, instead, celebrating being her true self. "We have to work, really, really hard at that whole self-confidence thing," one mommy blogger writes, in order, as she proudly explains she did, to transform ourselves from a "sorry mom," who is a "people-pleaser," "obsessed with doing everything perfectly," to "a sorry-not-sorry mom."[35] Similarly, the Authentic Mom website implores women to refuse "messages dictating how we should raise our children—and how we're expected to feel about it."[36] Such exhortations are part of and in turn contribute to larger changes in the meanings of motherhood, in ways that defy the "mommy myth," that is, the "highly romanticized and yet demanding view of motherhood in which the standards for success are impossible to meet."[37] This trend is evident, for example, in popular culture, in the emergence of unapologetically non-normative "aberrant" mothers, who are "unabashedly sexual" and who resist male control and normative familialism, or in the emerging cultural construction of the "mother behaving badly," who revels in "chaotic hedonism."[38] Such representations of mothers unashamedly defying the pressures of perfect mothering and reveling in chaos and loss of control proliferated on social media during the COVID-19 pandemic, for example, in memes of mothers rejoicing in excessive alcohol consumption ("mommy juice").[39]

Indeed, instead of seeking to adhere to and measure oneself by oppressive unattainable standards of mothering and femininity, much of the contemporary advice on mothering emphasizes authenticity, letting go, and being true to one's self—emphases that, as we have shown in previous chapters, are part and parcel of a popular feminist sentiment and the confidence cult. One of the most central themes within the "authentic/confident mother" imperative is body image. Numerous media texts, websites, blogs, organizations, and programs promulgate that women should love and celebrate their postnatal bodies. For example, in their study of Australian media portrayals of the childbearing body in celebrity stories in women's magazines, Roth, Homer, and Fenwick found that alongside the prominent message that women need to strive to regain a pre-pregnant body shape, there was a substantial number of stories about celebrities who appeared to embrace their changed but healthy postnatal body and advocated that women "refuse to bounce back."[40] Similar messages circulate in various mothering websites, blogs, and vlogs. For instance, in her study of mother blogs, Husbands discusses the highly trafficked website The Shape of a Mother, where mothers post images of their bodies and posts related to their feelings about their postnatal bodies. Though the site does not completely avoid reproducing dominant discourses and images of the perfect maternal body, Husbands writes, "it does successfully negotiate and contest popular cultural understandings of the pregnant and postpartum body," allowing for a more inclusive, positive, and realistic understanding of the maternal body.[41] In Sweden, under the hashtags #mammamage (mum tummy) and #mammakropp (mum body), women post on Instagram images of their post-birth bodies as a way to challenge oppressive body ideals and negotiate cultural expectations about postpartum bodies.[42] Along a similar vein, the creators of the comic digital video series *I Mom So Hard*, which we discuss later in this chapter, tackle the pressure on mothers'

4.2 Peanut advertisement

body images with humor and sarcasm, encouraging mothers to refuse and free themselves from these pressures.

Alongside the emphasis on refusing the quest to get back to one's prenatal body, a central exhortation is to preserve one's prenatal identity and realize and protect that non-maternal "authentic" identity as entirely separate from the maternal one. For example, the social media platform Peanut (launched February 2017), dubbed a "dating-app for mums" and founded by entrepreneur Michelle Kennedy, invites women to "meet as mamas, connect as women" (fig. 4.2).[43] Kennedy describes the motivation for her app as connecting mothers so that they do not feel isolated and, crucially, so that they do not lose their prenatal identity: "Motherhood is amazing, but that's not all I am. And I think that there are a lot of women who that will resonate with. To feel like you've lost your identity and you're just this tag of 'mum' is quite scary."[44]

Similar calls to women to not let motherhood "steal their identity" or to "get it back" and "rediscover themselves" if it has been "stolen" proliferate on mothering websites and social media.[45] Preservation of one's prenatal identity is couched in these sites as active resistance against the stigmatization that reduces women only to mothers and the loss of one's true identity. However, the onus of resisting the "tag of 'mum'" is the women's only. The societal structures and cultural pressures that encourage women to take on the role of the "foundation parent" at the expense of their other roles and identities, and that participate in and propel the stigmatization, undervaluing, and suppression of women's "prenatal identity"—related primarily to the world of waged work—are let off the hook entirely.[46] The resistance that mothers are exhorted to perform is directed entirely inward, through following a series of behavioral steps that are strikingly similar to those advocated to women in relation to other "crises": make time for the things you enjoy, incorporate self-care, ditch the guilt, accept yourself the way you are, and so on.

Positive Affect

As with other confidence culture domains, so, too, mothering is characterized by the dominance of positive affect and positivity. Tellingly, Peanut is marketed in a putatively feminine aesthetic: young and (normatively) beautiful women, dressed in reds and pinks, are seen engaging in stereotypically "girly" talk (reinforced by a "Girl Gang" sticker-like text displayed in one of the images), on four phone-like frames, and all against pink backgrounds (fig. 4.2). Similarly, the image accompanying the advice of the mummy blogger cited earlier, who cajoles women to become a "sorry-not-sorry mom" (echoing Demi Lovato's confidence cult anthem "Sorry Not Sorry") is of a young, white, beautiful mother in pink trousers and red vest joyously caressing her baby girl (fig. 4.3).

A number of studies show how the proliferation of such parenting social media platforms has facilitated the explosion of mothers' expressions of the ambivalence, difficulties, frustrations, anger, and disappointments of motherhood, which, previously, were largely inexpressible.[47] However, the branding of these platforms rarely contains any trace of these "negative" feelings. Furthermore, as some studies have shown, the policing of negative affect and the promotion of this type of "pink positivity" are present also in the actual communication taking place between and among mothers on these sites.[48] For example, in her study of discussion threads from an online parenting forum, Ranjana Das examines the range of discursive strategies employed to silence difficult stories and promote positive accounts of childbirth, showing that "the space available to speak freely about childbirth difficulties, or feelings of disappointment," remains highly limited.[49] Along similar lines, Wilson and Yochim observe that the American mothers they studied, who engage intensively in the online "mamasphere," invest significant affective labor in routing their "bad, unhappy affects" into "just not being angry."[50] Happiness, the authors conclude, drawing on Ahmed, shuts down possibilities for alternative sensibilities of who and what these mothers might become.[51] Thus, paradoxically, while the emphasis in confident mothering discourses, practices, and technologies is on authenticity and being true to one's feelings and identity, the version of

4.3 "How to Become a
Sorry-Not-Sorry Mom"

authentic confidence that they favor is predicated on suppressing "negative"
feelings and maintaining an upbeat, "positive" outlook.

Heteronormative, Middle-Class, White Femininity

The look of the confident mother is also far less diverse than the rhetorical encouragement to "be you" and refuse external and oppressive pressures
might suggest. In the Peanut ad, for example, we see several white women
and one Black woman with a distinctively Afro hairstyle—emblematic of the
confidence culture's "postracial" tenor that we discussed in previous chapters. Nevertheless, all of the women in the ad conform conspicuously to narrow heteronormative beauty standards, signifying the stereotypical middle-
class "yummy mummy."[52] Therefore, while the app's founder highlights the
significance of the platform in reflecting that "we're not all the same, every
woman is different, [and] every mother is different," its visual branding tells
a different story.[53]

An ad by the UK women and children's fashion brand Boden is another example of the visual construction of the confident mum.[54] A dark-skinned, South Asian–looking, young beautiful woman dressed in a floral dress is seen sitting on a bench in what looks like the sort of trendy kitchen associated with middle-class private homes, while her contented toddler is shown behind her wearing a space costume. "Wear it like a mum," the ad cajoles women, "as in your terms, in your way, how YOU like. Your style, and how you wear it, is something to be championed—because mum is a title to be proud of." Yet, against the discursive reiteration of the expression of one's unique and authentic identity, style, and preferences, the visual construction reveals that "wearing it like a mum" requires subscribing to very specific and narrow terms of heteronormative feminine beauty and middle-class aesthetics and, crucially, showing no traces of messiness or struggle.

As Kathryn Jezer-Morton observes about online motherhood, on the one hand, the current dominant trend on social media is of the "perfectly imperfect"—a rebuttal to the beauty and lifestyle ideals that characterize traditional women's media representations of beauty and success and the perfect Instagram mommy influencers. At the same time, "most images that are tagged with #perfectlyimperfect or #motherhoodunplugged represent conventionally 'perfect' women—attractive, carefully groomed, usually white, posing for selfies that reinforce many of the same old beauty and femininity norms that have dogged women since the dawn of time." The perfectly imperfect mom is still very beautiful, "on the inside AND on the outside. She's caffeinated, motivated, hyperorganized, yet also soulful and vulnerable. She is all of these things and then some."[55]

In contradistinction to the perfectly imperfect (white) middle-class motherhood that contemporary media exhort women to embrace, a notable and important development in the context of Black Lives Matter in the US is that of "mothering while Black." It refers to the increasing visibility in popular discourse of voices and bodies that expose the anxieties, fears, and vulnerability of Black mothers and other women of color about mothering amid Black maternal crisis, precarity, and injustice.[56] Of course, Black mothers have long expressed and contested the injustices, inequalities, and risks they and other women of color who mother experience, and they have continuously engaged in negotiating, navigating, and resisting what Patricia Hill Collins termed white "controlling images." However, it is only more recently that celebrities such as Beyoncé, Serena Williams, and Cardi B have brought the experience of Black motherhood into wider popular conversation.[57] Their voices have played an important role in expanding the popular discussion about mothering and motherhood, to include racially centered accounts of Black maternal crisis and precarity. However, these celebrity voices continue to overshadow the more mundane, quotidian, and diverse experiences of women of color, whose lives may diverge from the overarching themes of Black celebrity.

Yet in recent years, and especially in the wake of the killing of George Floyd and the ensuing reinvigoration of Black Lives Matter, more and more voices and accounts of ordinary Black women have entered public discussions on social media, as well as mainstream media and books. They expose and highlight the consequences of racism that Black mothers face, including maternal mortality and their profound anxieties that they cannot guarantee the safety of their children in contemporary America.[58] Jennifer Nash discusses how in accounts by writers like Claudia Rankin and Emily Bernard, memoirs such as *Rest in Power: The Enduring Love of Trayvon Martin*, and speeches made in the wake of state disavowals of Black death in the US, "black motherhood is imagined as a life-giving practice of radical anti-state care-work."[59] Thus, many of these contemporary maternal accounts poke a hole in the edifice of confident mothering and its postracial character, the notion that maternal confidence is a parenting style or attitude that one can and should adopt through individualized work on the self. Rather, these voices highlight that for Black mothers the meanings of being a "confident mother" diverge radically. As Dasia Moore observes, "while helicopter moms are busy multiplying their children's privilege and advantages, many black moms are fighting to protect their children from the structural disadvantages that keep opportunity just out of reach."[60]

Affective and Aesthetic Labor

The Boden ad we discussed above and similar texts hide the considerable labor required of women in order to become confident and authentic mothers, and the resources needed to be able to "wear it like a mum." To identify what is "most important to you" and to champion "your own terms," women are urged to engage in multiple activities, to monitor their thinking, feeling, and behavior, to seek the advice of experts, and, importantly, to purchase self-help tools and various fashion and cosmetic products. For example, the mommy blogger who advocates becoming the "sorry-not-sorry mom" lists on her blog six things that are necessary for transformation into that desirable maternal subject. They include inspirational exhortations similar to those we have seen in other domains, such as "tell yourself you're awesome," "be authentic," or "do something you're afraid of and see what happens," all involving intense introspection and constant monitoring of one's feelings. So, for instance, to "tell yourself you're awesome" requires the woman to make a list of the things she is and was good at: "If you remember the school art project on time, write that crap down. If you are really good at making your kids wash their hands before dinner, write it down. If you didn't yell for one hour straight, write it down. Tallying up your strengths will help you realize that you're pretty amazing." This 24/7 labor is cast as individualized and not relational: "Don't get your self-esteem from other people. (Not even your kids)," the blogger urges. And, as if the labor involved in loving oneself is not enough, the number one piece of advice for mothers who want to transform from insecure, apologetic to authentic, empowered women is to have more kids (!): "If you want to become that mom that doesn't apologize, simply have. more. kids. Because then they'll be in control anyway. Not you."[61]

This blog's advice might seem atypically extreme. However, it is characteristic of the messages found on numerous confidence culture sites addressing mothers or mothers-to-be. The "refusal" to "surrender" to oppressive expectations of perfect mothering involves constant self-work and self-governance through adherence to a series of instrumental DIY advice on how to change your body, talk, behavior, thinking, and feeling, often requiring the purchase of certain "aid tools," such as books and apps, registration on mailing lists, and attendance at certain groups and conferences. Thus, it is not surprising, but is deeply disturbing, that mothers, like those whose experiences were studied by Wilson and Yochim, become "exceedingly flexible abilities-machines for their families," working constantly to elevate their families' lives above the risks and threats of the precarious ordinary *and* to elevate themselves.[62]

The demand to perform all this invisible affective and aesthetic labor is frequently cast in terms of self-love and self-empowerment. For example, during the COVID-19 pandemic, numerous messages on social media, in magazines, in the news, and on other websites exhorted mothers to "let go" and "self-care" by performing ongoing psychological and physical work: revisit your values, exercise self-compassion, turn the news off, take a walk, meditate, indulge in stress baking—to mention just a few of the multifarious "tips" addressed to mothers.[63] However, crucially, this labor is also, and perhaps primarily, oriented to benefiting others. As a *Psychology Today* advice column adjures: "Mama, take care of yourself. Prioritize yourself and your self-care so that it is on your list of 'to-do's each day. . . . *Your goal is to take care of yourself so that you can keep your home ship sailing* until we see this to the end."[64]

The injunction to mothers to perform as a confident role model for their children, and especially daughters, was illustrated most vividly in a CNN article reviewing (and praising) *The Confidence Code for Girls*. In this article, CNN digital correspondent and editor-at-large Kelly Wallace lists five advice points from Kay Shipman (one of the book's authors) on "how to build up our daughters."[65] One of these is the call to women to "role model failure and struggle." Wallace notes that one of the most surprising results from the poll Shipman and Kay commissioned for their book is that "fathers seem to be better at recognizing a lack of confidence in their daughters than mothers: They were found to be 26% more likely to accurately estimate their child's confidence than moms were." This is, Shipman observes, because mothers "don't see their daughters' behavior as unusual," whereas fathers "find it genuinely strange." This rather gender-essentialist observation leads to an important takeaway: "Let them see us, especially mothers, dealing with failure and struggle and taking risks." Shipman relates how she models this takeaway herself. When she's upset about something, she allows her daughter to "see how she's feeling and then raises the question whether she's overreacting and figures out how she's going to deal with it—all in front of her daughter." One of the striking things in this example is that the onus of role-modeling confidence is exclusively the mother's. The father is cast in the role of the referee, determining the "abnormal" levels of confidence in his daughter but totally exempt from responsibility for correcting it. By the same token, the *Guardian* writer Cerys Howell notes in her account of her postnatal depression that all the baby apps she downloaded (and later deleted) "only mentioned dads as a subsection, like a type of buggy."[66] Notably, the focus in these discussions about mothers' "duty" to model confidence to their daughters is heteronormative, implying the existence of a mother and a father. Injunctions to mothers to instill confidence in their daughters largely ignore the huge number of single mothers raising their children and the existence of families with two mothers.

Thus, to demonstrate confidence to her daughter, the mother has not only to monitor her own difficult feelings but also to share them and how she overcomes them. It is the mother's responsibility to both overcome her own confidence crisis and nurture resilient and confident children. It is her failure, and hers alone, if confidence is not properly instilled in the next generation.

Self-Worth Is an Echo from Me to Them: Raising Confident Daughters

As noted earlier, a growing body of research highlights the ever more pronounced preoccupation in contemporary culture with building girls' confidence and the rise of a "market of empowerment" that aims to tackle girls' "crises" and empower girls within a context of commodified girl power.[67] This can be seen in hundreds of organizations, corporate campaigns, advertisements, YouTube vlogs, and political and policy discourses (especially those related to body image and girls' exclusion at school from STEM subjects) urging girls to become more confident.[68] For example, Banet-Weiser examines the "Confidence Coalition" in the United States, which situates confidence as an individual commodity—something you can carry via the Confidence Coalition "Go Confidently" handbag collection—and the campaigns of the consumer brands Always and CoverGirl, which mobilize individualized confidence messages to sell their products to an audience of girl consumers.[69]

While these messages, programs, and products hail girls directly, they simultaneously, albeit often implicitly, target their parents, especially mothers, who are the fundamental backbone facilitating the economic viability of this market. In what follows we highlight how mothers are positioned as mainly, if not exclusively, responsible for both their daughters' confidence crisis *and* its resolution. We use four illustrative examples to highlight the central features of this construction of mothers: Dove's "legacy" ad, a YouTube video by *I Mom So Hard*, tennis player Serena Williams's "Letter to My Mom," and the website of the doll brand American Girl.

Dove: Legacy

The "Dove: Legacy" 2014 film, which is part of the brand's campaign celebrating "real beauty" and female self-esteem, shows five women who were asked to write what they like and do not like about the way they look, and it shares some of what they listed. We then see them reading extracts from their daughters' lists in response to similar questions. The film dwells on the mothers' reactions when they realize the striking similarity between what they and their daughters listed that they dislike about their bodies: disheartened, the mothers sigh in discomfort and, significantly, guilt. Several are shown explaining their daughters' lack of confidence as a direct result of their own low self-confidence. The film concludes with mother-to-mother confidence exhortations: "Just be confident with yourself and just realize how you can influence your child," says one; "Self-worth and beauty . . . is an echo from me to them," says another; "How I feel about myself really affects how she feels about herself," confesses yet another. The girls are then seen sitting next to their mothers or on their mothers' laps recounting what they do like about their bodies. Accompanied by a cheerful tune that is gradually amplified, Dove's final address to mothers appears in a caption at the center of the screen: "The way a girl feels about her beauty starts with how you feel about yours." Unsurprisingly, nowhere in the ad are there hints about the influence of various societal and structural factors—including the cosmetic industry of which Dove is part—and their culpability for producing low self-esteem in women and girls in the first place. As we have argued in chapter 1, so many of the companies promoting LYB, such as Dove, are deeply invested in maintaining female body dissatisfaction in order to sell their products, while casting themselves as if they were entirely disconnected from the problem.[70]

Thus, the project of making confident mothers relies on a contradictory impetus. On the one hand, couched in feminist language, it encourages women to challenge and refuse to surrender to oppressive societal expectations about the significance of body look, size, or shape and promises to free them from societal norms and prescriptions of "good mothering" by unapologetically "believing in themselves" and being their true selves.[71] At the same time, this very technology of confidence relies on and in turn reproduces deep-seated historical discourses of mothers' guilt and practices of blaming women, implying that the insecure mother is a bad mother and demanding women take full and exclusive responsibility for addressing the problem for which they are being blamed. As Barak-Brandes and Lachover note about the mother-daughter Dove campaign, it centers the mother as the key and crucial figure for building up her daughter's self-esteem and body image against the background of Western culture's narrow and oppressive model of beauty.[72] Here, too, as in other messages discussed before, fathers or any other parents are glaringly absent.

I Mom So Hard

This contradictory impetus of "empowering" mothers to be their true selves and love their bodies while simultaneously blaming them for their potential harmful effect on their daughters, is not characteristic only of marketing efforts that, arguably, exploit women's manufactured guilt to sell them products. Rather, this contradiction can be found in various social media sites created by mothers for mothers. For example, a video in the *I Mom So Hard* comic digital video series (#IMomSoHard) attracted over seventeen million views; its creators, Kristin Hensley and Jen Smedley, tackled the embarrassment and discomfort mothers experience wearing swimsuits on the beach. The video hilariously mocks the ridiculous and completely impractical and uncomfortable swimsuits mothers are cajoled to wear and, by wearing some of these swimsuits themselves in the video, Hensley and Smedley encourage viewers to feel good in their bodies and refuse to give in to marketing pressure: "Nobody thinks that they look perfect ever, let's just all go to the beach and be the same . . . and have a good time!" they exclaim. However, the video concludes on a serious note, with Hensley stressing her personal responsibility for role-modeling body confidence to her daughter. "I want my daughter to love her life and to love herself and she's not going to do it because I tell her to do it, she's going to do it because I teach her to do it," she says.[73]

As in other confidence domains, so too in that of parenting, both the problem and its solutions are located in women's psyches. The message is that the only way to challenge the confidence crisis effectively is for women to internalize both responsibility for the problem and the actions required to resolve it. What is distinctive about the domain of mothering, however, is the *double* affective burden that women are demanded to shoulder. Women are asked to inhabit a constant simultaneous awareness of the (assumed) direct effect of their self-confidence level on their daughters' and, therefore, to monitor and regulate themselves with a mind to improving and "fixing" themselves *and* their daughters simultaneously. This move cements the woman's primary affective role as a mother, since everything she feels, thinks, and does implicates her daughter: she continuously has to govern herself and monitor her feelings and behavior and internalize the notion that—as one of the women in the Dove ad puts it—her self-worth and beauty are an "echo" to her daughter.

Serena Williams's "Letter to My Mom"

The centering of the woman as the primary if not exclusive affective laborer, charged with responsibility for raising confident girls, is notable in another example that received a lot of publicity: an open letter posted on Reddit written by the tennis champion Serena Williams to her mother after the birth of Williams's first child. In her letter, the American tennis player, who is a symbol of "Black excellence," muses on the problems related to raising a confident and strong Black girl able to endure the hardships of growing up in a world that is likely to disparage her and fail "to understand the power of a black woman."[74] Williams's emotional letter foregrounds her painful experience of being denigrated as not belonging in women's sport because of her masculine physique and subjected to racist stigmas about Black women. She praises her mother for being a role model of an extremely strong and confident woman, who instilled in her pride and fortitude, and expresses her anxious hope that she will be able to follow her mother's lead and cultivate in her baby girl the same qualities.

Unlike *The Confidence Code for Girls* and the Dove ad, Williams's letter goes some way toward confronting structural inequalities and, specifically, the toxic cocktail of racism and sexism experienced by Black women. In many of Williams's other media appearances—in particular after the egregious racist 2018 *Herald Sun* cartoon that depicted her jumping in the air and "spitting the dummy" after losing a match to Naomi Osaka—and following the killing of George Floyd in 2020, Williams has connected female confidence and success, and its lack thereof, to racism and sexism in sports and beyond. More broadly, as Jennifer Nash argues, Williams's performance of Black maternal aesthetics has systematically linked "personal and political discontent."[75] However, like many of the other examples we discussed, Williams's "Letter to My Mom" adopts an individualized approach to addressing the structural conditions, which it identifies as the *exclusive* responsibility of her mother and now of herself. Nowhere in the letter is there a mention of Williams's partner's potential role in preparing their daughter to face the hardships awaiting her with confidence, nor is there a mention of the pivotal role played by Williams's own father, who homeschooled her and her sister, tennis player Venus Williams, and at one time was her official coach.

American Girl

The imperative to "repair" girls' confidence crisis is seen in numerous parenting advice books and programs, where the address, frequently, is to parents, rather than mothers specifically. However, the linking of mothers' and girls' confidence—as seen in the examples discussed thus far—and the broader persistent prioritization of mothers as "foundation parents" in contemporary culture work to justify the gendering of the imperative to raise confident girls, with fathers and paternal responsibility overwhelmingly absent from this address.[76]

This is clearly seen on the website of the popular doll brand American Girl. At the time of writing, the website's front page promoted a line of toys, clothing, and books called "Truly Me," accompanied by the slogan "self-expression becomes self-confidence" (see fig. 4.4). The brand's ethos was described as follows:

We believe in creating girls of strong character.
Because character counts.

4.4 American Girl main website page

Facing fears, running into roadblocks, and learning from mistakes? That's life. Responding with optimism and resilience? That's character—the kind we build in girls everywhere, every day through stories and experiences both timely and timeless.[77]

In appealing to parents, American Girl capitalizes on the self-confidence discourse and its sister qualities of character, resilience, grit, and gumption— the key dispositions highlighted as necessary to survive and thrive in neoliberal societies.[78] Building character in girls is framed as a universal, constant, and never-ending project—"everywhere, every day"—and as a collective commitment enjoining parents and the company. It is to be exercised through the supposedly effortless, casual, and intuitive activities of "stories and experiences."

However, beneath this "universal," "collective," and "effortless" project, the numerous products sold on the website and their marketing to parents reveal a highly individualized, formulaic, laborious, and financially expensive enterprise that almost exclusively targets mothers. For example, the website's "advice library" includes books such as *A Smart Girl's Guide: Liking Herself*, whose subtitle reads "the secrets to trusting yourself, being your best & never letting the bad days bring you down," or *The Care and Keeping of You: The Body Book for Girls* (number 1 aimed at younger girls and number 2 at older ones). There is also one of the library's award-winning books (winner of a 2011

4.5 *The Care and Keeping of Us*

National Parenting Publications Award) entitled *A Smart Girl's Guide: Knowing What to Say*, which is a manual of words "to fit any situation," for example, "25 things to say after 'hi,'" "25 questions to know someone better," and "what to say if a friend lets you down." Geared toward self-improvement, these supposedly empowering American Girl texts are chillingly redolent of Victorian advice, conduct, and etiquette books for young women, which emphasize "feminine qualities" such as cheerfulness, politeness, humility, and grace.

The library's other award winner is *The Care and Keeping of Us: A Sharing Collection for Girls and Their Moms* (fig. 4.5). This best seller includes two books, one for the girl (aged 8+) and one for her mother, filled with dozens of "how-to-say-it" scripts. "These scripts," the book's description states, "give girls the words to talk about all the big topics from body basics, hygiene, and healthy habits to friends, first crushes, clothing, and more. And mom's book gives her the actual words to respond to her girl's questions, as well as scripts to initiate important conversations with her daughter." The kit includes a "sharing journal," in which both the mother and her daughter are invited to record their thoughts, and two bookmarks "to guide each other to the latest entry or point out something they don't want the other to miss."[79] Thus, the kit invites mother and daughter to enroll in an intensive program of linguistic "reprogramming," which will bring into being not one but two newly upgraded, confident selves—a mother and a daughter who care about themselves and each other.

Conclusion: Confident Mothering
and the Reframing of Feminism

The examples discussed in this chapter, including Shipman's modeling of how to overcome upset feelings and act confidently, the Dove ad, *I Mom So Hard* vlogs, Serena Williams's letter, and the American Girl website, display how the confidence cult "does" motherhood with a double whammy. These examples also contribute to and illustrate a radical re-articulation of the meanings of feminism, in four significant ways.

First, they acknowledge the difficulties and struggles mothers and daughters experience, related to, for instance, eating, weight, and health. However, instead of mobilizing this important recognition into a collective vision of addressing the structural sources of and solutions to these struggles, they individualize these experiences, suggesting that it is up to girls and their mothers to change how they feel, think, and talk about them. As we have discussed, some accounts, especially of Black motherhood (as well as queer and other non-normative mothering, which we have not addressed here), challenge the individualization of mothering and direct increasing attention to the structural conditions of contemporary motherhood. Nevertheless, as we have shown, confident mothering is fundamentally about turning mothers' and daughters' struggles into cheerful, positive experiences, free of "negative" feelings.

Second, as we have seen in other domains, becoming an empowered, self-caring feminine subject demands an intense, affective regime of self-regulation. Both mother and daughter are required to engage in intense work on the self, by monitoring and learning the "right" way to communicate their feelings. In the Dove ad the moral is that mothers must be constantly on the watch because their feelings, thinking, and behavior are an echo to their daughters. And the exercise on which the ad is based, of asking mothers and girls to list the things they like and do not like about their bodies, demonstrates to the young girls that the female body is inherently "difficult to love" and that their feelings about it must, therefore, constantly be regulated.[80] *I Mom So Hard* rejects the fashion industry's demands for mothers' self-regulation of their bodies, only to reinforce their obligation to self-police their levels of confidence for the sake of their daughters. Serena Williams concludes her letter with a promise to labor tirelessly—"I am trying, though, and God is not done with me yet. I have a LONG way to go"—in order to teach her daughter fortitude. Although of all the examples we discussed it is the least focused on self-regulation, it nevertheless ends on a self-deprecating note that commits to working on *her* self to secure *her* daughter's confidence in this world: "I'm not sure if I am as meek and strong as you are yet. I hope to get there one day." The *Care and Keeping of Us* book requires mothers and daughters to follow detailed instructions about what words and sentences to use to communicate feelings related to particular topics and situations and to record and monitor their feelings in the joint journal. Couched in feminist rhetoric of "freeing" oneself from the shackles of society's oppressive mothering scripts, confident mothering enjoins women to enlist in a non-stop laborious "project of the self" with the goal of improving themselves *and* their daughters.

Third, as is evident in all examples, the mother is the *exclusive* subject responsible for securing her daughter's development into an empowered and confident girl. Fathers, co-parents, friends, and other family members who might plausibly affect the girl's physical and emotional well-being are glaringly absent. Thus, as Wilson and Yochim note in another context, the mother is suspended between contradictory sensibilities: she is regarded as the sole self-responsible agent of her child while simultaneously being cast as "potential deficient gender subject(s) in need of perpetual government."[81] In a troubling and contradictory manner, then, the confidence culture in the domain of mothering is cast as a feminist project but is simultaneously predicated on and reproduces an unequal gendered division of labor. It reproduces and cements the unequal division of affective labor in heterosexual parenting, leaving fathers almost exempt from shouldering the responsibility of building their daughters' confidence.

Finally, it is noteworthy that one of the fundamental thrusts of feminist psychoanalysis has been cultivation of mothers' and daughters' capacities for separation and disidentification. This separation is seen as crucial for the daughter's capacity to achieve her desire for autonomy and form her own identity (and arguably confidence!) and for the mother to free herself from experiencing her daughter as her "double."[82] However, what we see in examples such as *The Care and Keeping of Us*, the Dove ad, the advice of the authors of *The Confidence Code for Girls*, and many other contemporary texts and parenting advice and coaching programs is a strange reverse move, reinforcing and encouraging a lack of separation between mother and daughter.[83] This is encapsulated perhaps best by the title of the book *The Care and Keeping of Us*, the inclusion of a joint rather than separate private diaries, and the illustration on its cover, which shows a happy and calm mother and daughter, standing with arms linked, while holding the letters "US" (which can, of course, be read also as the United States).

5

confidence
without borders

IN SEPTEMBER 2019, the former Duchess of Sussex, African American actress Meghan Markle, visited South Africa with her husband, Prince Harry, as part of the couple's royal Africa tour. After watching a self-defense class for girls, organized by the human rights organization Justice Desk in the Nyanga township of Cape Town, Markle gave a brief speech to the young people there. She spoke about the importance of preventing gender-based violence through education and praised her audience for standing firm in their "core values of respect, dignity, and equality." Quoting the civil rights activist and poet Maya Angelou, who said that "each time a woman stands up for herself, without knowing it, possibly without claiming it, she stands up for all women," Markle then concluded her talk: "And just on one personal note, may I just say that while I am here with my husband as a member of the Royal family, I want you to know that I am here as a mother, as a wife, as a woman, as a woman of color, and as your sister. I am here with you and I am here for you and thank you for showing us your Ubuntu [spirit of togetherness]."[1]

Markle's speech, and her personal message in particular, quickly went viral. It was overwhelmingly applauded on social media and media outlets as "powerful," "feminist," and "empowering."[2] Many commended Markle's words for resonating with and inspiring women around the world and for their strong universal message of sisterhood. Indeed, Markle did not just speak about sisterhood, she performed it: she danced with local women in Cape Town, hugged many of them and their children, and joined in their food preparations in a community cooking activity. Redolent of celebrities such as Angelina Jolie, through foregrounding her multiple feminine roles and identities and highlighting her embodied and affective intimacy of being "here with you" and "for you," Markle displayed her role as a humanitarian charity "do-gooder" and her compassion for "the afflicted."[3] In turn, her hosts displayed gratitude: the young women and girls welcomed her with excitement, and the Nobel Prize–winning, anti-apartheid movement champion Archbishop Desmond Tutu praised the royal couple: "Thank you for your concern and interest in the welfare of our people. It's very heartwarming to realize that you really, genuinely are caring people" (in reply to which Prince Harry said, "We all try to make things better").[4]

Markle's solidarity with her South African "sisters" is inseparable from her mediated depiction as a symbol of female empowerment and confidence and a fashion icon. The week before the royal couple embarked on their Africa tour, Markle launched her clothing collection for the charity Smart Works, an organization that helps disadvantaged women secure employment. Only a few weeks earlier she served as guest editor of a special issue of the women's magazine *Vogue*, entitled "Forces for Change," for which Markle invited many confidence cult champions to participate, including body positivity advocate and actor Jameela Jamil, actor Salma Hayek Pinault, and courage/vulnerability guru Brené Brown.[5] Thus, perhaps unsurprisingly, although Markle's speech was directed at the women and girls in one of South Africa's most poverty-ridden and dangerous townships, her speech was quickly appropriated as (yet another) injunction of confidence to women in the global North. For example, writing in the American business magazine *Forbes*, the careers and leadership writer Terina Allen used Markle's inspirational words to offer tips to female readers on how to "celebrate the courage and confidence that women display when they embrace their own power."[6] Similarly, the red beaded bracelet reading "Justice," which was given to Markle by a local boy at the start of her South Africa visit, and which she wore throughout her tour, quickly became a much-sought-after item that sold for $35 and was marketed to consumers in the UK and the US as a way to express their care and support for their less well-off sisters.[7]

The turn from confidence to vulnerability, which we discussed in the previous chapters, plays an important role in the construction of Markle's heartfelt intimacy with her South African "sisters." An African American woman and a former actress who married into the British royalty, Markle is marked, by definition, as a *foreign* princess—a position that made her subject to intense media scrutiny and repeated attacks, which ultimately led to her departure from the UK in January 2020 and with it her distancing from her royal obligations. The representation of her own mother, Doria Ragland, as a Black American mother on the global stage intersects uncomfortably with histories of Black maternal absence, silence, and suffering at the hands of systemic injustice.[8] Thus, Markle's care for global injustice appears as inextricably connected to and validated by her personal experiences. Her ability to empathize and connect with her South African audience is implicitly authorized by her personal vulnerability and her identification as a woman of color. In a similar way, confessions of celebrities like Angelina Jolie or Melinda Gates about their personal insecurities and vulnerabilities serve to authenticate and authorize their work in the space of international development and humanitarian aid. Thus, for example, coinciding with the launch of her 2019 book *The Moment of Lift*, which advocates a philanthrocapitalist approach to empowering women, the cofounder of the Bill and Melinda Gates Foundation gave a series of confessional interviews and wrote on her LinkedIn Influencer account about her struggles with lack of confidence, self-doubt, and fear and how she overcame them. Similarly, Jolie's admission of her difficulties and struggles over the years—from coping with breast cancer to undergoing divorce—and her consequent embrace of confidence and resilience have worked intertextually to license her role as a UN ambassador and endow it with authenticity and authority, especially in the context of growing criticisms of celebrity advocacy as self-interested and inauthentic.[9]

Returning to Markle, her performed intimacy with her Nyangan "sisters" works to obfuscate the crucial historical role of the British monarchy in South Africa's colonial history. In her speech she marginalizes her role as a member of the royal family and invokes motherhood, wifehood, femininity, and race as universalizing links for global feminist solidarity. Yet Markle's presence there, "with" and "for" her South African "sisters," was as a representative of the British monarchy. Echoing her deceased mother-in-law, Princess Diana, Markle performs the role of the "global mother": a role whose politics is "predicated upon a transnational love that offers the promise of a history and color-blind cosmopolitanism."[10] The invocation of what Raka Shome calls "global motherhood," typical of feminist ethical capitalism initiatives, "circulates familial desires that shore up white heterosexual patriarchal kinship structures and in doing so erase the masculinist violence of western colonialisms that have destroyed familial domesticities in so many nations in the global south."[11] Indeed, Markle's speech, and her mediated figure more broadly, neatly operates in and in turn reinforces a postracial facade (discussed in chapter 1), where race is dissociated from its historical and material context to promote a fantasy of egalitarianism—here, in the form of solidarity, transnational intimacy, and sisterhood. As Rachael McLennan notes, Markle has been used by biographers, the media, and the monarchy itself as a tool for ironing out and smoothing "the wrinkle" of race and a symbol of transcending it.[12] In late 2019, before her exit from royal duties, surrounded by a captivated audience of young South African women, Markle performs an ideological role akin to the famous *Paris-Match* cover, discussed by Roland Barthes, in which a young Algerian man salutes the French flag: in that moment, she signifies that Britain, the (former) great empire, embraces all her daughters, without any discrimination. To paraphrase Barthes, "there is no better answer to the detractors of an alleged colonialism than the zeal shown" by Britain's African American feminist princess and by the empire's former subjects.[13] Indeed, the indebtedness expressed by her South African hosts offers approval of Markle's focus on the "here and now"; their affective gratitude signals "moving on" and a seeming erasure of the violence inflicted in the past by the British monarchy and the empire on the colonies. However, as Mimi Nguyen points out, such feelings of gratitude have been central to the manufacture of structures of feeling within and between empire subjects, as part of imperial statecraft.[14]

The cultural texts and commodities circulating around Meghan Markle's South Africa visit encapsulate some of the central issues we unpack in this chapter concerning the ways in which female confidence is mobilized in relation to women and girls in the global South. Specifically, the chapter focuses on the *flow* of confidence discourses and technologies across and between the global North and South, highlighting the neocolonial dimensions of social enterprises and corporate initiatives dedicated to spreading confidence to girls and women in the global South. Following Shome, we understand the global South not just as a place but also as a placeholder for the conditions of dispossession and survival.[15] Crucially, we understand the global South in terms of "its historical antecedents, the historical legacy of colonialisms, and the ensuing period of decolonization" and as "an outcome or effect of the excessive economic accumulation and geopolitical power and privileges of the Global North."[16] This approach emphasizes the need to understand the North and South in relational terms. As Shome observes, "the exploitation of Southern conditions is always connected to larger global relations. The dispossession of the South is intimately linked to geopolitics (colonialisms—past and present) and global capitalism."[17]

In this chapter we explore how the confidence cult is situated within these dynamics. The remainder of the chapter is divided into three broad sections. The first considers how the confidence cult(ure) is positioned in relation to trends of corporatization, celebritization, and post-humanitarianism. The second explores how confidence is promoted transnationally through commodity activism, in which the purchase (or sometimes recycling) of commodities in the global North is said to give the "gift" of confidence to girls and women everywhere—obfuscating deep-rooted geopolitical power relations and injustices. In the third part we discuss how confidence is increasingly seen as a desirable quality to be exported and sold to women in the global South, creating an ideal of "confidence without borders" in which inequalities are refigured as individual deficits in self-esteem.

Empowering Our Southern Sisters
While Boosting Our Confidence (and CV)

Over the last few decades, the private sector has become centrally involved in global crises and particularly in foreign aid. The rise in the privatization of aid has been closely connected to the ongoing erosion of the welfare state and the deepening of poverty associated with neoliberal policies of the 1980s. The World Bank, other international institutions, and governments—notably under Reagan in the US and Thatcher in the UK—adopted new frameworks for promoting private-sector responsibility and leadership for addressing social ills. This resulted in increasing transfer of administration of matters of public concern to private hands and the reconfiguration of the modalities of international development assistance through "brand aid."[18] In this process, celebrities have come to play an increasingly important role in "deciding who and what are worthy of being 'saved' or 'developed,' how and in what ways to respond to various disasters and 'crises' of development, and which particular causes are important for us as citizens, consumers and audience members to focus our attention, donations and shopping on."[19]

These transformations have been accompanied by and in turn contributed to intensifying public disillusion with humanitarian aid and NGOs' efficacy and legitimacy (exacerbated and exemplified by criticisms of campaigns such as Live Aid in the 1980s and Make Poverty History in the early 2000s). Public criticism, distrust, and scrutiny of humanitarian organizations add to continuing pressure on humanitarian and international development organizations to raise funds.[20] They have led NGOs to increasingly adopt a corporate logic in their humanitarian communication, influenced by business, advertising, and branding models.[21] Recently, in the wake of #MeToo, revelations about sexual abuse scandals engulfing international NGOs (INGOs) such as Oxfam and Save the Children have further fueled a mistrust in these organizations and a move away from transnational aid organizations toward foundations with deep corporate histories and links.

In particular, philanthrocapitalism, epitomized by the Bill and Melinda Gates Foundation, which has been involved in global development for more than two decades, has become hegemonic within the field of international development.[22] Recent years have seen a proliferation of international development and humanitarian philanthrocapiatlist initiatives predicated on the mainstreaming of the idea that the private sector is the most effective vector to eradication of global inequalities.[23] The majority of these initiatives, some of which we will discuss in this chapter, position the individual as the solution to social ills and identify individual pursuit of happiness and empowerment as the most effective approach to social change.[24] For example, the Living Proof campaign, funded by the Bill and Melinda Gates Foundation, relies on individual success stories of triumph over poverty and a "positive deviance" approach.[25]

As many scholars and commentators have observed, the adoption of the logic of global market capitalism has fundamentally depoliticized humanitarian and international development communication. The latter increasingly relies on and fosters neoliberal ideas of self-responsibilization and consumerist forms of engagement, shifting focus from the distant other inward onto the supporter in the global North and instrumentalizing solidarity as a profitable choice that consumers are invited to make.[26] The new "post-humanitarian" paradigm "privileges privatized action rather than grand ethical and political changes that seek to dismantle global structures of injustice. It is [predicated on] an ethics of click, donate, and (possibly) forget it."[27]

Girl Power and Confidence Culture

It is in this context of "post-humanitarianism" that female empowerment and confidence have emerged as central, perhaps even paradigmatic, dispositions. Girls, in particular, have come to embody this model, as both agentic and "empowered" beneficiaries of aid *and* donors and advocates.[28] In the global South, women and girls have been positioned simultaneously as at-risk and can-do subjects, whose self-reliance, self-responsibilization, and self-confidence can lift them out of poverty and allow them to escape the social ills of their societies. In the global North, philanthropic organizations, corporations, and celebrities call on women and girls to help their Southern "sisters" and act as "transnational caretakers."[29] Thus, the girl "trades on and reproduces connotations of the 'ideal victim' historically employed by NGOs in their communications, and shown (or believed) to elicit compassion and monetary donation: innocence, vulnerability, authenticity, blamelessness, and 'pure' untroubled femininity. Simultaneously, the figure of the girl is now also potent for the way in which she mobilises ideas and motifs of the post-humanitarian regime: empowerment, newfound freedoms, orientation to the future, self-responsibilisation, resilience and economic productivity."[30]

The Nike Foundation's Girl Effect, which was launched in 2008, has provided the blueprint for numerous subsequent projects and campaigns in the sphere of what Ofra Koffman and Rosalind Gill call "the girl powering of international development."[31] The campaign's leading promotional video, which to date has attracted 1.8 million views, urges viewers in the global North to "invest in a girl and she will do the rest."[32] This logic, which has been espoused by a wide range of transnational organizations and celebrities involved in international development, regards investment in women and girls as a means for facilitating "development on the cheap," by placing responsibility for lifting themselves out of poverty firmly on the shoulders of adolescent girls.[33] It relies on constructing binary North-South oppositions, whereby Northern women are cast as ethical and free saviors of oppressed, "backward," and benighted Southern women.[34] As Kalpana Wilson notes in her analysis of the use of "positive" and active images of "poor women in developing countries" in international development campaigns by Oxfam Unwrapped, the Nike Foundation, and Divine Chocolate, the message is that these women "have the potential to be the individual instruments of change if only 'we'—the intended viewers—recognise it and give it shape and direction."[35] Reminiscent of exhortations to self-confidence in other realms, such as work (chapter 2) or sex and relationships (chapter 3), where women are called on to release and realize their "full potential," here the consumer in the global North is positioned as responsible for unleashing and directing the unrealized agency of her sister in the global South through "entrepreneurial" labor. Empowerment and self-confidence are mobilized to reaffirm the structure of colonial discourses of civilization: the consumer in the global North is endowed with the role of the "rescuer" or the "white savior," which simultaneously infantilizes her female victims and imposes on them a moral responsibility for self-improvement and redemption by becoming entrepreneurial subjects.[36]

This logic was manifested incisively in the Girl Up campaign, launched in 2010 by the Washington, DC–based United Nations Foundation. The campaign encouraged girls in the global North to exploit "the opportunity to channel their energy and compassion" toward supporting girls in the global South by setting up clubs and fundraising for the education of their global South "sisters" and by consuming Girl Up merchandise.[37] As Koffman et al. argue, Girl Up's address to girls is characterized by a post-humanitarian and postfeminist "selfie gaze."[38] Drawing on "girl power" discourses, Northern and especially American girls are invited to stand up for their disempowered Southern sisters through self-promotion. For example, for one of the Girl Up action days, girls in the US were invited to express their solidarity with girls in the global South by donating a digital self-portrait. Another activity called on them to tweet an answer to the question "Why do you stand up for girls around the world?"[39]

In similar fashion, on the second International Day of the Girl (IDG) in 2013, the international charity Plan held a public event in London's Trafalgar Square to promote awareness of the plight of the millions of girls around the world who are denied access to the basic right to education. The event centered on the unveiling of a massive billboard erected in front of the National Gallery displaying an image of girls working at sewing machines, signifying a sweatshop. Speakers gathered around this billboard and reiterated "girl power" and "sisterhood" rhetoric in self-congratulatory addresses. These included Plan UK's CEO, who began by encouraging all the girls and young women who had joined the morning's event to celebrate the IDG and to "give yourself a great cheer!," a call that drew cheers, applause, and exclamations from the audience. The UK TV presenter Gillian Joseph then invited the Trafalgar Square audience to repeat after her (echoing a therapeutic self-help meeting) the mantra "I am a girl and I matter," while young Plan UK members spoke about their desire to share their happiness with their faraway sisters in the developing world.[40] As Shani Orgad and Kaarina Nikunen's analysis of the event shows, "this individualized rhetoric simultaneously promotes a blurring of the difference between western and southern girls and obfuscates the radical differences in their life experiences, conditions and structures."[41] The event culminated in an invitation to the Trafalgar Square audience, comprising predominantly UK girls and young women, to approach the billboard and *erase* the image of the Southern girls in the sweatshop. The

5.1 Scratching the surface, Plan UK event, 2013 International Day of the Girl (IDG), Trafalgar Square, London

participants scratched the surface off to reveal a full-color "happier" image of these same girls sitting in a classroom (see fig. 5.1). This makeover act by girls in London simultaneously "transformed" the docile black-and-white bodies of their Southern sisters in a sweatshop into colorful, happy, proud learners in a classroom *and* their own selves: it was constructed as an act of self-transformation that allowed the Northern girls to recognize their own value and worth: "I am a girl and I matter." Yet ironically, this very act neatly illustrates the superficiality of "scratching the surface": it is a short-term, low-intensity, feel-good engagement that does little to address (let alone erase, as the event's slogan goes) the structural barriers to education and justice for girls in the global South.

Rosie Walters's ethnographic study of Girl Up club members in the UK, US, and Malawi presents a somewhat different evaluation of this type of international development initiative addressing girls in the global North.[42]

Chapter Five

Drawing on interviews with Girl Up members, Walters insists that their participation in these clubs should be seen as feminist political activism that defies neoliberal and instrumentalist discourses of international development. She shows how girls' participation in these clubs inspired attendance at feminist demonstrations and how the girls were able to subvert discourses of rescue and white saviorism in order to facilitate their activism within their own communities. However, at the same time, Walters's analysis confirms that girls' participation in spaces of this ilk is significantly inward-looking. For the majority of girls, the main purpose of the Girl Up club was about "giving each other support and encouragement" and "discussing the challenges they were facing."[43] As one of the girls Walters interviewed describes it, Girl Up is "a place to 'vent' with like-minded people."[44]

Perhaps nowhere is the inculcation of Northern girls' self-confidence through an act framed as aiding their Southern counterparts more palpable than in Girl Up's "Teen Advisor" scheme. Teen Advisors are promised that the role will enhance their leadership skills and self-confidence—a promise that seems to be confirmed by various testimonies published on Girl Up's website. For instance, a testimony entitled "What Being a Girl Up Teen Advisor Means to Me" recounts its author's transformation from a shy, insecure girl who worried about what other people thought of her to a confident public speaker who had "found" her voice. "As long as you believe in yourself, nothing should discourage you," the American Teen Advisor writes, echoing the confidence mantras discussed in previous chapters.[45] Thus, "helping others is intimately connected to entrepreneurial projects of the self, and is increasingly figured less in terms of redistribution or justice than in terms of a makeover of subjectivity for all concerned."[46] While initiatives such as Girl Up may encourage girls in the global North to develop empathy and care for distant others in need and to participate in demonstrations, the concern with global injustice is simultaneously turned into an individualized opportunity for entrepreneurial personal growth—increasingly a form of growth built around the development of dispositions like confidence.

A related iteration of the neocolonial tendencies of many development programs is the volunteer tourism (or voluntourism) industry. More than 70 percent of volunteer tourists are women, and white female participants have been the most visible subjects in popular depictions of voluntourism.[47] Similar to initiatives such as Girl Up, which are framed as opportunities for global North girls to invest in their entrepreneurial selves and boost their self-confidence while helping their sisters overseas, "for young western middle-class women, volunteer tourism provides the means to participate in transformational activities that give rise to aspirational and entrepreneurial investments in the self, which is promoted by neoliberal subjectivities."[48] For example, the ME to WE movement, dedicated to empowering local communities in Kenya, Ecuador, and India, cajoles its website's visitors to engage in volunteer travel, which not only will help others in need but also crucially will leave you with a better understanding of *yourself*: "If you're itching to explore the globe, learn new skills and make a difference in the lives of others, then you're in for the trip of a lifetime. Leap headfirst into culture and a different way of life as you volunteer on a sustainable development project alongside community members. From taking part in centuries-old traditions to embarking on one-of-a-kind excursions, you'll leave with a better understanding of global citizenship and yourself."[49]

While volunteer tourism has been criticized extensively for reproducing and normalizing the privilege of Western voluntourists, as Wearing et al. point out, these critiques often problematically regard the individual female volunteer as the primary offender.[50] Yet they fail to account for the broader structural industry of volunteer tourism and the neoliberalization of international development within which young women are positioned. Girls in the global North are positioned by this industry (and the numerous images and posts circulating on social media in its support) as agents of change, who by "rescuing" the unfortunate Other go through a self-transformation, which boosts their self-esteem, confidence, and happiness. Specifically, helping to boost the volunteer's self-confidence is repeatedly cited on voluntourism websites as one of the benefits of volunteering abroad. For example, an article on the Go Volunteer Abroad (GVA) website, an online platform for various international and US organizations, explains: "When we commit ourselves to serve others, and we know that we have the capability to make a difference in someone's life—it eventually boosts our self-confidence! Your role as a volunteer can also give you a sense of pride, and strengthen your sense of identity. And the better you feel about yourself, the more likely you are to have a positive view of your life and future goals."[51]

Similarly, the website of the UK voluntourism organization GVI promotes the organization's sports program, where participants engage in a variety of sporting activities to help children from the local communities in which the organization works, as "a great boost to individual confidence."[52] While GVI addresses both men and women, the images on its website are overwhelmingly of young female volunteers and beneficiaries, mirroring the clear gendered bias of the industry. Indeed, on these and many other websites and social media platforms, one can find numerous testimonials of young women, recounting their experience of voluntourism as self-transformational and highlighting the positive role it played in building their self-confidence.[53]

Transnational Solidarity, Commodities, and Confidence

A central aspect of the confidence programs addressing girls and women in the global North as "transnational caretakers" is commodity activism.[54] As mentioned in chapter 4, Sarah Banet-Weiser analyzes how the proliferation and consolidation of US girls' empowerment organizations are intimately linked to, and based on, commodification.[55] In a similar vein, Lisa Daily shows how initiatives such as the fashion collection Born Free Africa (aimed at combating mother-to-child HIV transmission) and the brand THINX (which sells "period-proof" panties) promote a global feminist empowerment that is enacted through commodities.[56] THINX is dedicated to eliminating period poverty and breaking the stigma of menstruation and is targeted toward African, especially Ugandan, girls. Its slogan, "We bleed for female empowerment," promises the consumer in the global North that in purchasing a pair of $34 THINX period-proof panties she contributes to the empowerment of a less fortunate woman, while simultaneously protecting her "own menstruating body from unsightly period accidents."[57] As Daily notes, "to bleed for female empowerment simultaneously calls forth a dedication to the cause—concern over the bodies of other women—while also enabling the cause to become embedded within the bodies of the entrepreneurs and the consumer-activists."[58]

It is interesting to note how the "love your body" discourses discussed in chapter 1 are being inserted into the post-humanitarian landscape. Like THINX, many "feminist" commodity activism projects call women in the global North to help empower less fortunate women in the global South by centering their own individual female body as an object of pride and self-esteem. For example, in the UK, Oxfam and the retailer Marks and Spencer (M&S) have been collaborating since 2012 on a "Shwopping" scheme, where customers can bring back any clothes, whether fully intact or damaged, to be recycled via Oxfam. "Love your boobs and recycle your bra," the M&S website exhorts its female customers, mobilizing the body-confidence imperative in the service of making a "massive difference" for the fight against poverty around the world.[59] Another initiative is the Edinburgh-based charity Smalls For All, which is dedicated solely to distributing unworn underwear donated by women in the UK to women and girls in Africa. The organization helps vulnerable women living in orphanages, slums, and internally displaced person camps and schools, as well as providing underwear to hospitals. Here confidence is evoked as the gift that the women in the global North who recycle their underwear give their less fortunate sisters in the South: bras "are hugely important as a status symbol which at the one end gives confidence (to girls at school in mixed classrooms) and at the other end of the spectrum, purportedly reduce attacks and rapes on women," says Emma Sinclair, a tech entrepreneur from London who promotes the campaign.[60]

These and many other similar initiatives call on women in the global North to engage in commodity activism as a way of "giving back": to purchase something as a way of advancing the empowerment of women "in need," who are typically constructed in racialized terms. The commodity— be it period-proof panties, a bracelet, a T-shirt, a recycled bra, or a handbag— mediates social relations of "sisterly solidarity" between women, engendering an imagined unity with the faraway other in need.[61] As Mimi Nguyen observes about the nonprofit organization V-Day (founded by the *Vagina Monologues* playwright Eve Ensler), which promoted to American women the purchase of a blue mesh Swatch watch as part of a fundraising campaign for Afghan women: "This fantasy of substitution and subtraction, in which we might imagine that every swatch purchased here in the 'free' West led to the decrease of burqas elsewhere, thus enacts a symbolic unveiling of the Afghan woman, returning her to beauty, freedom and the world."[62] In this way, confidence, commodity, and activism converge in inculcating a "savior" psychological mindset. Purchasing or consuming a commodity is imagined and marketed as a form of a psychic saviorism, an act of rescuing the faraway, at-risk girl, through which she (the recipient in the global South) and the donor (the girl in the global North) are transformed into confident, empowered subjects.

In the context of an intensifying self-tracking that individuals are encouraged to perform over their bodies and psyches,[63] consumers in the global North increasingly are being offered the possibility also to track the impact of the commodity they purchased or money they donated on the faraway people in need in the global South. For example, the ME to WE organization mentioned earlier, which encourages women and girls to shop as a way of turning "gifting into do-gooding," explains in its website's "Shop" section: "When you give a ME to WE gift, you're part of something so much bigger than a simple gesture. You're part of a sustainable cycle of good. *And through our Track Your Impact promise, you get to see where and how you changed lives, with stories about the people and places behind every purchase.*"[64] Thus, the project of enhancing one's self-confidence in the global North, which, as we have shown, is addressed primarily to women and girls and is performed intensely in and mediated through self-tracking and self-governing, is extended here to tracking the impact of one's consumption on the lives of one's "sisters" in the global South.

However, this relational imaginary of self (in the North) and Other (in the South), which is mediated through commodities and self-tracking programs, completely obscures the historical legacy of colonialisms, the violence inflicted on the colonized and the accumulation of immense geopolitical power and privilege in the global North. It implies that girls in the global North simply "happen" to be more fortunate than their Southern counterparts and they are therefore encouraged to help empower their sisters in need through consumption. For example, one of the many commodities promoted on the ME to WE website is the "Unstoppable Rafiki Bracelet," which was designed by the Disney singer and actress Sofia Carson and is handmade by women in Kenya.

The webpage shows Carson in a pose that reminds one of the (endlessly appropriated) iconic Rosie the Riveter image, wearing the Rafiki bracelets and a pink T-shirt with the slogan "Here's to strong women: May we know them, may we be them, may we raise them" (fig. 5.2). The text under the image reads: "Break the barriers and change lives with the all-new Unstoppable Rafiki Bracelet—created with singer and actress Sofia Carson, star of the Disney Channel franchise *Descendants* and *Pretty Little Liars: The Perfectionists*. Sofia is passionate about making sure every young girl feels empowered, and was inspired to create this bold new Rafiki after going on a ME to WE Trip to Kenya and seeing the power of education firsthand. Every bracelet you purchase gives young girls access to education in our WE Villages partner communities."

5.2 Unstoppable Rafiki on ME to WE website

Capitalizing on "girl power" and female confidence discourses, the $10 bracelet is constructed as a magical tool that will make its girl consumers in the global North feel "unstoppable" *and* give young girls in the global South access to education, because "education is our greatest super power."[65] The profound difference between the "magic" required to empower girls in the global North and their less fortunate counterparts in the WE partner communities in the global South is obscured by the universal promise to make "every young girl feel empowered." Why some girls do not possess the "super power" of education is neither mentioned nor discussed. Thus, the dispossession of girls in the global South is entirely decontextualized and ahistoricized, with abdication of the West's historical responsibility for its creation. However, the alleviation of their dispossession is conceived as dependent on individual girl and women consumers in the global North, reduced to the act of purchasing a $10 bracelet.[66]

Exporting the Confidence Imperative to the Global South

We turn now to the deliberate "export" of confidence to the global South. The intersection between female confidence and so-called ethical capitalism in the global South is manifested vividly in the global initiative launched by the hygiene brand Always, aimed at raising awareness of the challenges posed to women and girls by menstruation. Capitalizing on its earlier work in the global North, which positioned the brand as a champion of girls' body confidence (e.g., the Always #LikeAGirl campaign; see chapter 1), the Always initiative has been extended to education about menstruation and provision of menstrual products in seventy countries. The campaign centers the commodity (Always menstrual products or "femcare") as the solution not just to the global problem of period poverty but to the obstacles constraining girls around the world. In 2018, following the Saudi prince's announcement of the lifting of the ban on women driving, Always launched its #WeAre-TheGenerationOfFirsts campaign. Exploiting the excitement about this and other "revolutionary" steps to relax rules governing Saudi women's lives (e.g., granting women passports and permission to travel abroad without the consent of their male guardians and allowing women to attend sports events in stadiums, hold senior government posts, and participate in football games), Always produced a video intended to "pay tribute to this Generation of Firsts, as well as support & share their achievements, showing girls everywhere that everything starts with a first step."[67] Produced by an all-female Saudi crew and cast, the video showcases Saudi women who have achieved a "first" in their own right in different fields: Dhoha Abdullah, the first Saudi woman head chef in a Riyadh hotel; Rayouf Alhumedhi, who developed the first hijab emoji; and Fatima Baatouk, "who wanted to give girls like her the opportunity to be confident while playing sports" and became the country's first female gym owner.[68] In the second phase of the campaign, Always invited Saudi women to share their "first" experiences.

On the one hand, the #WeAreTheGenerationOfFirsts campaign appears to draw on and celebrate local female expertise, in terms of both the women it showcases and the fact that this was the first film to be produced by Saudi women. The "we" in its hashtag stands for the generation of Saudi women who are celebrating their newfound freedoms. On the other hand, the campaign is underpinned and, in turn, reinforces what Mimi Nguyen calls "the biopower and biopolitics of beauty," which are deeply embedded in geopolitical interests and colonial histories. The "other," Nguyen writes, often comes to signify and be signified as the ugly, while beauty is linked intimately to a civilizational project. In her study of the establishment of the Kabul Beauty School by the NGO Beauty Without Borders, sponsored in large part by the US fashion and beauty industries, Nguyen highlights how beauty is entangled with both humanitarian imperialisms and global feminisms: "Only with lipstick and eyeliner . . . does the Afghan woman achieve legible personhood. . . . The Afghan woman who desires beauty thus desires a democratic future of movement, choice, and independence, where beauty is imagined to live."[69]

By the same token, in the #WeAreTheGenerationOfFirsts video, Saudi women are called on to esteem themselves and to maintain their personhood implicitly through the consumption of Always "femcare" products and—explicitly and crucially—by embracing the neoliberal "feminist" confidence cult(ure). Always exhorts Saudi women to overcome their inner fears and doubts in order to take the first steps to becoming confident, assertive, and empowered economic subjects. In an action shot in the gym, we see Fatima Baatouk on a static bicycle dressed in a fashionable Nike Pro Hijab sports outfit, recounting how the "pounding voice" (paralleled by the pounding music in the gym) overtook her voices of doubt. Similarly, we see Rayouf Alhumedhi inspecting herself in the mirror and then leaving her home, striding out and saying that this is the first time she has left her home no longer feeling like a child. We also hear Dhoha Abdullah confessing to her anxieties and insecurities—"Thousands of questions will run through your mind: what if it won't work?"—and then see her working passionately in her smart restaurant kitchen.[70]

In the same way that the NGO Beauty Without Borders groomed Afghan women to be agents of their own transformation, Always urges Saudi women to make over their insecure selves to become empowered and confident subjects, by buying Always products and espousing neoliberal normative notions of beauty, confidence, and empowerment. The campaign hails Saudi women as new feminist subjects on the grounds of new empowerment technologies and the notion of confidence as a universal good.[71] However, this "feel-good" celebration of women's newfound individual freedom and confidence, linked inextricably to consumption, deflects attention from and helps to obfuscate the enduring repressive and patriarchal guardian system that the Saudi government continues to enforce. This system "stipulates that women are not legal persons, and consequently, they have to be represented by male relatives to work, marry, study, travel, and seek medical care."[72] As Madawi Al-Rasheed argues powerfully, Saudi Arabia continues to be "a most masculine state."[73] While many Saudi feminists have pushed for recognition of Saudi women's right to be equal citizens, "the regime's nightmare is for this language [of rights and equality] to spread beyond its control, which is why so many vocal and courageous women have been silenced behind bars."[74] However, rather than critiquing this, the #WeAreTheGenerationOfFirsts campaign unambiguously shies away from the language of rights and from any allusion to women's structural inequality, endorsing instead techniques and dispositions that encourage women to govern themselves by finding their *own* voice and becoming part of the "generation of firsts."

A further extension to the export of confidence discourses and forms of expertise from the global North to the global South can be found in what Srila Roy discusses in relation to "empowerment workers."[75] In the context of the restructuring of international development under neoliberalism and the "NGOization of feminist activism," poor women in the global South have been "almost exclusively positioned to pick up the fallout of state withdrawal from key areas such as education, health and welfare provision in the Global South."[76] Roy shows how NGOs' work in the expanding space of women's empowerment in the global South relies heavily on "capacitating" local poor women to act as service providers in domains such as microfinance and microcredit, domestic violence, and education. In the face of the inability to tackle structural issues such as education, domestic violence, and employment, which should be the responsibilities of the state, Roy observes that those poor "empowerment workers" rely on models of self-sufficiency, self-reliance, and therapeutic self-help in order to confront gender inequality in their everyday lives. The NGOs for which those women work, mostly voluntarily, become significant spaces of personal transformation, spaces that allow them to disrupt their confinement to the home and to enter the traditionally male domain of employment. At the same time, their mostly unpaid participation in these spaces reproduces and helps to stabilize their precarity and inequality. The poor, rural, and Dalit women that Roy studied "remained attached to a lifeworld both made available and compromised by neoliberal development."[77]

Conclusion: Confidence without Borders

In this chapter we examined how the confidence cult(ure) is spreading out transnationally and, in particular, how confidence is increasingly mobilized within the humanitarian and international development field. We situated the rise of confidence within the broader shifts in contemporary approaches to and policies and practices of international aid and, in particular, the rise in the privatization of foreign aid, the public disillusion with humanitarian aid and public criticism of humanitarian organizations, and an increasing visibility of celebrities in the sphere of "philanthrocapitalism." We argued that in this context, over the last two decades, female empowerment and confidence have become central dispositions in what some call the "post-humanitarian" environment. We demonstrated how brands and NGOs promote female self-confidence as a unifying and universal strategy that ostensibly benefits and empowers girls and women in the global South, while offering their Northern "sisters" short-term, low-intensity, feel-good engagement and endowing them with a sense of solidarity, pride, and entrepreneurial skills. In the last part of the chapter we showed how the confidence imperative inculcates women and girls in the global South to become empowered and confident subjects.

We might consider the various examples discussed in this chapter as embedded in a wider movement of "Confidence without Borders": transnational forms of intervention in the field of international development, which, like Nguyen's Beauty Without Borders (referencing Doctors Without Borders), "adopt a borderless sense of space and an ethos of direct intervention" and promote confidence as a universal good, supposedly devoid of structural conditions and global configurations of power—or a way of magically overcoming them.[78] Confidence without Borders targets young women through transnational political agencies, transnational corporations, NGOs, and celebrities as the ideal subjects of entrepreneurial interventions, who through small-scale acts of self-empowerment and adoption of techniques and tools for the manufacture of self-confidence can solve global inequalities. Crucially, Confidence without Borders effectively obscures the roots of current global inequities in the historical legacy of colonialisms and decolonization, and it abjures state responsibility in both the global North and the global South for tackling these inequalities.

conclusion
beyond confidence

BY DRAWING TOGETHER the themes of the confidence injunctions across the five domains discussed in the book, in this conclusion we highlight the striking consistencies across and between those seemingly disparate realms. We discuss how confidence emerges as a gendered technology for remaking the feminine self, which simultaneously participates in the remaking of feminism in the context of its new visibility. Outlining the work of the confidence cult(ure), we also consider how current feminist identifications might move beyond confidence. Looking back at the domains of social life discussed in the book, and using the example of the popular African American artist Lizzo, we demonstrate the value and possibilities opened up by alternative articulations of feminism beyond confidence. We conclude by reflecting on how the project of *social justice*, which the confidence culture so often occludes, might be resurrected into the meanings of contemporary feminism.

The Confidence *Dispositif*

The ideas and techniques discussed in the previous chapters constitute what Foucault called *dispositif*: an assemblage of discourses, institutions, and regulatory modes and measures that is systematic and patterned, whose function at a given historical moment is to respond "to an urgent need."[1] As social and welfare structures that were designed to provide a safety net against social risks and ills are being aggressively dismantled—with the greatest costs of this process inflicted on women, children, people of color, disabled people, and the elderly—confidence emerges as a *gendered technology* of self, directed predominantly at women and requiring their intense labor. As we have shown throughout the book, confidence is mobilized as a device to manage the intensifying precarity and flexibility in the labor market and is a response to the increasing disinvestment in social welfare and the privatization and individualization of social risks. Confidence is an individualizing technology inculcating a self-regulating spirit, which works to reframe contemporary issues about social injustice in individual and psychological terms, locating responsibility for, blame for, and solutions to pain and injustice in women. Indeed, as we have shown throughout the many examples discussed in the book, the confidence cult(ure) exculpates social, economic, and political forces from their responsibility for producing and maintaining inequality, instead placing emphasis upon women self-regulating and finding the solutions to their problems within a newly upgraded form of confident subjectivity. Despite its apparently warm and affirmative address to women to believe in themselves, to lean in, to love their bodies, to focus on what is most important to them, to embrace imperfection and vulnerability, and to be confident across all spheres of life, the confidence cult(ure) works by locating the blame and responsibility for all difficulties and challenges in women themselves. In the wake of movements such as #MeToo and Black Lives Matter, which have spotlighted the prevalence of sexism, racism, and misogyny, and the ongoing destabilization of patriarchy and heteronormative gender binaries, the confidence cult redirects attention from the brutal effects of patriarchal capitalism to women's individual "self-inflicted wounds" and their responsibility for healing them. In the confidence cult(ure) women's individual "toxic baggage" is treated as self-generated and unconnected to a culture of normalized pathologization, objectification, surveillance, blame, and hate speech directed at women.

Confidence is offered as a one-size-fits-all solution, disavowing significant differences between and among women and contexts. The problem of low self-esteem is described in strikingly similar terms whether referring to a woman with a body designated as plus-size, a senior professional woman in the corporate workplace, an unemployed single mother, a young woman in a romantic relationship, or a girl in the global South with no access to education. The mission for all women is constructed in terms of overcoming the inner obstacles to becoming confident, empowered, and successful. The trajectory is always linear: from low to high self-esteem, from poor to high levels of confidence and resilience. Moreover, the solutions to the problem are highly standardized: they are often constructed as instrumental "steps," involving extraordinarily similar behavioral changes required to enable the building and boosting of confidence in women across a wide range of identities, ages, backgrounds, and contexts: "be mindful," "strike a pose," "fake it till you make it," "stop trying to be liked," "don't sweat it," "breathe," "be grateful," and so on.

The Turn to Confidence and the Remaking of Feminism

Unlike the *psy* complex, the state of esteem, or the "happiness industry,"[2] what is distinctive about the culture of confidence is how it is articulated as a feminist intervention. Against a background in which feminism has been routinely repudiated, mocked, or located in terms of "pastness," the prominence accorded to feminism in the confidence cult(ure) is striking.[3] This prominence is deeply implicated in the broader luminosity and popularity of feminism in popular culture in recent years. Feminist books top best-seller lists; glossy magazines promote "feminism issues"; musicians, politicians, and other celebrities proudly proclaim their feminist identities; and stories about unequal pay or sexual harassment, which a few years ago would have been dismissed, have become the stuff of newspaper headlines and primetime news broadcasts. Indeed, in confidence culture texts and practices, feminism is embraced, championed, and held up as an obvious good rather than being repudiated or disavowed.

So in putting to work a new type of feminine subject—a woman who turns inward and through self-work and self-governing embraces vulnerability and strengthens her confidence and resilience—how does the confidence cult(ure) contribute to the remaking of feminism? How does the confidence cult converge with, support, and expand the popular versions of feminism that circulate in contemporary media and culture?

First, in conjunction with the current luminosity of feminism and the continuing influence of postfeminism, the confidence culture promotes a version of feminism that emphasizes individualism, choice, and agency as dominant modes of accounting.[4] Like postfeminism, it is characterized by the muting of vocabularies to talk about both structural inequalities and cultural influence; the "deterritorialization" of patriarchal power and its "reterritorialization" in women's bodies and the beauty-industrial complex; the intensification and extensification of forms of surveillance, monitoring, and disciplining of women's bodies; and the influence of a "makeover paradigm" that extends beyond the body to constitute a remaking of subjectivity.[5] As we have shown throughout the book, confidence is a technology of self, which acknowledges female "injuries" only to rehabilitate or instrumentalize them, suggesting that a female confidence deficit rather than an unjust world is what needs to be challenged. It proposes and promotes an intensive program of individually based cognitive, behavioral, embodied, linguistic "reprogramming" that will bring into being a newly upgraded confident self, a protofeminist subject who has been "made over" and "brought into recovery." In this sense, confidence culture is continuous with the ongoing therapeutic remaking of feminism and the spread of postfeminism since the late 1980s and 1990s, except that rather than serving to disavow and repudiate feminism, all of its elements are taken up and rebranded as "feminist."

Second, the confidence culture contributes to the remaking of feminism by and through its "inclusive" address and postracial and postqueer tenor. In the domains we have examined, the addressee of the confidence culture is "every woman," across race, class, age, religion, sexuality, and location.[6] While *Lean In* and similar "feminist" manifestos such as Ann-Marie Slaughter's essay "Why Women Still Can't Have It All" have been criticized for addressing exclusively the white middle-class heterosexual professional woman,[7] the wider landscape of confidence injunctions appears broader and seemingly more inclusive, and, as we demonstrated in chapter 5, it seems to travel between and across the global North and the global South. Furthermore, as manifest by some of the examples we discussed, the confidence culture has a distinctly "postracial" tenor. Strikingly, however, the highly standardized way in which women of color and nonbinary and genderqueer people are addressed erases a long history of feminist struggle around difference, especially racial difference. Rather than recognizing difference as the basis for responding to women's particular needs and for insisting on the relevance of antiracist critiques, confidence culture expunges difference and the possibility of its critique. While it tries to construct a positive identification with what has been made abject—love your curls, love the skin you're in—it rarely expands the range of racial representations and the complexity of racial subjectivities. Thus, the confidence cult contributes to reshaping a version of feminism that takes difference "into account" only to be shown that attention to it is no longer necessary.

Third, the confidence culture participates in remaking feminism through its affective qualities. As we have shown in relation to a variety of texts, programs, and technologies that call on women to become confident, these exhortations reframe women's feelings and experience in a compulsory upbeat and positive manner, renouncing and delegitimizing anger, complaint, resentment, or bitterness—those bold emotions considered "political," which have historically propelled feminism. The appeal of the changes that women are encouraged to make in transforming themselves into confident subjects is that they are (supposedly) small, quick, easy, and, crucially, *not disruptive*. Indeed, the confidence culture is tied closely to the fantasy of happiness, proposing a positive version of feminism that goes along with, rather than challenges, existing structures and rules.[8] It demands that transformation occurs almost exclusively within women's psyches, while the capitalist structures and material realities conditioning these psyches are left unchanged.

This move, we suggest, is simultaneously political, psychological, and aesthetic. It links to a wider tendency within some versions of popular feminism—for example, that embraced by women's magazines—to figure feminism as an appealing and stylish, "cool," or "hot" identity rather than a political movement for change.[9] Its ostensible appeal resides in the construction of a highly aestheticized version of the feminist as someone who is individual, authentic, and "beautiful on the inside and the outside." Building on New Age/self-help discourses that promote enduringly feminine ideas of serenity, inner calm, warmth, "glow," success, and positive energy, the confidence culture rejects what are assumed to be the old aesthetics of feminism, associated with images of feminists as ugly, hairy-legged, and so forth, and with notions of feminism as "angry" or "judgmental." In this sense, the confidence culture abets the popular and troubling notion of generational divisions in feminism and the rejection and disparaging of older feminists and feminism.

Alternative Articulations

Having discussed how the culture of confidence acts as a powerful *dispositif* addressed to women in the twenty-first century, and the ways in which it contributes to the reconfiguration of feminism, we want to ask some critical questions about what, if anything, exists outside—or at least *resists*—the confidence cult(ure). There are, we suggest, still many examples of challenges to the confidence cult that frame questions of injustice in different terms. Across all the domains we have looked at, despite the prominence of psychologized discourses promoting dispositions such as confidence, resilience, or gratitude, there *are* alternatives.

In relation to the *body*, for example, TV shows such as *This Is Us* and *Shrill* rework discourses of body confidence related to fat female bodies. While a show like *Shrill* ostensibly "might read like a Dove ad, just another love-yourself affirmation,"[10] at the same time it refuses the compulsory upbeat and positive tone of so many confidence messages. In transforming herself into a more confident and happier subject, the lead character, Annie, refuses to continue to be sweet, nice, and easygoing. She is concurrently vulnerable and angry, soft but not sweet, and often egotistical. Meanwhile, Hannah Gadsby's phenomenally successful show *Nanette* (which later became a Netflix special) systematically takes apart and refuses feminine self-deprecation as a comedic mode, showing how such self-deprecation risks reinforcing lesbian marginality. But Gadsby also avoids the inverse: championing female self-confidence. Instead, and perhaps even more powerfully in her subsequent show *Douglas* (2019), she offers a feminist analysis in which subjectivity is understood as structurally and culturally shaped. "This is not an isolated incident," she riffs repeatedly—whether talking about not being taken seriously by her doctor or dealing with sexual harassment in the park. In a similar vein, on social media, there are more and more examples that push against and go beyond the confidence cult. One such example is influencer Leah Vernon's posts and her book *Unashamed: Musings of a Fat, Black Muslim*, which take on multiple forms of body-shaming as they relate to race, religion, body size, and appearance (see fig. C.1).[11] Another example is disabled comedians Rosie Jones and Francesca Martinez, who also subvert normative expectations about their low self-esteem, with riffs on the advantages of being disabled—including in intimate relationships.

In the domain of *work*, in contrast to many of the self-help/advice books we discussed in chapter 2, and to the confidence cult(ure) more broadly, important alternatives are emerging. One compelling example is the best-selling book *Slay in Your Lane: The Black Girl Bible*, a collection of essays based on the experiences of Black British authors Yomi Adegoke and Elizabeth Uviebinené and those of thirty-nine other Black women interviewees.[12] The motivation for writing the book was precisely the authors' frustration with the dominant *Lean In* popular narrative. They felt that it "failed to address the uniquely challenging experience faced by me and women like me."[13] Indeed, *Slay in Your Lane* is a collective project that, at least to an extent, refuses the individu-

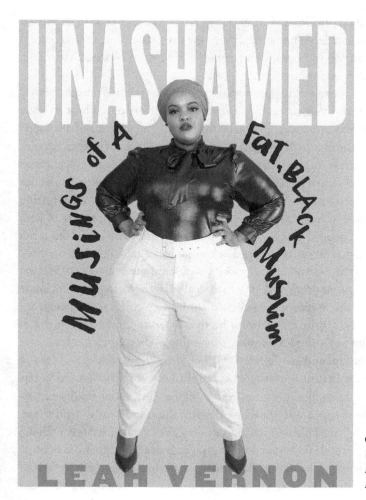

C.1 Cover of
*Unashamed:
Musings of a Fat,
Black Muslim*

alized tendencies characterizing much of the discussion about women and work. It points to some of the often-overlooked structural roots of women's struggles and obstacles, in particular sexism and racism. Moreover, *Slay in Your Lane* makes necessary the often-obscured connections between vulnerability and discrimination. Yomi Adegoke divulges her painful struggle with depression and the heightened pressure on Black people, and especially Black women, to treat emotional trauma as "a wasteful and self-indulgent distraction." She offers the example of Black rapper Lady Leshurr's struggles with depression and anxiety as an admirable deviation from the pervasive upbeat display of female confidence and strength. And she invites readers to expose their vulnerability but to understand it as crucially connected to structural inequality; to tackle vulnerability, then, means doing so at the structural level—for example, by creating state-funded services to address the specific mental health needs of minorities.

Slay in Your Lane rejects the postracial and postclass tenor of current gender and workplace discussions, highlighting the long history of feminist struggle around difference and especially racial difference, the salience of antiracist critiques, and the urgent need to attend to the experiences of women of color within this context. In the vein of Audre Lorde and the lineage of Black feminist activists, the authors highlight anger as a vital driving political force for change. Yet they also reflect candidly on the difficulties related to "navigating the 'angry black woman' stereotype" and criticize the white premise of *Lean In*: "Most black women have been 'leaning in' for years," they note, "but it has been at the cost of being stereotyped as 'too assertive' or 'angry.'"[14]

Turning to the domain of *relationships*, two stand-out recent TV series are *Sex Education* and *Atypical*, both of which deal with the struggles of intimate life without a single recourse to clichéd confidence culture messaging. *Sex Education* presents intimate relationships in an open and nuanced way that is sensitive to myriad complexities and differences as they crosscut class, race, sexual orientation, and gender identity. The show is bold, sex-positive, and funny, while facilitating empathy and identification with *multiple* characters and refraining from focusing on one point of view. Although bodily embarrassment and shame are repeated motifs and thus could easily lend themselves to confidence cult(ure) discourses, *Sex Education* deliberately eschews facile "love your body, love your self" messages. Indeed, a scene from season 1 has become iconic for the way the protagonists shut down "slut-shaming" after a sext of Ruby is circulated around the school. Attempts by the head teacher to reveal her identity in a school assembly are thwarted when person after person stands up to claim: "It's my vagina. No, it's *my* vagina"—initially starting with cis young women but eventually including almost everyone. This joyous collective response articulates, at least temporarily, a *refusal* of individualistically framed moves from shame to confidence.

Atypical is also groundbreaking in its portrayals of the nuclear family of four—so far so familiar in the sitcom genre—with parents Doug and Elsa, whose relationship is in crisis, and children Casey and Sam, who are teenagers exploring their sexualities and intimate relationships. Sam is autistic and is depicted in a nuanced way as he moves from school to college, acquires greater independence from his family, and figures out his relationship with on/off girlfriend Paige. Casey struggles with friendships as she moves schools and class milieux and is shown experiencing attraction to both male and female characters. Like *Sex Education*, *Atypical* offers much more nuanced portrayals of its characters' ambivalent experiences, none of which fit neatly into predefined categories. In fact, against this careful depiction of the struggles of intimate life, confidence messages and technologies appear crass and simplistic; there is no sense that the "problem" for any of the characters is a lack of confidence or resilience, or that self-help apps, gratitude diaries, or affirmations of self-belief would significantly change or improve their lives.

Attempts to move beyond individual confidence injunctions are also seen in a growing number of blogs and Instagram accounts focused on sex and disability. "Cripping Up Sex" is one example by Eva Sweeney, a queer disabled activist who has written a book entitled *Queers on Wheels*.[15] Sweeney's cerebral palsy means she uses a wheelchair and cannot use her hands or her voice, so she communicates via a laser pointer attached to her head and a letter board. She identifies as a sex educator in a world in which discussing sex and disability is still taboo, in which queer disabled sexualities are even more difficult to talk about, and in which queer disabled people feel excluded from both "mainstream" (non-disabled) LGBTQ+ communities and "mainstream" (heteronormative) disability organizations. Eva's work of educating doctors, social workers, and carers is significant, focused as it is upon communication, resources, and practical changes—for example, adaptations of sex toys. But what is also striking is her conviction that confidence is *not* the issue. Asked in an interview for the Queer Disability Project whether confidence in her own desirability is a problem, she responds categorically, "I have always had a good self-image and I think I am hot, so that aspect hasn't been a problem for me."[16]

Our relationship to or with ourselves is also being rethought beyond the individualistic confidence paradigm in a growing number of resources used in antiracist practice, particularly since 2016. Although Audre Lorde's much-circulated notion that "self-care . . . is an act of political warfare" has arguably been overused, exploited, stripped of its radical Black lesbian politics, commodified, and pressed into service for corporate interests and a generation of white, privileged Instagrammers, some people and organizations are reclaiming its subversive potential.[17] For example, among an extensive list of antiracism sources, a Harvard University website features examples of "anti-oppression therapy" that seek to *contextualize and politicize* issues of depression and low self-esteem.[18] Other resources—like the self-care app Shine; the organization The Nap Ministry, which "examines the liberating power of naps"; and the online space Therapy for Black Girls—are perhaps more consonant with the confidence messaging we have analyzed in this book, yet, like *Slay in Your Lane*, are simultaneously pushing at the familiar prescriptions of the confidence cult(ure) in both its individualistic analysis of emotional distress and its suggestions for healing.[19]

We also see the "double whammy" of discourses of confident *mothering* being increasingly challenged. As mentioned in chapter 4, blogs, websites, and social networking sites offer important spaces for mothers to express not just satisfaction, happiness, and confidence but also powerful emotions of frustration, disappointment, dissatisfaction, anxiety, anger, and ingratitude. Mothers describe, talk about, and critique the unpaid, undervalued, and onerous work of mothering. In popular culture, too, recent years have seen the emergence of unapologetically non-normative "aberrant" mothers," such as the "slummy mummy" and what Jo Littler calls "mothers behaving badly," who revel in "chaotic hedonism."[20] In this context, a particularly interesting recent development is the figure of the "rage mom." Writing for the *New York Times*, Lisa Lerer and Jennifer Medina describe how in the wake of the COVID-19 pandemic, the American "soccer mom" has given way to "rage mom," a term coined by Senator Patty Murray (at the time of writing the highest-ranking woman in Senate leadership). The struggle of millions of American families for childcare, education, and economic stability, Lerer and Medina write, has fueled "a political uprising, built on the anger of women who find themselves constantly—and indefinitely—expected to be teacher, caregiver, employee and parent."[21] "Rage moms" gathered in Facebook groups and other social media platforms, packed virtual town halls, and took to the streets to express their frustration and protest against school shutdowns and the lack of childcare. Meanwhile, across the Atlantic, Julia Llewellyn Smith describes the growing prominence of a similar figure: the "rage mum."[22] Unlike the "Worcester Woman," an archetypal middle England thirty-something mother-of-two, dreamed up in the late 1990s by Tony Blair's strategists, rage mums are mobilizing through campaigns such Black Lives Matter or Us for Them—the latter founded during the pandemic by four women campaigning on social media to have children return to school without social distancing.[23] Of course, mothers' activism is not a new phenomenon. Indeed, contemporary examples of maternal activism build on the long battles of women, and especially working-class women and women of color, for justice, care, survival, and peace. However, what is particularly noteworthy in the context of our book is how recent iterations of the "rage mom/mum" and of activism of mothers across race, class, sexuality, and age push against the individualized, upbeat, positivity-driven, and "authentic" trope of confident mothering that we identified in chapter 4.[24]

Finally, in the *global South*, there are examples of powerful alternatives and challenges to the trend we discussed in chapter 5, of brands and NGOs promoting female self-confidence as a universal strategy that ostensibly benefits and empowers girls and women both in the global South and in the global North. For example, in 2014, Radio Nissa, the first women's Arabic-speaking radio station in the Middle East, launched a fiction series entitled *Be 100 Ragl*. Translated in English as "Worth 100 Men," "Be 100 Ragl" is an Arabic expression used to describe influential high-achieving women. Based on research about the issues affecting women in the communities in which the program is broadcast, the popular radio fiction series, which later was developed into a social media animated cartoon series, centers on women's participation in economic and political life, their experiences of domestic violence and sexual harassment, and family relationships and romance, through the adventures of young radio journalist Noha.[25] While Noha displays defiance, assertiveness, and self-confidence, *Be 100 Ragl* significantly differs from the examples of "Confidence without Borders" we discussed in chapter 5 in its confrontation of some of the root causes of the inequalities, discrimination, and oppression that women face. Indeed, the broadcasting of the series in Palestine, Egypt, Iraq, Morocco, Saudi Arabia, Syria, Yemen, and Jordan has been accompanied by radio talk shows, social media debates, and face-to-face community conversations (in partnership with NGOs Womanity, Oxfam Novib, and several civil society organizations) about women's role in society, problems they encounter, and collective approaches to tackling them.

In a similar vein, in 2019, the digital content platform Khateera, which in Arabic means "dangerous" in the feminine form, launched a YouTube satirical series targeting Arab millennials (fig. C.2).[26] The series, *Smi'touha Menni*,

C.2 Khateera
website

aims to deconstruct common traditional stereotypes and narratives of gender in the Arab world by highlighting issues such as marriage, women in the workforce, parenting, and normative masculinity. The show is anchored by Maria Elayan, a Middle Eastern social influencer, who plays different roles, discussing controversial matters, such as honor, domestic violence, harassment, masculinity, gender and health, parenting, and menstruation, with humor.

These examples underscore that there is nothing inevitable about the triumph of the confidence cult(ure). Other worlds *are* possible, albeit often incorporated into the mainstream confidence imperatives we have interrogated in this book.

To develop this point, in the remainder of the chapter we briefly consider a case study that illustrates a move beyond confidence *within* popular culture, namely the singer Lizzo. We show how the mediated figure of Lizzo offers a more complicated and ambivalent articulation of those affects and ideas that the confidence cult(ure) repudiates and obscures. It can be read as repairing, even if only temporarily and restrictedly, the injurious limits of the confidence cult(ure). At the same time, we show that Lizzo's popular figure also remains—at least in some respects—attached to some of the tropes and pitfalls of the confidence culture. Thus, rather than constituting a complete or "perfect" alternative to the confidence *dispositif*, we explore Lizzo as a popular site that opens up a space for imagining ways of being, feeling, and comprehending that are *beyond* confidence if not entirely outside it.

Lizzo: "Me Just Existing Is Revolutionary"

No discussion of confidence would be complete without considering the phenomenally successful thirty-one-year-old African American artist Lizzo. After nearly a decade of performing shows while earning very little and living part of this time in her car, in 2019 Lizzo logged over one billion streams of her songs, was named *TIME* magazine's Entertainer of the Year, and earned eight Grammy nominations—the highest number awarded to any artist that year. Dubbed "the queen of self-love," "music's patron saint of self-care and self-love," and the "fat-a-bulous" "body-positive rapper who will change the world," Lizzo makes music that is effervescent, loud, fun, and catchy.[27] Her songs appear in various commercials, including ones for the American retailer Walmart and the food delivery company GrubHub. She has been featured in campaigns for the fashion brand Good American and the plus-size women's clothing brand Lane Bryant. Lizzo's lyrics expose her vulnerability and insecurities but at the same time are bawdy, funny, and steeped in relentless positivity alongside messages of self-care and self-growth. One of her most popular songs, "Truth Hurts," is a sassy, self-affirming anthem whose famous opening lyrics are "I just took a DNA test, turns out I'm 100% that bitch."[28] The TIME feature article describes how "attending a Lizzo concert feels like worshipping at the church of self-love, if your preacher was a pop star living joyfully in a big Black body, delivering a sermon of self-acceptance that's as frank as it is accessible. At a time when Instagrammers are shilling flat-tummy tea or pretending to eat a giant cheeseburger, Lizzo sells something more radical: the idea that you are already enough."[29]

Lizzo identifies as a proud "beautiful and fat" Black woman, a feeling she displays enthusiastically in her many mediated appearances and performances. She brazenly foregrounds her Black plus-size body: posting nude photos on her social media accounts, wearing revealing near-naked outfits and lingerie for her performances, and displaying visual elements such as a giant inflatable butt in her performances (at the 2019 Video Music Awards). About her Blackness Lizzo has said, "I am really just so honored to be graced with this identity. . . . I just love being a black woman, even in a world where [we] are statistically the least desirable. I am still here, and I still rise."[30]

While Lizzo has been performing for nearly a decade, it is largely the coalescing of the discourses, institutions, and regulatory modes and measures of female self-confidence which we have described in this book that has furnished the necessary context for her meteoric rise to fame at this particular moment. As she herself explains, "I've been doing positive music for a long-ass time . . . then the culture changed. . . . Body positivity, which at first was a form of protest for fat bodies and black women and has now become a trendy, commercialized thing. . . . Suddenly I'm mainstream!"[31]

Indeed, Lizzo epitomizes the confidence cult and its prominence in contemporary culture. She embodies and encourages a belief in self-love and body positivity. In her lyrics, media appearances, and social media posts, she vigorously emphasizes self-care, self-determination, and self-growth. She identifies unapologetically as "a fat bitch," promoting refreshingly different beauty standards from the narrowly normative ones that dominate contemporary culture.[32] Yet she also is open about and displays her vulnerability and insecurities, something that makes her highly relatable and much loved. Lizzo offers a way of being, feeling, thinking, and looking that is a corrective: a solution to "harmful" ways of relating to the female body—and particularly the Black female body—a bold and excited refusal of "the tyranny of perfect" and a celebration of inclusivity and self-acceptance in times of growing divisiveness, polarization, and exclusionary politics.[33] As Gerrick Kennedy wrote in 2019, "with tensions thick across the nation in the age of Trump, there's something exuberant about watching a curvy black woman win over America with witty, razor-sharp testimonies of liberation and self-care."[34]

At the same time that Lizzo epitomizes the confidence cult(ure), she seems to also push its boundaries in several significant ways. First, in contrast to the "hollow diversity" and the rather limited diversification of bodies which characterize the confidence cult, Lizzo represents and celebrates a radical deviation from the normative ideal of female attractiveness and the highly restrictive normative beauty standards that dominate this cult. Lizzo explicitly marks a space that privileges fat Black bodies and experiences—bodies typically excluded from participation in the confidence cult and popular culture more broadly. Catherine Connell describes a similar intervention enabled by *Fa(t)shion February*, an online virtual fashion community that represents fat, queer, and femme-identified bodies: "Fat bodies were not merely legitimized as participants in fashion but actively celebrated as purveyors of fashionable and desirable aesthetics."[35] Similarly, Lizzo's mediated appearances and persona go beyond simply displaying fat bodies as aesthetic, a radical act in and of itself; they challenge the highly policed boundaries of who may legitimately participate in the confidence cult and subvert traditional notions of how this participation takes form. Importantly, and unlike cultural sites such as *Fa(t)shion February*, which are largely on the margins of popular culture and are consumed by a limited audience, Lizzo's popularity, visibility, and reach are vast. She is, as she herself has declared, the mainstream.

Crucially, Lizzo subverts the pathologization of fatness as the "disease of obesity" that has to be eradicated through self-work and self-responsibilization. "I'm embracing the title," she says of her body-positive crown, "but it's not a label I wanted to put on myself. It's just my existence. All these fucking hashtags to convince people that the way you look is fine. Isn't that fucking crazy? I say I love myself, and they're like, 'Oh my gosh, she's so brave. She's so political.'" "Even when body positivity is over," she continues, "it's not like I'm going to be a thin white woman. I'm going to be black and fat. That's just hopping on a trend and expecting people to blindly love themselves. That's fake love. I'm trying to figure out how to actually live it."[36]

Second, unlike the postracial space in which many body confidence messages seem to operate (see chapter 1), Lizzo's performance and persona are inseparable from her experience of racism, sexism, and fat-shaming. For example, her popular music video "Bye Bitch," in which she plays a flute wearing a bodysuit and joyfully dances hitting the shoot onstage with her two dancers, was born out of Lizzo's experience of being treated unjustly during her university music studies when, during a sound check, a professor threatened to report her to campus police unless she showed her permit. Lizzo retells this story in interviews and to her audience, saying angrily, "The privilege that you have to walk up to young women, brown women, black women, and yell 'Do you have [a] permit to be here?' While we're clearly onstage with the microphones singing and dancing." "Me just existing is revolutionary," Lizzo exclaims often.[37] Having repeatedly encouraged her fans to "Vote Blue" in the US 2020 presidential election, in November 2020 Lizzo posted on her Instagram account a message expressing her criticism of racial capitalism and her hopes for US politics and society, and thanking her fans for voting. "When I think of this country," she writes, "I think about how we were raised to be patriotic of violence, propaganda & war. I think about how this country is owned by the oppressor and how the oppressed are locked in a valley of capitalism. . . . I believe in a country that teaches the true history so we can better understand where we live and how we can do better. . . . I believe in a country that listens to the cries of the protester and doesn't politicize death. . . . I believe in restoration of this beautiful land and respecting the communities of people who owned America before colonizers renamed it." Accompanying Lizzo's message was an image in which she is nude and the American flag is draped over half of her body (fig. C.3).[38]

The Instagram image, alongside Lizzo's entire mediated figure, disrupts what Janelle Hobson has criticized as Black women's overall investment in the "respectable body."[39] Rather, Lizzo centers her plus-size Black body as a political site of resistance: she refuses and subverts the strategic aesthetic and fashion choices that some Black women historically have made to convey both style and progressive Black political consciousness and to regain their dignity and assert their political agency.[40] At the same time, Lizzo's Black embodiment remains within the boundaries of a commercialized and highly sexualized spectacle. Her mediated appearances center her sexuality. Yet as Hobson contends, "A black beauty project must now grapple with a more complex examination of the intersections of race, gender, class, sexuality, and disability that can reframe black embodiment beyond commercialized spectacles and toward more diverse representations of liberated bodies."[41]

Third, Lizzo explicitly criticizes the inclusive veneer and self-love injunctions of many contemporary commercial campaigns and their hollow diversity, which we discussed in chapter 1. Referring to her empowerment self-confidence anthem "Truth Hurts," Lizzo says: "Could this song be in a Dove commercial? Yes, but it won't. They aren't thinking about everybody."[42] In

C.3 Lizzo's
Instagram
photo, November 2020

this context, Lizzo declined an invitation from Oprah Winfrey's team to use her inspirational song "Worship" in a Weight Watchers commercial. In an interview for *The Cut*, Lizzo recounts how her commitment to uplifting her community of fans trumped her desire to "push herself to national consciousness" through the inclusion of her song in such a prominent advertisement.[43]

Relatedly, through her multiple media appearances—on her social media accounts, in media interviews, and on stage—Lizzo continually makes it clear that self-love requires work. Describing herself as "doing work on the deep crevices" of herself, she talks openly about and details the amount of labor she performs to maintain her positive outlook.[44] For example, she talks frankly about having therapy and of taking her therapist on tour via Skype, of canceling shows if she realizes she is not taking care of herself, and of quoting herself to self-motivate.

Finally, against the limited license for women to express their vulnerability, namely, to be glimpsed briefly before re-emerging defiant, Lizzo seems unafraid to dwell on her vulnerability and admit to its ongoing nature. For example, on social media, Lizzo is notorious for not masking her moods or feelings. "Even as she preaches self-empowerment," writes Samantha Irby, "she's candid about the struggle." Irby continues: "Omnipresent as she may be, Lizzo is just a person who feels like garbage sometimes and lives on the same actively dying rock hurtling through space as the rest of us. She's not a walking inspirational infographic. She knows that part of being enough means acknowledging your imperfections."[45]

Against the repudiation of dependence as the "ugly" antonym of self-confidence, Lizzo highlights her dependence on others, for example, by crediting the group of friends and family who travel with her when she tours (musicians normally tour unaccompanied by friends and family) with helping her "mentally, spiritually and emotionally."[46] In this sense, Lizzo highlights interdependence, care, and relationality, rejecting the fantasy of the no-needs, self-made, and self-maintaining contemporary confident woman.

Resisting the Confidence Cult(ure)?

The examples we mentioned briefly earlier and the case of Lizzo are interesting and significant for the ways in which they disrupt the confidence cult(ure), but also for the ways in which they cannot fully move beyond its logics. They offer glimpses of the way in which social justice projects may be created beyond the confines of the confidence cult within popular culture. Yet they remain partial and uneven, often tugged back to the very discourses, representations, and affective practices we have critiqued throughout this book. As such, they indicate the ongoing force, pervasiveness, and seductiveness of the confidence cult(ure)—the difficulties of resisting, let alone refusing, its strictures. They also show how deeply its individual and psychological logics penetrate and, in so doing, the manner in which they make other ways of knowing oneself or of conceiving social transformation if not *un*thinkable then certainly—and we suggest *systematically*—harder to imagine.

Thus, we see the impact of the confidence cult not simply on the individual women who are its ideal subjects, nor yet on a culture that rewrites its understanding of gender injustice through the notion of a female confidence deficit, but also on feminist politics, which is being remade along neoliberal lines in which the psychological self is ever more prominent. This has such cultural power that even those people and texts that seek to resist these ideas are partly constrained by them. We include ourselves in this, and we return to the points we made at the start of the book about our own ambivalence about and complicity in the confidence cult(ure). Even as outspoken critics of the way that confidence has come to be mobilized in contemporary culture, we are ourselves entangled in it—often reluctantly, sometimes pleasurably, always ambivalently. It was this sense of the seductiveness—the cultural and psychic power—of confidence as a *dispositif* that inspired us to unpack and interrogate the confidence cult(ure).

In our critical interrogation of today's confidence cult(ure), we were reminded of the foundational feminist text *Our Bodies, Ourselves*, now more than half a century old. Written by the Boston Women's Health Book Collective, the book distinguishes between the "climate of doubt" that surrounds pregnancy and birth and increases women's anxiety and fear, and a "climate of confidence." The latter "reinforces women's power and minimizes fear" and crucially is dependent on collective and structural factors such as high-quality prenatal care, a safe work and home environment, childbearing leave, and skilled and compassionate health-care provision. Extended beyond the context of maternity, the notion of a "climate of confidence" seems highly suggestive for the argument of this book: it allows retaining the focus on female confidence and its significance but shifts the emphasis from the individualized and psychologized imperative to women and girls to work on and care for themselves (because no one else will), to the structural factors and resources required to nourish and sustain such a climate.

Conclusion: The Extraordinary Power of Confidence Culture

Having considered some examples that seek to resist and go beyond confidence imperatives, we want to ask what is happening to the confidence cult(ure) today. As we noted at the start of the book, the confidence cult seems to be growing rather than diminishing in force over time, as it spreads across multiple domains (only some of which we have considered here); materializes in novel discourses, images, and social and affective practices; and seemingly intensifies its hold as a gendered technology of self that rewrites social injustice in individualized and psychologized terms. As we were completing the writing of this concluding chapter, images of US vice president elect Kamala Harris were circulating everywhere, reminiscent of many of the features we discussed in the book, vividly embodying female self-confidence, resilience, and ambition. One highly visible image was of Harris striding forward in an elegant trouser suit, briefcase in one hand, alongside the shadow of six-year-old Ruby Bridges, one of four female students who in the 1960s entered the first desegregated classroom in a New Orleans school amid heated protest. The image quickly went viral and was inscribed on a variety of merchandise, accompanied by the caption: "Ruby walked so Kamala can run." Like so many other messages we discussed in this book, this image too equates individual female self-confidence with structural equality and celebrates the two.

Indeed, the confidence cult may be the latest development in the transformation of how women are incited to think and feel about themselves in a moment of ongoing crisis in which inequality and precarity are worsening and the state (particularly in the US and the UK) is dramatically cutting its role in welfare and care-taking of citizens—shifting those obligations to the individual. Going back to the example of Kamala Harris, while there is much to be celebrated about her trailblazing achievements as the first woman of color elected US vice president, it is crucial not to lose sight of the sobering reality of enduring racial, gender, and other inequalities, whose obfuscation the confidence cult(ure) continues to secure.

Against this backdrop, confidence emerges as a disciplinary technology of self par excellence, part of the trend toward "self-care" as a new and exploitative obligation in a broader shift from welfare to wellness,[47] which includes the contemporary emphasis upon positivity and resilience. The confidence cult(ure) is also ever more entangled with other contemporary discourses and imperatives to happiness, inspiration, resilience, affirmation, and gratitude. "New Age spirituality" is increasingly embedded in corporate culture and circulated more widely through smartphone apps and social media that traffic ideas about "positive mental attitude," the "law of attraction" (in which "the universe" is said to "have your back"), and capital-friendly McMindfulness programs.[48]

A tone of rebellion and rule-breaking characterizes many aspects of the confidence cult(ure), in what we have termed "hollow defiance." The confidence cult(ure) is both homogeneous and contradictory. Exhortations to "choose confidence" sit alongside those to "have the courage to be vulnerable"; suggestions to "dare greatly" coexist with instructions to "embrace failure"; meanwhile, advice not to "sweat the small stuff" and to "give up on being perfect" works toward instantiating imperfection as a new cultural ideal, alongside vulnerability—but only if it can be championed confidently and defiantly and in an aesthetically pleasing manner (i.e., with beauty or "hotness"). What unites so many of the self-help books, workplace policies and programs, advertising messages, celebrity proclamations, and development initiatives we have examined in this book is the idea that embracing female self-confidence is essentially "breaking the rules." In fact, as we have shown, the confidence cult(ure) is hegemonic: it is not *against* the system; it is the way "the system" now addresses women—a ubiquitous, unexamined, taken-for-granted assemblage performing powerful cultural, political, and psychological work.

In *Confidence Culture* we have begun the work of interrogating this—not to attack confidence per se but to question what its fetishization does. Our analysis has focused on the textual iterations of the confidence cult(ure), whether in ads, books, smartphone apps, blogs and social media posts, You-Tube videos, films, television shows, popular songs, policy documents, or NGO communicative practices. We have shown the extraordinary force of the confidence culture as a *dispositif* and the remarkable similarity of its "diagnoses" and "prescriptions" for change across disparate fields. What is now urgently needed are studies of the "reception" of the confidence cult(ure) and the way in which its ideas are being taken up, negotiated, and resisted by diverse groups of people. In this way, we will have a fuller understanding of the extent to which warm, "innocent," and affirmative injunctions to feel more confident are contributing to a politics in which the emphasis is upon changing women, rather than changing an unjust world.

notes

Introduction

1. See Vogue, "Congresswoman Alexandria Ocasio-Cortez's Guide to Her Signature Red Lip | Beauty Secrets," YouTube, August 21, 2020, https://www.youtube.com/watch?v=bXqZllqGWGQ.

2. For example, Chloe Brotheridge, *Brave New Girl: Seven Steps to Confidence* (London: Michael Joseph, 2019); Maria van Noord, *Self Esteem for Women: Proven Techniques and Habits to Grow Your Self Esteem, Assertiveness and Confidence in Just 60 Days* (self-published, 2018).

3. Rosalind Gill and Shani Orgad, "The Confidence Cult(ure)," *Australian Feminist Studies* 30, no. 86 (2015): 324–344; Rosalind Gill and Shani Orgad, "Confidence Culture and the Remaking of Feminism," *New Formations* 91 (2017): 16–34; Rosalind Gill and Shani Orgad, "The Amazing Bounce-Backable Woman: Resilience and the Psychological Turn in Neoliberalism," *Sociological Research Online* 23, no. 2 (2018): 477–495.

4. Sarah Banet-Weiser, *Empowered: Popular Feminism and Popular Misogyny* (Durham, NC: Duke University Press, 2018); Catherine Rottenberg, *The Rise of Neoliberal Feminism* (Oxford: Oxford University Press, 2018).

5. See Dominic Nicholls, "Army Chiefs Say Controversial 'Snowflake' Recruit-

ment Campaign Was Most Successful in a Decade as New Series Is Launched," *Telegraph*, January 2, 2020, https://www.telegraph.co.uk/news/2020/01/02/army -chiefs-say-controversial-snowflake-recruitment-campaign.

6. See also Jael Goldfine, "The Rise of the Vulnerable Heroine," *Paper Magazine*, April 3, 2019, https://www.papermag.com/vulnerable-heroine-kesha-lady-gaga -beyonce-2633185821.html; and Fredrika Thelandersson, *Sad Affects and Contemporary Women's Media* (PhD diss., Rutgers University, 2020).

7. Nikolas Rose, *Inventing Ourselves: Psychology, Power, Personhood* (Cambridge: Cambridge University Press, 1998).

8. Rottenberg, *Rise of Neoliberal Feminism*.

9. See his website, https://michaelserwa.com, accessed December 3, 2020.

10. Liz McLardy, "5 Ways to Make Managing Your Money an Act of Self-Love," *WellBeing*, August 1, 2018, https://www.wellbeing.com.au/mind-spirit/mind/5-ways -make-managing-money-act-self-love.html.

11. Jack Bratich and Sarah Banet-Weiser, "From Pick-Up Artists to Incels: Con(fidence) Games, Networked Misogyny, and the Failure of Neoliberalism," *International Journal of Communication* 13 (2019): 5003–5027; Alison Hearn, "Confidence Man: Breaking the Spell of Trump the Brand," *Soundings: A Journal of Politics and Culture* 66 (2017): 79–89.

12. Bratich and Banet-Weiser, "From Pick-Up Artists to Incels," 5010.

13. Rachel O'Neill, *Seduction: Men, Masculinity and Mediated Intimacy* (Cambridge: Polity, 2018).

14. Angela McRobbie, *The Aftermath of Feminism: Gender, Culture and Social Change* (London: Sage, 2009).

15. Rosalind Gill, "Post-postfeminism? New Feminist Visibilities in Postfeminist Times," *Feminist Media Studies* 16, no. 4 (2016): 610–630.

16. Coming to prominence (in the US at least) post-2008, the notion was intimately connected to Barack Obama's presidency and to an American fantasy of fairness and egalitarianism, in which a shameful and painful history was rhetorically laid to rest, with numerous proclamations of the end of race and of racism and other myth-making and "mystique." Catherine R. Squires, *The Post-racial Mystique: Media and Race in the Twenty-First Century* (New York: NYU Press, 2014). Despite the absurdity of the premise, it is striking how it took hold, influencing the operation of modes of racism.

17. David T. Goldberg, "Neoliberalizing Race," *Macalester Civic Forum* 1, no. 1 (2007), http://digitalcommons.macalester.edu/maccivicf/vol1/iss1/14; Roopali Mukherjee, Sarah Banet-Weiser, and Herman Gray, eds., *Racism Postrace* (Durham, NC: Duke University Press, 2019).

18. Roopali Mukherjee, "Antiracism Limited: A Pre-history of Post-race," *Cultural Studies* 30, no. 1 (2016): 51.

19. Mukherjee, "Antiracism Limited," 51.

20. Kate McNicholas Smith and Imogen Tyler, "Lesbian Brides: Post-queer Popular Culture," *Feminist Media Studies* 17, no. 3 (2017): 315–331. See also Lisa Duggan, "The New Homonormativity: The Sexual Politics of Neoliberalism," in *Ma-*

terializing Democracy: Toward a Revitalized Cultural Politics, ed. Russ Castronovo and Dana D. Nelson (Durham, NC: Duke University Press, 2012), 175–194; Jasbir Puar, "Rethinking Homonationalism," International Journal of Middle East Studies 45, no. 2 (2013): 336–339; Michael Warner, "Introduction: Fear of a Queer Planet," Social Text 29 (1991): 3–17.

21. Lyra McKee, "Lyra McKee: A Letter to My 14-Year-Old Self," Guardian, April 19, 2019, https://www.theguardian.com/commentisfree/2019/apr/19/lyra -mckee-letter-gay-journalism-northern-ireland.

22. Alison Kafer, Feminist, Queer, Crip (Bloomington: Indiana University Press, 2013).

23. Akane Kanai and Rosalind Gill, "Woke? Affect, Neoliberalism, Marginal-ised Identities and Consumer Culture," New Formations 102 (2020): 10–27, https:// doi.org/10.3898/NEWF:102.01.2020. As Micki McGee observes, in a world of ever-expanding demands for flexible productivity and sociability, what were formerly considered personality characteristics are now handicaps. See Micki McGee, "Neurodiversity," Contexts 11, no. 3 (2012): 12–13. More broadly, "new approaches by disability scholars and activists show that disability is not simply lodged in the body, but created by the social and material conditions that 'dis-able' the full participation of those considered atypical." Faye Ginsburg and Rayna Rapp, "Disability Worlds," Annual Review of Anthropology 42 (2013): 53.

24. "Improve Your Social Confidence," Psychologies, March 1, 2012, https:// www.psychologies.co.uk/self/social-confidence.html; cited in Sarah Riley, Adri-enne Evans, and Martine Robson, Postfeminism and Health (London: Routledge, 2018), 30.

25. For a similar point about neoliberal subjectivity generally, see Ulrich Bröck-ling, "Gendering the Enterprising Self: Subjectification Programs and Gender Dif-ferences in Guides to Success," Distinktion 11 (2005): 7–23.

26. This example is discussed also in Riley, Evans, and Robson, Postfeminism and Health.

27. Rose, Inventing Ourselves.

28. Eva Illouz, Saving the Modern Soul: Therapy, Emotions, and the Culture of Self-Help (Berkeley: University of California Press, 2008).

29. Micki McGee, Self-Help, Inc.: Makeover Culture in American Life (Oxford: Ox-ford University Press, 2005), 43.

30. Illouz, Saving the Modern Soul; McGee, Self-Help, Inc.; Sarah Riley, Adrienne Evans, Emma Anderson, and Martine Robson, "The Gendered Nature of Self-Help," Feminism and Psychology 29, no. 1 (2019): 3–18.

31. Heidi Marie Rimke, "Governing Citizens through Self-Help Literature," Cultural Studies 14, no. 1 (2000): 73, emphasis in original.

32. Richard Layard, Happiness: Lessons from a New Science (London: Penguin, 2011), 200.

33. Riley et al., "Gendered Nature of Self Help," 9; and see Rosalind Gill, Gender and the Media (Cambridge: Polity, 2007).

34. Lisa Appignanesi, Mad, Bad and Sad: A History of Women and the Mind Doctors

from 1800 to the Present (London: Virago, 2009); Elaine Showalter, *The Female Malady: Women, Madness, and English Culture, 1830-1980* (New York: Pantheon, 1985).

35. In art and self-help Shakespeare's character of Ophelia has been used as a symbol of and a site for challenging ideas about female psychology and sexuality. See Elizabeth Marshall, "Schooling Ophelia: Hysteria, Memory and Adolescent Femininity," *Gender and Education* 19, no. 6 (2007): 707–728; Elaine Showalter, "Ophelia, Gender and Madness," British Library, March 15, 2016, https://www .bl.uk/shakespeare/articles/ophelia-gender-and-madness. An example of a highly popular self-help book inspired by the character of Ophelia is Mary Pipher, *Reviving Ophelia: Helping You to Understand and Cope with Your Teenage Daughter* (New York: Penguin, 1995).

36. Anita Harris, *Future Girl: Young Women in the Twenty-First Century* (New York: Psychology Press, 2004).

37. McGee, *Self-Help, Inc.*

38. McGee, *Self-Help, Inc.*, 19.

39. For example, Lois McNay, *Foucault and Feminism: Power, Gender and the Self* (Cambridge: Polity, 1992); Elayne Rapping, *The Culture of Recovery: Making Sense of the Self-Help Movement in Women's Lives* (Boston: Beacon, 1997); Corrine Squire, "Empowering Women? The Oprah Winfrey Show," in *Feminist Television Criticism: A Reader*, ed. Charlotte Brunsdon, Julie D'Acci, and Lynn Spigel (Oxford: Oxford University Press, 1997), 98–113.

40. Janice Peck, "TV Talk Shows as Therapeutic Discourse: The Ideological Labor of the Televised Talking Cure," *Communication Theory* 5, no. 1 (1995): 75.

41. Meg Henderson and Anthea Taylor, *Postfeminism in Context: The Australian Postfeminist Imaginary* (New York: Routledge, 2018).

42. Diane Negra, *What a Girl Wants? Fantasizing the Reclamation of Self in Postfeminism* (London: Routledge, 2009).

43. Henderson and Taylor, *Postfeminism in Context.*

44. Riley et al., "Gendered Nature of Self Help," 9–10.

45. Eva Illouz, *Cold Intimacies: The Making of Emotional Capitalism* (Cambridge: Polity, 2007); Henderson and Taylor, *Postfeminism in Context.*

46. Stuart Hall, Doreen Massey, and Mike Rustin, eds., *After Neoliberalism? The Kilburn Manifesto* (London: Lawrence and Wishart, 2015).

47. Katherine Sender, *The Makeover: Reality Television and Reflexive Audiences* (New York: NYU Press, 2012).

48. Sam Binkley, "Governmentality and Lifestyle Studies," *Sociology Compass* 1, no. 1 (2007): 111–126.

49. Laurie Ouellette, *Lifestyle TV* (New York: Routledge, 2016), 77.

50. David Harvey, *A Brief History of Neoliberalism* (Oxford: Oxford University Press, 2005), 2.

51. Jo Littler, *Against Meritocracy: Culture, Power and Myths of Mobility* (London: Routledge, 2018), 2.

52. Wendy Brown, *Undoing the Demos: Neoliberalism's Stealth Revolution* (Cambridge, MA: MIT Press, 2015); Michel Foucault, *The Birth of Biopolitics: Lectures at*

the *Collège de France, 1978–1979,* translated by Graham Burchell (London: Springer, 2008); Thomas Lemke, "'The Birth of Bio-politics': Michel Foucault's Lecture at the Collège de France on Neo-liberal Governmentality," *Economy and Society* 30, no. 2 (2001): 190–207; Nikolas Rose, *Governing the Soul: The Shaping of the Private Self* (London: Taylor and Francis/Routledge, 1990).

53. Brown, *Undoing the Demos.*

54. Barbara Cruikshank, "Revolutions Within: Self-Government and Self-Esteem," *Economy and Society* 22, no. 3 (1993): 327–344.

55. Christina Scharff, *Repudiating Feminism: Young Women in a Neoliberal World* (Farnham, UK: Ashgate, 2013); Christina Scharff, "The Psychic Life of Neoliberalism: Mapping the Contours of Entrepreneurial Subjectivity," *Theory, Culture and Society* 33, no. 6 (2016): 107–122.

56. Akane Kanai, *Gender and Relatability in Digital Culture* (London: Palgrave Macmillan, 2019).

57. Riley et al., "Gendered Nature of Self Help," 7.

58. Barbara Ehrenreich, *Bright-Sided: How Positive Thinking Is Undermining America* (New York: Macmillan, 2010), 8.

59. Sam Binkley, *Happiness as Enterprise: An Essay on Neoliberal Life* (New York: State University of New York Press, 2015); William Davies, *The Happiness Industry: How the Government and Big Business Sold Us Well-Being* (London: Verso, 2015); Carl Cederström and Andre Spicer, *The Wellness Syndrome* (Cambridge: Polity, 2014); Barbara Ehrenreich, *Natural Causes: Life, Death and the Illusion of Control* (London: Granta, 2018).

60. Kim Allen and Anna Bull, "Following Policy: A Network Ethnography of the UK Character Education Policy Community," *Sociological Research Online* 23, no. 2 (2018): 438–458.

61. Tracey Jensen, "Against Resilience," in *We Need to Talk about Family: Essays on Neoliberalism, the Family and Popular Culture,* ed. Roberta Garrett, Tracey Jensen, and Angie Voela (Cambridge: Cambridge Scholars, 2016), 76–94; Gill and Orgad, "Amazing Bounce-Backable Woman."

62. Lynne Friedli and Robert Stearn, "Positive Affect as Coercive Strategy: Conditionality, Activation and the Role of Psychology in UK Government Workfare Programmes," *Medical Humanities* 41, no. 1 (2015): 40–47.

63. Allen and Bull, "Following Policy"; Gill and Orgad, "Amazing Bounce-Backable Woman"; Jensen, "Against Resilience."

64. Illouz, *Cold Intimacies.*

65. Raymond Williams, *The Long Revolution: An Analysis of the Democratic, Industrial, and Cultural Changes Transforming Our Society* (New York: Columbia University Press, 1961).

66. Laura Favaro, "'Just Be Confident Girls!': Confidence Chic as Neoliberal Governmentality," in *Aesthetic Labour: Rethinking Beauty Politics in Neoliberalism,* ed. Ana Sofia Elias, Rosalind Gill, and Christina Scharff (London: Palgrave Macmillan, 2017), 283–299.

67. Michel Foucault, *Technologies of the Self: A Seminar with Michel Foucault,* ed.

Luther H. Martin, Huck Gutman, and Patrick H. Hutton (London: Tavistock, 1988).

68. Foucault, *Technologies of the Self*, 18.

69. Michel Foucault, *The Use of Pleasure*, vol. 2 of *The History of Sexuality*, translated by Robert Hurley (Harmondsworth, UK: Penguin, 1987), 122; our emphasis.

70. Rebecca Hazleden, "Love Yourself: The Relationship of the Self with Itself in Popular Self-Help Texts," *Journal of Sociology* 39, no. 4 (2003): 413–428.

71. Judith Butler, *The Psychic Life of Power: Theories in Subjection* (Stanford, CA: Stanford University Press, 1997).

72. Susan Bordo, *Unbearable Weight: Feminism, Western Culture, and the Body* (Berkeley: University of California Press, 1993); Judith Butler, *Gender Trouble: Feminism and the Subversion of Identity* (New York: Routledge, 1990); Teresa De Lauretis, *Technologies of Gender: Essays on Theory, Film, and Fiction* (Basingstoke, UK: Macmillan, 1989); McRobbie, *Aftermath of Feminism*; Hilary Radner, "Introduction: Queering the Girl," in *Swinging Single: Representing Sexuality in the 1960s*, ed. Hilary Radner and Moya Luckett (Minneapolis: University of Minnesota Press, 1999), 1–36; Adrienne Evans and Sarah Riley, *Technologies of Sexiness: Sex, Identity, and Consumer Culture* (Oxford: Oxford University Press, 2015); Gill and Orgad, "Confidence Cult(ure)"; Gill and Orgad, "Confidence Culture and the Remaking of Feminism."

73. Robert Goldman, Deborah Heath, and Sharon L. Smith, "Commodity Feminism," *Critical Studies in Mass Communication* 8, no. 3 (1991): 333–351. See also Robert Goldman, *Readings Ads Socially* (London: Routledge, 1992).

74. Susan J. Douglas, *Where the Girls Are: Growing Up Female with the Mass Media* (Harmondsworth, UK: Penguin, 1994), 247–248. More recently, Nancy Fraser writes of feminism having been "abducted" by neoliberal capitalism. See Nancy Fraser, "Feminism, Capitalism and the Cunning of History," *New Left Review* 56 (2009): 97–117.

75. Cited in Caroline West, "The Lean In Collection: Women, Work, and the Will to Represent," *Open Cultural Studies* 2, no. 1 (2018): 433, https://doi.org/10.1515/culture-2018-0039.

76. Giorgia Aiello and Katy Parry, *Visual Communication: Understanding Images in Media Culture* (London: Sage, 2020).

77. Jessica Valenti, "Sad White Babies with Mean Feminist Mommies," *Jessica Valenti* (blog), accessed December 9, 2020, https://jessicavalenti.tumblr.com/post/25465502300/sad-white-babies-with-mean-feminist-mommies-the.

78. West, "Lean In Collection," 434. Interestingly, West also notes that there is only one single reference to feminism across 16,000 images—and it is a reference to a series of three images that depict a harried white father precariously balanced with bags, phone, and toddler. This has the possible implication, we suggest, that in this contemporary visual habitat men are given dispensation to struggle, to be vulnerable and overwhelmed, while confidence, as a marker of success (among other things), has become "compulsory" for women. We return to issues of vulnerability throughout this book.

79. Kirsten Kohrs and Rosalind Gill, "Confident Appearing: Revisiting *Gender Advertisements* in Contemporary Culture," in *Routledge Handbook of Language,*

Gender, and Sexuality, ed. Jo Angouri and Judith Baxter (London: Routledge, 2021), 528–542; Erving Goffman, *Gender Advertisements* (New York: Harper and Row, 1979).

80. Arlie Hochschild with Anne Machung, *The Second Shift: Working Families and the Revolution at Home* (New York: Penguin, 1989), 1.

81. For example, a 2020 advertisement for Geox (Respira) shoes depicts a woman striding, her hands in her trouser pockets, her head held high. A similar image is used in an ad for Marks and Spencer: the woman's hair blows behind her to signify the speed and purposefulness of her gait, her confidence emphasized by the copy "Always walk tall, even in flats."

82. Arlie Hochschild, "Emotion Work, Feeling Rules, and Social Structure," *American Journal of Sociology* 85, no. 3 (1979): 551–575.

83. Patricia Ticineto Clough and Jean Halley, eds., *The Affective Turn: Theorizing the Social* (Durham, NC: Duke University Press, 2007).

84. Lauren Berlant, *Cruel Optimism* (Durham, NC: Duke University Press, 2011); Robert Seyfert, "Beyond Personal Feelings and Collective Emotions: Toward a Theory of Social Affect," *Theory, Culture and Society* 29, no. 6 (2012): 27–46.

85. Sara Ahmed, *The Cultural Politics of Emotion* (London: Routledge, 2004).

86. Imogen Tyler, *Revolting Subjects: Social Abjection and Resistance in Neoliberal Britain* (New York: Zed Books, 2013).

87. John Clarke, "A Sense of Loss? Unsettled Attachments in the Current Conjuncture," *New Formations: A Journal of Culture/Theory/Politics* 96, no. 1 (2019): 132–146; Kirsten Forkert, *Austerity as Public Mood: Social Anxieties and Social Struggles* (London: Rowman and Littlefield, 2017); Lawrence Grossberg, "Cultural Studies in Search of a Method, or Looking for Conjunctural Analysis," *New Formations: A Journal of Culture/Theory/Politics* 96/97 (2019): 38–68.

88. Margaret Wetherell and David Beer, "The Future of Affect Theory: An Interview with Margaret Wetherell," *Theory, Culture and Society*, October 15, 2014, https://www.theoryculturesociety.org/the-future-of-affect-theory-an-interview -with-margaret-wetherall; Margaret Wetherell, "Trends in the Turn to Affect: A Social Psychological Critique," *Body and Society* 21, no. 2 (2015): 139–166.

89. Wetherell and Beer, "Future of Affect Theory."

90. Wetherell, "Trends in the Turn."

91. Nick Couldry, "Theorising Media as Practice," *Social Semiotics* 14, no. 2 (2004): 115–132; Rosalind Gill, "Surveillance Is a Feminist Issue," in *Routledge Handbook of Contemporary Feminism*, ed. Tasha Oren and Andrea L. Press (New York: Routledge, 2019), 148–161.

92. Ann Swidler, "What Anchors Cultural Practices?," in *The Practice Turn in Contemporary Theory*, ed. Theodore R. Schatzki, Karin Knorr Cetina, and Eike von Savigny (London: Routledge, 2001), 74–92.

93. In his essay on multisited ethnography as a research strategy, George Marcus lists various techniques to trace the objects of study within different settings of a complex cultural phenomenon. See George Marcus, *Ethnography through Thick and Thin* (Princeton, NJ: Princeton University Press, 1998). See also Shani Orgad, *Heading Home: Motherhood, Work, and the Failed Promise of Equality* (New York: Co-

lumbia University Press, 2019), for a discussion of how the principle of "following the object" is applied to the study of cultural representations and discourses.

94. Jonathan Potter, "Discourse Analysis and Constructionist Approaches: Theoretical Background," in *Handbook of Qualitative Research Methods for Psychology and the Social Sciences*, ed. J. Richardson (Leicester, UK: British Psychological Society, 1996), 125–140.

95. Goldfine, "Rise of the Vulnerable Heroine."

One. Body Confidence

1. Maxine Leeds Craig, *Ain't I a Beauty Queen? Black Women, Beauty, and the Politics of Race* (New York: Oxford University Press, 2020).

2. Chanel (@Chanelofficial), "Forget foundation. Choose confidence," Instagram, accessed January 29, 2020, https://www.instagram.com/p/BtOeHK-nsqX; "Goodbye Resolutions: Hello Empowerment," television advertisement, *Sweaty Betty*, dir. Nicola Pearl and Studio BLVD, 2019.

3. Sabrina Barr, "Love Island Criticised as New Figures Reveal Impact of Reality TV on Body Image," *Independent*, June 3, 2019, https://www.independent.co.uk/life-style/health-and-families/love-island-2019-mental-health-body-image-reality-tv-itv-a8940856.html.

4. "Beauty and the Muse," accessed January 29, 2020, http://www.beautyandthemuse.net; Leah Vernon, *Unashamed: Musings of a Fat, Black Muslim* (Boston: Beacon, 2019).

5. Leah Lakshmi Piepzna-Samarasinha, *Care Work: Dreaming Disability Justice* (Vancouver, BC: Arsenal Pulp, 2018).

6. Andrew Pulrang, "Self-Help or Activism: A Fundamental Divide in the Disability Community," *Forbes*, February 23, 2020, https://www.forbes.com/sites/andrewpulrang/2020/02/23/self-help-or-activism-a-fundamental-divide-in-the-disability-community/.

7. Alice Wong, *Disability Visibility: First-Person Stories from the Twenty-First Century* (New York: Vintage, 2020).

8. Marcia Darvell and Ahmed Elsharkawy, *Eating Disorders, Body Image and the Media* (London: British Medical Association, 2000).

9. Darvell and Elsharkawy, *Eating Disorders*.

10. See, for example, "Body Dysmorphia," Centre for Clinical Interventions, Government of Western Australia, last updated December 16, 2019, https://www.cci.health.wa.gov.au/Resources/Looking-After-Yourself/Body-Dysmorphia; Jill Andrew, "Inspire Body Positivity with the Body Confidence Canada Awards," Canadian Women's Foundation, March 18, 2016, https://canadianwomen.org/blog/body-confidence-canada-awards-2016; "Body Image," Department of Health, Government of Western Australia, https://gdhr.wa.gov.au/-/media-and-body-image; *A Proposed National Strategy on Body Image* (Canberra: National Advisory Group on Body Image, 2009).

11. See Body Positive, "About Us," accessed June 9, 2021, https://thebodypositive

.org/about-us/; see also Sarah Banet-Weiser, "'Confidence You Can Carry!': Girls in Crisis and the Market for Girls' Empowerment Organizations," *Continuum: Journal of Media and Cultural Studies* 29, no. 2 (2015): 182–193.

12. Emma A. Jane, "'Your a Ugly, Whorish, Slut': Understanding E-bile," *Feminist Media Studies* 14, no. 4 (2014): 531–546.

13. Prince's Trust, "L'Oréal Paris," accessed January 29, 2020, https://www .princes-trust.org.uk/about-the-trust/success-stories/loreal-paris.

14. Weight Watchers, "Discover WellnessWins," accessed January 29, 2020, https://www.weightwatchers.com/uk/wellnesswins.

15. Dove, "School Workshops on Body Image: Confident Me," accessed January 29, 2020, https://www.dove.com/uk/dove-self-esteem-project/school-workshops -on-body-image-confident-me.html.

16. Sarah Banet-Weiser, "'Free Self-Esteem Tools?': Brand Culture, Gender, and the Dove Real Beauty Campaign," in *Commodity Activism: Cultural Resistance in Neoliberal Times*, ed. Roopali Mukherjee and Sarah Banet-Weiser (New York: NYU Press, 2012), 39–56.

17. Dove, "The CROWN Act: Working to Eradicate Race-Based Hair Discrimination," 2020, https://www.dove.com/us/en/stories/campaigns/the-crown-act.html.

18. Dove, "The CROWN Act." As Sarah Banet-Weiser argues, in this market, "self-esteem is crafted as a commodity, positioning the girls who are seen to be suffering as particular sorts of vulnerable consumers. This in turn marks these girls as would-be consumers for the self-esteem market which then works to trivialise and contain these discourses as individual, market-based problems whose solutions are consumerist." Sarah Banet-Weiser, "Am I Pretty or Ugly? Girls and the Market for Self-Esteem," *Girlhood Studies* 7, no. 1 (2014): 90. It constitutes a cyclical process, in which brands become intimately entangled with other organizations such as think tanks and NGOs and with political action and intervention. This is captured by notions of "cause marketing" and "commodity activism," in which particular political goals—such as raising girls' self-esteem—become rendered as requiring *consumer solutions* (Mukherjee and Banet-Weiser, *Commodity Activism*).

19. Danielle Egan, *Becoming Sexual: A Critical Appraisal of the Sexualization of Girls* (Cambridge: Polity, 2013); Rosalind Gill, "The Sexualisation of Culture?," *Social and Personality Psychology Compass* 6, no. 7 (2012): 483–498; Dove, "The CROWN Act"; Unilever, "Unilever Says No to 'Normal' with New Positive Beauty Vision," March 9, 2021, https://www.unilever.com/news/press-releases/2021/unilever-says-no-to -normal-with-new-positive-beauty-vision.html.

20. A corollary of the way that Black women may be marked as "always already angry" is the difficulty of recognizing their vulnerability.

21. John St., "Jane St.," YouTube, November 4, 2015, https://www.youtube.com /watch?v=fGJlrbpFa4k.

22. Rewa Murphy and Sue Jackson, "Bodies-as-Image? The Body Made Visible in Magazine Love Your Body Content," *Women's Studies Journal* 25, no. 1 (2011): 17–30; Dara Persis Murray, "Branding 'Real' Social Change in Dove's Campaign for Real Beauty," *Feminist Media Studies* 13, no. 1 (2012): 83–101.

23. Murray, "Branding 'Real' Social Change."

24. Meghan Lynch, "Blogging for Beauty? A Critical Analysis of Operation Beautiful," *Women's Studies International Forum* 34, no. 6 (2011): 582–592; Rewa Murphy, "(De)Constructing 'Body Love' Discourses in Young Women's Magazines" (PhD diss., Victoria University of Wellington, 2013).

25. Judith Butler, *Excitable Speech: A Politics of the Performative* (New York: Routledge, 1997); McRobbie, *Aftermath of Feminism*.

26. Katie Martell, "Femvertising: The Illusion of Progress in Marketing to Women," accessed January 29, 2020, https://www.katie-martell.com/femvertising.

27. "Lululemon Diaries: My Life in an Exploitative Libertarian Happiness Cult," *Jezebel*, July 15, 2015, https://jezebel.com/lululemon-diaries-my-life-in-an -exploitative-libertari-1717441616.

28. Martell, "Femvertising."

29. Sara Rodrigues, "Undressing Homogeneity: Prescribing Femininity and the Transformation of Self-Esteem in *How to Look Good Naked*," *Journal of Popular Film and Television* 40, no. 1 (2012): 42–51; Shaira Kadir and Joanna Tidy, "Gays, Gaze and Aunty Gok: The Disciplining of Gender and Sexuality in *How to Look Good Naked*," *Feminist Media Studies* 13, no. 2 (2011): 177–191.

30. Joanna Whitehead, "New Mothercare Campaign Encourages Mothers to Feel Confident about Their Bodies," *Independent*, February 25, 2019, https://www .independent.co.uk/life-style/health-and-families/mothercare-body-confidence -proud-mums-campaign-birth-pregnancy-a8792406.html.

31. Whitehead, "New Mothercare Campaign."

32. Missguided, "Keep on Being You," accessed January 31, 2020, https://www .missguided.eu/campaign/keep-on-being-you.

33. Olivia Petter, "Missguided Celebrates Female 'Flaws' in Latest Campaign," *Independent*, May 10, 2018, https://www.independent.co.uk/life-style/fashion /missguided-female-flaws-imperfections-celebration-campaign-body-positivity -fashion-a8345176.html.

34. Chelsea Ritschel, "Nike Uses Plus-Size Mannequins in Store," *Independent*, June 5, 2019, https://www.independent.co.uk/life-style/nike-plus-size-mannequin -london-store-niketown-a8946196.html.

35. Statistics show that the average UK woman weighs more than 150 pounds and is a dress size 16. More than 45 percent of women in the UK are a size 16 or above. See Rachel Hosie, "How Women's Bodies Have Changed since 1957," *Independent*, March 16, 2017, https://www.independent.co.uk/life-style/health-and -families/womens-body-changes-since-1957-self-image-fashion-weight-health -sizes-positive-a7633036.html.

36. Ana Sofia Elias, Rosalind Gill, and Christina Scharff, eds., *Aesthetic Labour: Rethinking Beauty Politics in Neoliberalism* (London: Palgrave Macmillan, 2017); Meghan Murphy, "Femininity Is No Joke: On the #nomakeupselfie and #manup-andmakeup," *Feminist Current*, March 21, 2014, https://www.feministcurrent.com /2014/03/21/femininity-is-no-joke-nomakeupselfie-and-manupandmakeup%E2 %80%AC.

37. Sofie Hagen (@SofieHagen), "Amy Schumer is blonde," Twitter, February 9, 2018.

38. Sara De Benedictis, Bridget Conor, and Rosalind Gill, "Feminist Gloss" (unpublished manuscript).

39. Stuart Hall, "The Spectacle of the 'Other,'" in *Representation: Cultural Representations and Signifying Practices*, ed. Stuart Hall (London: Sage, 1997), 223–279; Anne McClintock, *Imperial Leather: Race, Gender and Sexuality in the Colonial Contest* (London: Routledge, 1995).

40. Dove (@Dove), "An image we recently posted," Twitter, October 7, 2017, https://twitter.com/dove/status/916731793927278592?lang=en.

41. Mukherjee, Banet-Weiser, and Gray, *Racism Postrace*; Francesca Sobande, "Woke-Washing: 'Intersectional' Femvertising and Branding 'Woke' Bravery," *European Journal of Marketing* 54, no. 11 (2019): 2723–2745, https://doi.org/10.1108/EJM-02-2019-0134.

42. Lisa Nakamura, *Digitizing Race: Visual Cultures of the Internet* (Minneapolis: University of Minnesota Press, 2008).

43. Banet-Weiser, *Empowered*.

44. The Prince's Trust and L'Oréal Paris, "#AllWorthIt," YouTube, February 23, 2017, https://www.youtube.com/watch?v=iyHPD8dM3o4.

45. The Prince's Trust and L'Oréal Paris, "#AllWorthIt."

46. Marc Jacobs, "Introducing Our New Fragrance, PERFECT MARC JACOBS," YouTube, July 15, 2020, https://www.youtube.com/watch?v=CnOK1WTKLJY.

47. Mukherjee, "Antiracism Limited," 61.

48. L'Oréal, https://www.loreal-paris.co.uk/podcasts. All the L'Oreal Affirmations podcasts can be accessed via Spotify at the following link: https://open.spotify.com/show/1t2yj8OZAGii7hbIDWvZ8.

49. Pantene UK, "Pantene x Katie Piper—The Power of Hair Commercial," YouTube, August 7, 2019, https://www.youtube.com/watch?v=holH_W4sBws.

50. Anandi Ramamurthy and Kalpana Wilson, "'Come and Join the Freedom-Lovers': Racism, Appropriation and Resistance in Advertising," in *Colonial Advertising and Commodity Racism*, ed. Wulf D. Hund, Michael Pickering, and Anandi Ramamurthy (Zurich: Lit Verlag, 2013), 69–89.

51. Andreas Chatzidakis, Jamie Hakim, Jo Littler, Catherine Rottenberg, and Lynne Segal, "From Carewashing to Radical Care: The Discursive Explosions of Care during Covid-19," *Feminist Media Studies* 20, no. 6 (2020): 889–895; Francesca Sobande, "'We're All in This Together': Commodified Notions of Connection, Care and Community in Brand Responses to COVID-19," *European Journal of Cultural Studies* 23, no. 6 (2020): 1033–1037, published ahead of print June 22, 2020, https://doi.org/10.1177%2F1367549420932294.

52. Goldman, Heath, and Smith, "Commodity Feminism"; Rosalind Gill, "Beyond the 'Sexualisation of Culture' Thesis: An Intersectional Analysis of 'Six-packs,' 'Midriffs' and 'Hot Lesbians' in Advertising," *Sexualities* 12, no. 2 (2009): 137–160.

53. Wanna Thompson, "How White Women on Instagram Are Profiting off

Black Women," *Paper Magazine*, November 14, 2018, https://www.papermag.com /white-women-blackfishing-instagram-2619714094.html.

54. Alisha Gaines, *Black for a Day: White Fantasies of Race and Empathy* (Chapel Hill: University of North Carolina Press, 2017).

55. See, e.g., Naila Kabeer, *The Power to Choose: Bangladeshi Women and Labour Supply Decision-Making in London and Dhaka* (New York: Verso, 2005).

56. Jilly Boyce Kay and Helen Wood, "Culture and Commoning in a Time of Coronavirus: Introduction to a *Cultural Commons* Special Section on COVID-19," *European Journal of Cultural Studies* 23, no. 4 (2020): 630–634, https://doi.org/10.1177 %2F1367549420928360. See also Tammy E. Hoskins, *Stitched Up: The Anti-capitalist Book of Fashion* (London: Pluto, 2014).

57. Rosalind Gill, *Feeling Judged: Posting Perfect Lives on Social Media* (Cambridge: Polity, 2021).

58. Kanai and Gill, "Woke?"

59. Banet-Weiser, *Empowered*.

60. Safiya Noble, *Algorithms of Oppression: How Search Engines Reinforce Racism* (New York: New York University Press, 2018).

61. Jenny Kleeman, "SNL Producer and Film-Maker Are Latest to Accuse YouTube of Anti-LGBT Bias," *Guardian*, November 22, 2019, https://www.the guardian.com/technology/2019/nov/22/youtube-lgbt-content-lawsuit -discrimination-algorithm.

62. See images shared by @InfluencerPayGap on Instagram, https://www .instagram.com/influencerpaygap.

63. McRobbie, *Aftermath of Feminism*; Angela McRobbie, "Notes on the Perfect: Competitive Femininity in Neoliberal Times," *Australian Feminist Studies* 30, no. 83 (2015): 3–20; Heather Widdows, *Perfect Me* (Princeton, NJ: Princeton University Press, 2018).

64. Gill, *Gender and the Media*, 255.

65. Elias, Gill, and Scharff, *Aesthetic Labour*.

66. Gill, *Feeling Judged*.

67. Katherine Morton, "Emerging Geographies of Disciplining the Ageing Body: Practising Cosmetic Technologies in the Aesthetic Clinic," *Gender, Place and Culture* 22, no. 7 (2015): 1041–1057.

68. Bordo, *Unbearable Weight*.

69. Kristin Denise Rowe, "'I Love This Cotton Hair!': Black Women, Natural Hair, and Re(constructions) of Beauty" (master's thesis, Michigan State University, 2015).

70. Ana Sofia Elias, "Beautiful Body, Confident Soul: Young Women and the Beauty Labour of Neoliberalism" (PhD diss., King's College London, 2016).

71. Ana Sofia Elias and Rosalind Gill, "Beauty Surveillance: The Digital Self-Monitoring Cultures of Neoliberalism," *European Journal of Cultural Studies* 21, no. 1 (2017): 59–77.

72. Elias's female interviewees also felt themselves subject to constant evaluation from other people, particularly women. One woman vividly described her

feeling that there was a "checklist gaze" enacted by most women she met, which involved a quick but sweeping scrutiny of her entire body, checking from her footwear to the top of her head and forming an instant evaluation. Alison Winch coined the term "gynaeoptic surveillance" to talk about the "girlfriend gaze," in which women and girls police each other's looks and behaviors in a way characterized simultaneously by judgment, affection, and "normative cruelties." See Alison Winch, *Girlfriends and Postfeminist Sisterhood* (London: Palgrave Macmillan, 2013); Jessica Ringrose and Emma Renold, "Normative Cruelties and Gender Deviants: The Performative Effects of Bully Discourses for Girls and Boys in School," *British Educational Research Journal* 36, no. 4 (2010): 573–596.

73. Brooke Erin Duffy, *(Not) Getting Paid to Do What You Love: Gender, Social Media, and Aspirational Work* (New Haven, CT: Yale University Press, 2019); Shirley Tate, "Black Beauty: Shade, Hair and Anti-racist Aesthetics," *Ethnic and Racial Studies* 30, no. 2 (2007): 300–319.

74. Lauren Valenti, "Watch Liv Tyler Do Her 25-Step Beauty and Self-Care Routine," *Vogue*, July 25, 2019, https://www.vogue.com/article/liv-tyler-beauty-skin -self-care-secrets-tricks-techniques.

75. Jenna Drenten and Lauren Gurrieri, "Social Media, the 'Bikini Bridge' and the Viral Contagion of Body Ideals," *The Conversation*, December 3, 2017, https:// theconversation.com/social-media-the-bikini-bridge-and-the-viral-contagion -of-body-ideals-87262.

76. Natalie Morris, "The Underboob Bikini Is the Next Big Instagram Trend," *Metro*, May 13, 2019, https://metro.co.uk/2019/05/13/underboob-bikini-next-big -instagram-trend-9506261.

77. Michelle M. Lazar, "'Seriously Girly Fun!': Recontextualising Aesthetic Labour as Fun and Play in Cosmetics Advertising," in Elias, Gill, and Scharff, *Aesthetic Labour*, 51–66.

78. Sara De Benedictis and Shani Orgad, "The Escalating Price of Motherhood: Aesthetic Labour in Popular Representations of 'Stay-at-Home' Mothers," in Elias, Gill, and Scharff, *Aesthetic Labour*, 101–116; Imogen Tyler, "Pregnant Beauty: Maternal Femininities under Neoliberalism," in *New Femininities: Postfeminism, Neoliberalism and Subjectivity*, ed. Rosalind Gill and Christina Scharff (Hampshire, UK: Palgrave Macmillan, 2011), 21–36.

79. McRobbie, *Aftermath of Feminism*.

80. YMCA, "The Curate Escape," May 13, 2019, https://www.ymca.org.uk /research/the-curate-escape; "Girls' Attitudes Survey," *Girlguiding*, 2019, http:// www.girlguiding.org.uk/girls-making-change/girls-attitudes-survey.

81. Dove US, "Dove Real Beauty Sketches: You're More Beautiful Than You Think," YouTube, April 14, 2013, https://www.youtube.com/watch?v=XpaOjMXyJGk.

82. Dove, *Dove: Patches*, April 10, 2014, https://www.dove.com/us/en/stories /campaigns/patches.html.

83. Cause Marketing, "Pantene 'Sorry, Not Sorry' Commercial," YouTube, March 12, 2017, https://www.youtube.com/watch?v=TcGKxLJ4ZGI.

84. McRobbie, "Notes on the Perfect."

85. Gillette Venus, "Things Have Changed," 2018, accessed September 20, 2019, https://abancommercials.com/gillette-venus/things-have-changed-my-skin-my-way-ad-commercial/45567/ (video no longer available).

86. Breanne Fahs, "Dreaded 'Otherness': Heteronormative Patrolling in Women's Body Hair Rebellions," *Gender and Society* 25, no. 4 (2011): 451–472.

87. There is a growing body of writing about the white appropriation of Black aesthetics and "glow." For example, Thompson, "How White Women on Instagram."

88. Madison Magladry, "Fitspiration or Fitsploitation: Postfeminism, Digital Media and Authenticity in Women's Fitness Culture" (PhD diss., Curtin University, Australia, 2019).

89. "Cheesy Tunes to Help You Get Your Sweat On," *Evening Standard* (London), September 16, 2019.

90. Increasingly, there are changing practices within the advertising industry. For example, Ad Age now has a regular blog that monitors advertisers' and brands' responses to racial issues: Ad Age, "A Regularly Updated Blog Tracking Brands' Responses to Racial Injustice," January 13, 2021, https://adage.com/article/cmo-strategy/regularly-updated-blog-tracking-brands-responses-racial-injustice/2260291.

Two. Confidence at Work

1. McKinsey and Company, *Women Matter, Time to Accelerate: Ten Years of Insights into Gender Diversity*, October 2017, https://www.mckinsey.com/featured-insights/gender-equality/women-matter-ten-years-of-insights-on-gender-diversity.

2. Sheryl Sandberg, *Lean In: Women, Work, and the Will to Lead* (New York: W. H. Allen, 2013); Katty Kay and Claire Shipman, *The Confidence Code: The Science and Art of Self-Assurance—What Women Should Know* (New York: HarperCollins, 2014).

3. See, for example, the activities and educational programs promoted by Lean In: www.leanin.org. The online sphere contains numerous accounts from women of the influence these books have had on their lives. For example, Mackenzie Charlotte, "The Book That Changed My Life: Lean In," April 2013, http://mackenziecharlotte.blogspot.co.uk/2013/04/the-book-that-changed-my-life-lean-in.html; and Susan Rosenzweig, "There's a Time to Lean In, and a Time to Lean Out," *Huffington Post*, May 14, 2014, http://www.huffingtonpost.com/susa-rosenzweig/theres-a-time-to-lean-in-and-a-time-to-lean-out_b_4932013.html.

4. See also Emily Zemler, "20 Strong Women Who Kick Ass on TV," *Elle*, March 21, 2018, https://www.elle.com/culture/movies-tv/g19496038/20-strongest-women-on-tv.

5. Sandberg, *Lean In*, 8.

6. Sandberg, *Lean In*, 49.

7. West, "Lean In Collection," 433.

8. Sandberg, *Lean In*, 172. For critics, see Banet-Weiser, *Empowered*; Gill and Orgad, "Confidence Cult(ure)"; Angela McRobbie, "Feminism, the Family and the New 'Mediated' Materialism," *New Formations: A Journal of Culture/Theory/Politics* 80 (2013): 119–137; Orgad, *Heading Home*; Rottenberg, *Rise of Neoliberal Feminism*.

9. Rottenberg, *Rise of Neoliberal Feminism*; Sarah Ahmed, *The Promise of Happiness* (Durham, NC: Duke University Press, 2010).

10. West, "Lean In Collection."

11. Brown, *Undoing the Demos*, 133, cited in West, "Lean In Collection," 434.

12. Sandberg, *Lean In*, 33.

13. Gill and Orgad, "Confidence Cult(ure)."

14. For example, the World Bank's 2012 World Development Report on gender equality "advocates interventions 'to encourage positive thinking'" by women and urges them to "nurture their ambition" (Sydney Calkin, "'Tapping' Women for Post-crisis Capitalism: Evidence from the 2012 World Development Report," *International Feminist Journal of Politics* 17, no. 4 [2015]: 624). In the UK, a 2014 white paper on women in leadership published by the Chartered Management Institute (CMI) stresses the need to develop in women confidence as a crucial skill "needed to realise their potential" (Chartered Management Institute, "Women in Management: The Power of Role Models," 2014, https://www.managers.org.uk /knowledge-and-insights/research/the-power-of-role-models/). In 2014, the French government launched Leadership Pour Elles, a smartphone app designed to address the national gender wage gap by boosting women's self-confidence. The app invites women to take a range of tests, and based on their answers, it directs the women to the appropriate modules, simulations, and recommendations (Orgad, *Heading Home*, 37).

15. Valentina Zarya, "The World's Most Successful Women Share Their Best Career Advice," World Economic Forum, October 5, 2017, https://www.weforum .org/agenda/2017/10/the-worlds-most-successful-women-share-their-best-career -advice.

16. Barbara A. Carlin, Betsy D. Gelb, Jamie K. Belinne, and Latha Ramchand, "Bridging the Gender Gap in Confidence," *Business Horizons* 61 (2018): 765–774. See also, for example, Valerie Young, "Keynotes & Seminars," Imposter Syndrome, accessed June 10, 2021, https://impostorsyndrome.com/keynotes-seminars; Women Talk Design, "Designing Confidence: A Workshop for Dealing with Imposter Syndrome," April 26, 2015, https://womentalkdesign.com/talks/designing-confidence- a-workshop-for-dealing-with-impostor-syndrome; Deloitte, "Embracing Inclusion and Well-Being, Deloitte Hosts Dialogue with Leaders Series on Women of Impact," press release, September 14, 2018, https://www2.deloitte.com/cn/en/pages /about-deloitte/articles/pr-women-of-impact-event.html.

17. Renee Morad, "5 Ways Women Can Boost Their Confidence during the COVID-19 Pandemic," *NBC News*, October 28, 2020, https://www.nbcnews.com /know-your-value/feature/5-ways-women-can-boost-their-confidence-during -covid-19-ncna1245139.

18. Aiden Wynn, "Confidence at Work: Why Are We All Feeling So Down on Ourselves at the Moment?," *Stylist*, accessed November 5, 2020, https://www .stylist.co.uk/life/careers/confidence-at-work-wfh-uncertainty/442157.

19. Examples include the School of Self-Love (https://theschoolofself.love /private) and My Confidence Matters (https://www.myconfidencematters.com

/about) in the UK, RiSe Women (https://www.risewomen.com/about-rise-women) in Australia, The Brave Hearted (http://www.thebravehearted.ch) in Switzerland, and Own the Room (https://owntheroom.com) and The Confidence Factor for Women (http://www.theconfidencefactorforwomen.com) in the US. See Annie May Noonan, "The $11.6bn Coaching Industry Continues to Boom, and It's Being Led by Women for Women," Real Business, March 26, 2019, https://realbusiness.co.uk/female-coaching-industry-uk.

20. See Rosalind Gill and Shani Orgad, "Get Unstuck! Pandemic Positivity Imperatives and Self-Care for Women," *Cultural Politics* (forthcoming).

21. Kay and Shipman, *Confidence Code*.

22. West, "Lean In Collection."

23. Kay and Shipman, *Confidence Code*, xix.

24. Katty Kay and Claire Shipman, "Gender Discrimination Isn't Fair, but It's No Reason to Give Up on Self-Confidence," *Guardian*, April 30, 2014, https://www.theguardian.com/commentisfree/2014/apr/30/gender-discrimination-self-confidence-gap.

25. Kay and Shipman, *Confidence Code*, 164.

26. "Katty Kay and Claire Shipman Launch 'Your Confidence Code' Online Course," *Elle*, October 22, 2020, https://www.elle.com/culture/books/a34452278/confidence-code-katty-kay-claire-shipman.

27. Robert Walters, "Empowering Women in the Workplace," accessed January 14, 2020, https://www.robertwalters.co.uk/empowering-women/career-advice/top-tips-for-career-confidence.html.

28. Lin Grensing-Popha, "Ways for Women to Build Confidence in the Workplace," *HR Daily Advisor*, August 2, 2018, https://hrdailyadvisor.blr.com/2018/08/02/ways-women-build-confidence-workplace.

29. See, for example, Sharmadean Reid, "How Can I Boost My Confidence at Work?," *Guardian*, March 5, 2018, https://www.theguardian.com/money/2018/mar/05/how-can-i-boost-my-confidence-at-work; Kathryn Wheeler, "How to Rebuild Confidence Post-lockdown," Happiful, June 5, 2020, https://happiful.com/how-to-rebuild-confidence-post-lockdown.

30. Philip Salter, "Don't Stress: This Female Entrepreneur Has a New App Boosting Sleep, Calm and Confidence," *Forbes*, April 5, 2018, https://www.forbes.com/sites/philipsalter/2018/04/05/dont-stress-this-female-entrepreneur-has-a-new-app-boosting-sleep-calm-and-confidence.

31. Amy Cuddy, "Your Body Language May Shape Who You Are," TED Talk, June 2012, 19:33, https://www.ted.com/talks/amy_cuddy_your_body_language_may_shape_who_you_are?language=en. While Cuddy's TED talk and her power-posing theory are seemingly gender neutral and address both women and men, this neutrality is undercut by various signifiers of gender (as well as race and class), including her use of the image of Wonder Woman, as well as of her own personal story as a young woman who was trained as a ballet dancer and later suffered a brain injury following a car accident.

32. McGee, *Self Help, Inc.*, 12.

33. "Effortless": Sandberg, *Lean In*, 33; "honest": Kay and Shipman, *Confidence Code*, 19.

34. Sandberg, *Lean In*, 28.

35. Anne-Sylvaine Chassany, "Christine Lagarde Shows How to Deal with Imposter Syndrome," *Financial Times*, July 8, 2019, https://www.ft.com/content/13720bc4-a16e-11e9-a282-2df48f366f7d.

36. Kay and Shipman, *Confidence Code*, 101.

37. Kay and Shipman, *Confidence Code*, 103.

38. Kay and Shipman, *Confidence Code*, xviii, xvii, 100, 144.

39. Gill and Orgad, "Confidence Cult(ure)"; Gill and Orgad, "Confidence Culture and the Remaking of Feminism."

40. Reshma Saujani, *Brave, Not Perfect* (London: HQ, 2019); Ruth Soukup, *Do It Scared: Finding the Courage to Face Your Fears, Overcome Adversity, and Create a Life You Love* (Grand Rapids, MI: Zondervan, 2019); Romi Neustadt, *Get Over Your Damn Self: The No-BS Blueprint to Building a Life-Changing Business* (San Diego, CA: LiveFullOut Media, 2016).

41. Rachel Hollis, *Girl, Stop Apologizing: A Shame-Free Plan for Embracing and Achieving Your Goals* (New York: HarperCollins, 2019), 13. The book is a sequel to Hollis's previous bestseller, *Girl, Wash Your Face* (2018).

42. Hollis, *Girl, Stop Apologizing*, 36, xx, 94.

43. Hollis, *Girl, Stop Apologizing*, xxiii–xxiv.

44. Hollis, *Girl, Stop Apologizing*, 199.

45. Hollis, *Girl, Stop Apologizing*, 11.

46. Hollis, *Girl, Stop Apologizing*, xii.

47. Lisa Blackman, "Self-Help, Media Cultures and the Production of Female Psychopathology," *European Journal of Cultural Studies* 7, no. 2 (2004): 223.

48. Helena Morrissey, *A Good Time to Be a Girl: Don't Lean In, Change the System* (London: William Collins, 2018). Following a similar format and style to other titles in this genre, Morrissey blends memoir, "manifesto," and practical advice, which is supported by selected psychological studies, to discuss gender diversity in business, and specifically the goal of getting more women into the boardroom.

49. Morrissey, *Good Time*, 12, 57, 15, 192, 161.

50. Morrissey, *Good Time*, 18.

51. Morrissey, *Good Time*, 193.

52. Morrissey, *Good Time*, 43.

53. Morrissey, *Good Time*, 83, 59.

54. Sian Leah Beilock, "How Women Can Banish Self-Doubt at Work," *Financial Times*, February 6, 2019, https://www.ft.com/content/d154b5a0-287a-11e9-9222-7024d72222bc.

55. Rose, *Inventing Ourselves*.

56. Dawn Foster, *Lean Out* (London: Repeater, 2016); McRobbie, "Feminism, the Family"; Rottenberg, *Rise of Neoliberal Feminism*.

57. Hollis, *Girl, Stop Apologizing*, 22, 23.

58. Stephanie Taylor and Susan Luckman, *The New Normal of Working Lives: Crit-*

ical Studies in Contemporary Work and Employment (London: Palgrave Macmillan, 2018).

59. Shani Orgad, "The Cruel Optimism of *The Good Wife*: The Fantastic Working Mother on the Fantastical Treadmill," *Television and New Media* 18, no. 2 (2017): 165–183.

60. Rosalind Gill and Ngaire Donaghue, "Resilience, Apps and Reluctant Individualism: Technologies of Self in the Neoliberal Academy," *Women's Studies International Forum* 54 (January–February 2016): 91–99; Maria do Mar Pereira, *Power, Knowledge and Feminist Scholarship: An Ethnography of Academia* (London: Routledge, 2019).

61. Jia Tolentino, "The Gig Economy Celebrates Working Yourself to Death," *New Yorker*, March 22, 2017, https://www.newyorker.com/culture/jia-tolentino /the-gig-economy-celebrates-working-yourself-to-death.

62. Shani Orgad, "Working 9-to-5 Then 5-to-9: 'Hustle Culture' for Women during a Global Pandemic," LSE Blog, February 11, 2021, https://blogs.lse.ac.uk /medialse/2021/02/11/working-9-to-5-then-5-to-9-hustle-culture-for-women -during-a-global-pandemic/.

63. Sheryl Sandberg and Adam Grant, *Option B: Facing Adversity, Building Resilience, and Finding Joy* (London: W. H. Allen, 2017), 114.

64. See also Gill and Orgad, "Confidence Culture and the Remaking of Feminism."

65. Louise Chunn, "Women Are at Breaking Point Because of Workplace Stress: Wellbeing Survey from Cigna," *Forbes*, March 26, 2019, https://www.forbes .com/sites/louisechunn/2019/03/26/women-are-at-breaking-point-because-of -workplace-stress-wellbeing-survey-from-cigna.

66. See, for example, Victoria Masterson, "Why COVID-19 Could Force Millions of Women to Quit Work—and How to Support Them," World Economic Forum, October 20, 2020, https://www.weforum.org/agenda/2020/10/women -work-gender-equality-covid19; McKinsey and Company and Lean In, *Women in the Workplace 2020*, September 2020, https://wiw-report.s3.amazonaws.com /Women_in_the_Workplace_2020.pdf.

67. Shirley Leung, "Five Ways the Pandemic Can Ultimately Make the Workplace Better for Women," *Boston Globe*, November 6, 2020, https://www .bostonglobe.com/2020/11/06/magazine/five-ways-pandemic-can-ultimately-make -workplace-better-women.

68. Hugh Son, "New Goldman CEO's Advice to Help Remake a Wall Street Titan: Be Vulnerable," *CNBC*, July 27, 2018, https://www.cnbc.com/2018/07/27 /goldman-sachs-ceo-explains-how-to-be-more-effective-be-vulnerable.html.

69. Patrick Williams, "The Importance of Being Courageously Vulnerable at Work," *Forbes*, August 29, 2018, https://www.forbes.com/sites/forbescoaches council/2018/08/29/the-importance-of-being-courageously-vulnerable-at-work. See, for example, Emma Seppälä, "What Bosses Gain by Being Vulnerable," *Harvard Business Review*, December 11, 2014, https://hbr.org/2014/12/what-bosses -gain-by-being-vulnerable; Angus Chen, "Invisibilia: How Learning to Be

Vulnerable Can Make Life Safer," NPR, June 17, 2016, https://www.npr.org/sections
/health-shots/2016/06/17/482203447/invisibilia-how-learning-to-be-vulnerable
-can-make-life-safer.

70. Williams, "Importance of Being."

71. Catherine Bennett, "Is Impostor Syndrome Just for Women? There Are
Some Men I Can Think Of . . . ," *Guardian*, December 16, 2018, https://www
.theguardian.com/commentisfree/2018/dec/16/is-impostor-syndrome-just-for
-women-there-are-some-men-i-can-think-of.

72. Melinda Gates, "How Melinda Gates Learned to Overcome Fear," *Teen
Vogue*, May 31, 2019, https://www.teenvogue.com/story/how-melinda-gates
-learned-to-overcome-fear; Melinda Gates, *The Moment of Lift: How Empowering
Women Changes the World* (London: Blue Bird, 2019).

73. Gates, "How Melinda Gates."

74. Taylor Dua, "Vulnerability Is a Key Component of Management Say PwC
Execs Talking Diversity and Inclusion," *The Drum*, July 16, 2019, https://www.the
drum.com/news/2019/07/16/vulnerability-key-component-management-say-pwc
-execs-talking-diversity-and-inclusion.

75. Hollis, *Girl, Stop Apologizing*, 175.

76. Gill and Orgad, "Confidence Culture and the Remaking of Feminism," 27;
Kanai, *Gender and Relatability*.

77. Blackman, "Self-Help, Media Cultures."

78. Hollis, *Girl, Stop Apologizing*, 40.

79. Helen Walters, "Vulnerability Is the Birthplace of Innovation, Creativity
and Change: Brené Brown at TED2012," *TED Blog*, March 2, 2012, https://blog.ted
.com/vulnerability-is-the-birthplace-of-innovation-creativity-and-change-brene
-brown-at-ted2012.

80. Brené Brown, "Leading from Hurt versus Leading from Heart," *Brené
Brown* (blog), December 4, 2018, https://brenebrown.com/articles/2018/12/04
/leading-from-hurt-versus-leading-from-heart.

81. For example, see Brené Brown and Ibram X. Kendi, "Brené with Ibram X.
Kendi on How to Be an Antiracist," June 3, 2020, in *Unlocking Us*, podcast, 1:01:36,
https://brenebrown.com/podcast/brene-with-ibram-x-kendi-on-how-to-be-an
-antiracist; "Brené Brown: How to Have Difficult Conversations about Race," *Today*, September 11, 2020, https://www.today.com/video/bene-brown-how-to-have
-difficult-conversations-about-race-91526213661; msrcellaINC, "Brene Brown on
Black Lives Matter in her new book Braving the Wilderness quote," Pinterest,
https://www.pinterest.co.uk/pin/138767232252010111.

82. McRobbie, "Notes on the Perfect."

83. See Brené Brown, "Downloads," https://brenebrown.com/downloads.

84. Blackman, "Self-Help, Media Cultures," 232; Brené Brown, "Courage over
Comfort: Rumbling with Shame, Accountability, and Failure at Work," *Brené
Brown* (blog), March 13, 2018, https://brenebrown.com/articles/2018/03/13
/courage-comfort-rumbling-shame-accountability-failure-work.

85. Brown, "Courage over Comfort."

86. "'Speak Your Truth. Follow Your Wild Heart': How Brené Brown Learned to Cope with Cruelty Online," *Vogue*, August 21, 2019, https://www.vogue.co.uk/arts-and-lifestyle/article/brene-brown-writes-for-vogue.

87. Gates, "How Melinda Gates."

88. Sarah Banet-Weiser, "'Ruined' Lives: Mediated White Male Victimhood," *European Journal of Cultural Studies* 24, no. 1 (2021): 60–80.

89. Laura Favaro and Rosalind Gill, "'Emasculation Nation Has Arrived': Sexism Rearticulated in Online Responses to Lose the Lads' Mags Campaign," *Feminist Media Studies* 16, no. 3 (2016): 379–397; Glen Jankowski, "The Sexism of Men's Body Dissatisfaction Accounts," *Psychology of Women and Equalities Review* 2, no. 1 (2019): 38–54; Julie Whiteman, "Enduring Notions of Heterosexuality: A Study in Contemporary Sex and Relationships" (PhD thesis, University of Birmingham, 2020), https://etheses.bham.ac.uk/id/eprint/10412/7/Whiteman2020PhD.pdf.

90. Foster, *Lean Out*.

91. Shani Orgad and Rosalind Gill, "Safety Valves for Mediated Female Rage in the #MeToo Era," *Feminist Media Studies* 19, no. 4 (2019): 596–603.

Three. Confident Relating

1. "How to Kick Up Your Confidence," *Cosmopolitan*, September 18, 2014, https://www.cosmopolitan.com/health-fitness/how-to/a30202/how-to-kick-up-your-confidence.

2. "Sleep School, Mental Health Chats with Frankie Bridge and Sexual Confidence Classes: Join GLAMOUR and Boots for a Digital Wellness Event like No Other," *Glamour*, October 2, 2020, https://www.glamourmagazine.co.uk/article/glamour-and-boots-digital-wellness-event; *EnFemenino* cited in Laura Favaro and Rosalind Gill, "'Pump Up the Positivity': Neoliberalism, Affective Entrepreneurship and the Victimhood/Agency Debate," in *Re-writing Women as Victims: From Theory to Practice*, ed. María José Gámez Fuentes, Sonia Núñez Puente, and Emma Gómez Nicolau (London: Routledge, 2019), 161.

3. In *Cosmopolitan* magazine and across social media. See, for example, "10 Ways to Boost Your Confidence: Feel like the Queen of Confidence with These Expert Tips," *Cosmopolitan*, February 24, 2014, https://www.cosmopolitan.com/uk/body/health/a25435/tips-to-boost-confidence-happiness/.

4. Cited in Favaro and Gill, "'Pump Up the Positivity,'" 160.

5. Laura Favaro, "Transnational Technologies of Gender and Mediated Intimacy" (PhD diss., City, University of London, 2017).

6. Cate Mackenzie, "How to Have a Healthy Summer Fling," *Psychologies*, September 16, 2019.

7. Kajal Pandey, "11 Ways to Improve Your Relationship with Yourself," *HuffPost*, June 3, 2016, https://www.huffpost.com/entry/11-ways-to-improve-your-r_b_10269696; Grant Hilary Brenner, "12 Keys to a Great Self-Relationship, Starting Now," *Psychology Today*, May 25, 2017, https://www.psychologytoday.com/gb/blog/experimentations/201705/12-keys-great-self-relationship-starting-now.

8. Paris Lees, "From the Archive: Emma Watson on Being Happily 'Self-Partnered' at 30," *Vogue*, April 15, 2020, https://www.vogue.co.uk/news/article /emma-watson-on-fame-activism-little-women. See also Kinneret Lahad and Michal Kravel-Trovi, "Happily-Ever After: Self-Marriage, the Claim of Wellness, and Temporal Ownership," *Sociological Review* 68, no. 3 (2020): 659–674, published ahead of print November 15, 2019, https://doi.org/10.1177%2F0038026119889479.

9. Mark Manson, *The Subtle Art of Not Giving a F*ck: A Counterintuitive Approach to Living a Good Life* (New York: HarperOne, 2016); Lotta Sonninen, *The Little Book of Bad Moods* (London: Bloomsbury, 2018); Elizabeth Day, *How to Fail: Everything I've Ever Learned from Things Going Wrong* (London: HarperCollins, 2019).

10. Melissa Tyler, "Managing between the Sheets: Lifestyle Magazines and the Management of Sexuality in Everyday Life," *Sexualities* 7, no. 1 (2004): 81–106.

11. This can be seen even at the level of getting ready for a date when, as Rachel Wood notes in her analysis of *Cosmopolitan* magazine, routine preparations suggested to women "can appear onerous," involving the following steps: manicure, pedicure, full bikini wax, attention to weight, muscle tone, skin smoothness and moisture, lingerie, makeup, clothes, and hairstyle—and continuing with advice on how to set up lighting and adopt positions that draw attention away from "problem areas" such as a fat tummy or thighs. See Rachel Wood, "Look Good, Feel Good: Sexiness and Sexual Pleasure in Neoliberalism," in Elias, Gill, and Scharff, *Aesthetic Labour*, 317–332. Corresponding advice targeted at men rarely goes beyond the instruction to have a shower and turn up on time. See Meg-John Barker, Rosalind Gill, and Laura Harvey, *Mediated Intimacy: Sex Advice in Media Culture* (Cambridge: Polity, 2018). This disjuncture in expectations is also seen in the communication skills required, in the emotional labor demanded of different genders, and in the sexual labor—where a vast media instruct women on "53 things women can learn from porn stars."

12. Laura Harvey and Rosalind Gill, "Spicing It Up: Sexual Entrepreneurs and the Sex Inspectors," in *New Femininities: Postfeminism, Neoliberalism and Subjectivity*, ed. Rosalind Gill and Christina Scharff (London: Palgrave Macmillan, 2011), 52–67; Tyler, "Managing between the Sheets."

13. Rosalind Gill, "Mediated Intimacy and Postfeminism: A Discourse Analytic Examination of Sex and Relationships Advice in a Women's Magazine," *Discourse and Communication* 3, no. 4 (2009): 345–369.

14. Favaro, "'Just Be Confident Girls!'"

15. Favaro, "'Just Be Confident Girls!'"

16. Favaro, "'Just Be Confident Girls!'"

17. Cited in Favaro and Gill, "'Pump Up the Positivity.'"

18. Favaro, "'Just Be Confident Girls!'"

19. Female First, "My Husband Ogles at Other Women!," September 26, 2012, https://relationships.femalefirst.co.uk/yin-and-yang/anonymous+asks-259038 .html.

20. Favaro, "'Just Be Confident Girls!'"

21. Cited in Favaro and Gill, "'Pump Up the Positivity.'"

22. Barker at al., *Mediated Intimacy*; Gill, "Mediated Intimacy"; Wood, "Look Good."

23. Cited in Favaro and Gill, "Pump Up the Positivity," 157.

24. "Love and Sex: Health and Tips for Your Sex Life, Relationships and Love Life Whatever Your Sexuality, Sexual Orientation, Gender Identity, and Star Sign," *Cosmopolitan*, accessed February 9, 2020, https://www.cosmopolitan.com /uk/love-sex; emphasis added.

25. "8 Ways to Orgasm on Your Own That You May Not Have Thought Of . . . Because #Selfcare," *Glamour*, May 7, 2021, https://www.glamourmagazine.co.uk /article/how-to-orgasm-on-your-own.

26. Banet-Weiser, *Empowered*.

27. Catriona Harvey-Jenner, "Body Confidence: The Women Who Show Us Numbers and Sizes Mean Nothing," *Cosmopolitan*, April 16, 2020, https://www .cosmopolitan.com/uk/body/health/g14469299/numbers-weight-sizes-mean -nothing-health-fitness-body-confidence.

28. "How to Have a Good Date—Even If You Don't Fancy Them," *Marie Claire*, April 15, 2016, https://www.marieclaire.co.uk/life/sex-and-relationships/how-to -have-a-good-date-11486.

29. Gill, "Post-postfeminism?"

30. "14 Positivity Hacks That'll Turn Your Frown Upside Down," *Cosmopolitan*, December 15, 2014, https://www.cosmopolitan.com/uk/body/health/a31955 /positive-thinking-tips.

31. Demi Lovato, "Simply Complicated," Philymack Productions, 2017.

32. Birmingham LGBT, "On Body Confidence in the Bedroom," *Diva*, April 5, 2019, https://divamag.co.uk/2019/04/05/on-body-confidence-in-the-bedroom.

33. Christina Mitchell, "VIEWS/DATING: How to Be Your Ideal Self," *Diva*, March 30, 2020, https://divamag.co.uk/2020/03/30/views-dating-how-to-be -your-ideal-self. But see Barker, Gill, and Harvey, *Mediated Intimacy*, for more detailed discussion of advice targeted at a range of differently identifying audiences.

34. Cited in Favaro, "'Just Be Confident Girls!,'" 286.

35. Cited in Favaro, "'Just Be Confident Girls!,'" 286.

36. Cited in Favaro and Gill, "'Pump Up the Positivity,'" 162. Another example can be found in the September 2019 *Vogue* special edition that Meghan Markle edited. In her guest editor letter Markle framed the special issue as being "about the power of the collective" and as marked by the "power of inclusivity." At the same time, she added, "There is one caveat for you to remember: this is a magazine. It's still a business, after all. I share that to manage expectations for you: there will be advertising sections that are requisite for every issue, so while I feel confident that you'll feel my thumbprint on most pages, please know that there are elements that just come with the territory. The overall sentiment I hope you'll find, however, will be one of positivity, kindness, humour and inclusivity." See Meghan Markle, "HRH the Duchess of Sussex Introduces the September Issue in Her Own Words," *Vogue*, July 29, 2019, https://www.vogue.co.uk/article/meghan-markle-editors

-letter-september-2019-issue. Here, too, the magazine is let off the hook; it is the reader's responsibility to remain focused on the positive and inclusive "thumb-print" and ignore the rest, which "comes with the territory."

37. Joanne Baker, "Claiming Volition and Evading Victimhood: Post-feminist Obligations for Young Women," *Feminism and Psychology* 20, no. 2 (2010): 190.

38. Christopher Lasch, *The Culture of Narcissism: American Life in an Age of Diminishing Expectations* (New York: Norton, 1979).

39. Emma Dowling, *The Care Crisis: What Caused It and How Can We End It?* (London: Verso, 2021).

40. "Self-Care Apps Are Booming—TechCrunch," April 2, 2018, https://techmongo.com/2018/04/02/self-care-apps-are-booming-techcrunch.

41. Rachel Diebner, Elizabeth Silliman, Kelly Ungerman, and Maxence Vancauwenberghe, "Adapting Customer Experience in the Time of Coronavirus," McKinsey and Company, April 2, 2020, https://www.mckinsey.com/business -functions/marketing-and-sales/our-insights/adapting-customer-experience -in-the-time-of-coronavirus.

42. They are defined differently by different organizations; see, for example, Sensor Tower (https://sensortower.com) and Apptopia (https://apptopia.com).

43. While many of these apps also include broader health and "wellness" material, as well as mindfulness techniques and meditations, we have excluded those that take these as their primary focus.

44. Dwan Nafus and Jamie Sherman, "This One Does Not Go Up to 11: The Quantified Self Movement as an Alternative Big Data Practice," *International Journal of Communication* 8 (2014): 1784–1794; Deborah Lupton, *Data Selves: More-than-Human Perspectives* (Cambridge: Polity, 2019); Jill W. Rettberg, *Seeing Ourselves through Technology: How We Use Selfies, Blogs and Wearable Devices to See and Shape Ourselves* (London: Springer, 2014).

45. Deborah Lupton, "Beyond the Quantified Self: The Reflexive Monitoring Self," *This Sociological Life*, July 28, 2014, https://simplysociology.wordpress.com /2014/07/28/beyond-the-quantified-self-the-reflexive-monitoring-self.

46. Deborah Lupton, "Quantified Sex: A Critical Analysis of Sexual and Reproductive Self-Tracking Using Apps," *Culture, Health and Sexuality* 17, no. 4 (2015): 440–453; Deborah Lupton and Gareth M. Thomas, "Playing Pregnancy: The Ludification and Gamification of Expectant Motherhood in Smartphone Apps," *M/C Journal* 18, no. 5 (2015), https://doi.org/10.5204/mcj.1012.

47. See "Digital Wellness Preview, Lockdowns Give 'Self-Care' Apps a Boost," ACG New York, July 28, 2020, https://www.acg.org/nyc/news-trends/news /digital-wellness-preview-lockdowns-give-self-care-apps-boost.

48. Christine Lehmann, "'Self-Care' Urged for Women Caregivers amid Pandemic," WebMD, September 16, 2020, https://www.webmd.com/lung/news /20200916/self-care-urged-for-women-caregivers-amid-pandemic.

49. Jane McGonigal, "Gaming Can Make a Better World," TED Talk, February 2010, 19:47, https://www.ted.com/talks/jane_mcgonigal_gaming_can_make_a _better_world?language=en.

50. Raka Shome, *Diana and Beyond: White Femininity, National Identity, and Contemporary Media Culture* (Champaign: University of Illinois Press, 2014), 181.

51. Shome, *Diana and Beyond*, 187.

52. The app reminds those of us who have not yet signed up to Shine Premium that it "also includes access to the Shine Squad digital community, Shine's award-winning self-care programs, and over 500+ meditations."

53. For example, My Confidence Coach goes in for alliteration, and alongside its "priceless podcasts" are shopping opportunities via its "brilliant boutique."

54. Shine app, accessed November 11, 2020.

55. L'Oréal Paris, "Tom Daley: My Body Achieves What My Mind Believes," 2019, https://soundcloud.com/loreal-paris-uk/tom-daley-my-body-achieves-what-my-mind-believes.

56. L'Oreal, "Because You're Worth It," April 27, 2021, https://www.lorealparis usa.com/about-loreal-paris/because-youre-worth-it.aspx.

57. Shine app content, biographies of Shine hosts, accessed November 11, 2020.

58. Allen and Bull, "Following Policy"; Erica Burman, "(Re)Sourcing the Character and Resilience Manifesto: Suppressions and Slippages of (Re)Presentation and Selective Affectivities," *Sociological Research Online* 23, no. 2 (2018): 130–151.

59. Fredric Jameson, *Postmodernism, or, The Cultural Logic of Late Capitalism* (Durham, NC: Duke University Press, 1991); bell hooks, *Black Looks: Race and Representation* (Boston: South End, 1992).

60. Ruth Williams, "Eat, Pray, Love: Producing the Female Neoliberal Spiritual Subject," *Journal of Popular Culture* 47, no. 3 (2014): 613–633. The idea is that happiness and well-being are choices: as Resilient puts it, "staying positive is simply a matter of choosing an optimistic attitude and mindset regardless of the situation. . . . It can help to have regular reminders."

61. Lena Dunham, *Not That Kind of Girl: A Young Woman Tells You What She's "Learned"* (London: HarperCollins, 2015).

62. Rosalind Gill, "'Doing Her Best with What She's Got': Authorship, Irony, and Mediating Feminist Identities in Lena Dunham's *Girls*," in *Reading Lena Dunham's "Girls": Feminism, Postfeminism, Authenticity and Gendered Performance in Contemporary Television*, ed. Meredith Nash and Imelda Whelehan (Basingstoke, UK: Palgrave Macmillan, 2017), 225–242.

63. Dunham, *Not That Kind of Girl*, 87–98.

64. Gill, "'Doing Her Best.'"

65. Rob Haskell, "Selena Gomez on Instagram Fatigue, Good Mental Health, and Stepping Back from the Limelight," *Vogue*, March 16, 2017, https://www.vogue.com/article/selena-gomez-april-cover-interview-mental-health-instagram.

66. Lauren Valenti, "Selena Gomez on Acne, Mental Health, and Her Day-to-Night Make-Up Strategy," *Vogue*, September 4, 2020, https://www.vogue.co.uk/beauty/article/selena-gomez-beauty-secrets-skincare-makeup.

67. Sophie Hannah, *How to Hold a Grudge: From Resentment to Contentment—the Power of Grudges to Transform Your Life* (London: Hodder and Stoughton, 2018); Haemin Sunim, *Love for Imperfect Things: How to Accept Yourself in a World Striving for*

Perfection (London: Penguin, 2019); Karen Rinaldi, *It's Great to Suck at Something: The Unexpected Joy of Wiping Out and What It Can Teach Us about Patience, Resilience, and the Stuff That Really Matters* (New York: Atria, 2019).

68. Ellie Broughton, "Move Over Mindfulness: It's Time for 'Finefulness,'" *Guardian*, February 20, 2019, https://www.theguardian.com/books/2019/feb/20/move-over-mindfulness-its-time-for-finefulness-self-help.

69. Sonninen, *Little Book of Bad Moods*.

70. Oliver Burkeman, *The Antidote* (Edinburgh: Canongate, 2012).

71. Emma Brockes, "Yes, I Do Give a Sh*t about These Sweary Book Covers," *Guardian*, February 7, 2019, https://www.theguardian.com/commentisfree/2019/feb/07/emma-brockes-self-help-books; Broughton, "Move Over Mindfulness."

72. Mahika Banerji, "A Take on *The Subtle Art of Not Giving a Fuck*: Male Chauvinist as Hell," *Feminism in India*, April 13, 2018, https://feminisminindia.com/2018/04/13/the-subtle-art-of-not-giving-a-fuck-review.

73. Banerji, "A Take on *The Subtle Art of Not Giving a Fuck*."

74. Micki McGee, "Capitalism's Care Problem: Some Traces, Fixes, and Patches," *Social Text* 142 (2020): 39–65.

75. Day, *How to Fail*, 76.

76. Day, *How to Fail*, 122.

77. Day, *How to Fail*, 122.

78. Day, *How to Fail*, 128.

79. Day, *How to Fail*, 84–86.

80. Day, *How to Fail*, 138.

81. Day, *How to Fail*, 138.

82. Micki McGee, personal communication with Shani Orgad, November 1, 2019.

83. See also Orgad, *Heading Home*.

84. Day, *How to Fail*, 74.

85. Day, *How to Fail*, 188.

86. Day, *How to Fail*, 190–191.

87. For example, Becky Barnes, "I Live Alone. This Is My Survival Guide for the Second Lockdown," *Huffington Post*, November 6, 2020, https://www.huffingtonpost.co.uk/entry/live-alone-lockdown-survival-guide_uk_5fa101aec5b6128c6b5be4df. See, for example, Elizabeth Day, "Life Lessons from a Serial Failure," *Mail Online*, September 12, 2020, https://www.dailymail.co.uk/home/you/article-8694349/Life-lessons-serial-failure.html.

88. Marie-Claire Chappet, "Everyone's Favourite Podcast Host, Elizabeth Day, Reveals How You Can *Learn* from Your Failures in the Most Empowering Way," *Glamour*, October 1, 2020, https://www.glamourmagazine.co.uk/article/elizabeth-day-failosophy.

1. Katty Kay and Claire Shipman, *The Confidence Code for Girls: Taking Risks, Messing Up, and Becoming Your Amazingly Imperfect, Totally Powerful Self* (New York: HarperCollins, 2018).

2. See the book's page on the HarperCollins website, accessed April 28, 2021, https://www.harpercollins.com/pages/childrens-confidence-code-for-girls.

3. Banet-Weiser, "'Confidence You Can Carry!'"

4. Confidence Code Girls, "Why Now," accessed April 28, 2021, https://www.confidencecodegirls.com/why-now.

5. Charlotte Faircloth, "Intensive Fatherhood? The (Un)Involved Dad," in *Parenting Culture Studies*, ed. Ellie Lee, Jennie Bristow, Charlotte Faircloth, and Jan Macvarish (London: Palgrave Macmillan, 2014), 184–199; Tracey Jensen, *Parenting the Crisis: The Cultural Politics of Parent-Blame* (Bristol, UK: Policy Press, 2018); Sonia Livingstone and Alicia Blum-Ross, *Parenting for a Digital Future: How Hopes and Fears about Technology Shape Children's Lives* (Oxford: Oxford University Press, 2020).

6. Frank Furedi, "Parental Determinism: A Most Harmful Prejudice," *Spiked*, May 21, 2012, https://www.spiked-online.com/2012/05/21/parental-determinism-a-most-harmful-prejudice/.

7. Laura Briggs, *How All Politics Became Reproductive Politics: From Welfare Reform to Foreclosure to Trump* (Oakland: University of California Press, 2017); Ranjana Das, *Early Motherhood in Digital Societies: Ideals, Anxieties and Ties of the Perinatal* (London: Routledge, 2020); Sara De Benedictis, "'Feral' Parents: Austerity Parenting under Neoliberalism," *Studies in the Maternal* 4, no. 2 (2012): 1–21; Jensen, *Parenting the Crisis*; Wahneema Lubiano, "Black Ladies, Welfare Queens, and State Minstrels: Ideological War by Narrative Means," in *Race-ing Justice, En-Gendering Power: Essays on Anita Hill, Clarence Thomas, and the Construction of Social Reality*, ed. Toni Morrison (New York: Pantheon Books, 1992), 323–363; Shani Orgad and Sara De Benedictis, "The 'Stay-at-Home' Mother, Postfeminism and Neoliberalism: Content Analysis of UK News Coverage," *European Journal of Communication* 30, no. 4 (2015): 418–436; Orgad, *Heading Home*; Jacqueline Rose, *Mothers: An Essay on Love and Cruelty* (London: Faber and Faber, 2018); Julie A. Wilson and Emily Chivers Yochim, *Mothering through Precarity: Women's Work and Digital Media* (Durham, NC: Duke University Press, 2017).

8. Allen and Bull, "Following Policy"; Jensen, *Parenting the Crisis*; Roberta Garrett, Tracey Jensen, and Angie Voela, eds., *We Need to Talk about Family: Essays on Neoliberalism, the Family and Popular Culture* (Cambridge: Cambridge Scholars, 2016); Val Gillies, Rosalind Edwards, and Nicola Horsley, *Challenging the Politics of Early Intervention* (Bristol, UK: Policy Press, 2017).

9. Val Gillies, "Childrearing, Class and the New Politics of Parenting," *Sociology Compass* 2/3 (2008): 1080.

10. Ruth Cain, "The Court of Motherhood: Affect, Alienation and Redefinitions of Responsible Parenting," in *Regulating Family Responsibilities*, ed. Jo Bridgeman and Heather Keating (Farnham, UK: Ashgate, 2011), 67.

11. Tim Ross, "David Cameron Plans Parenting Classes for All Families,"

Telegraph, January 10, 2016, https://www.telegraph.co.uk/news/newstopics
/eureferendum/12091327/David-Cameron-plans-parenting-classes-for-all-families
.html.

12. Dorothy Bottrell, "Responsibilised Resilience? Reworking Neoliberal Social
Policy Texts," *M/C Journal* 16, no. 5 (2013), https://doi.org/10.5204/mcj.708.

13. Allen and Bull, "Following Policy," 452.

14. Wilson and Yochim, *Mothering through Precarity*; Jensen, *Parenting the Crisis*;
Lee et al., *Parenting Culture Studies*; Rachel Thomson, Mary Jane Kehily, Lucy Hadfield, and Sue Sharpe, *Making Modern Mothers* (Bristol, UK: Policy Press, 2011); Orgad, *Heading Home*; Ana Villalobos, *Motherload: Making It All Better in Insecure Times*
(Oakland: University of California Press, 2014).

15. Marianne Cooper, *Cut Adrift: Families in Insecure Times* (Oakland: University of California Press, 2014). See also Briggs, *How All Politics*; Wilson and Yochim,
Mothering through Precarity; Villalobos, *Motherload*.

16. Jessica Grose, "Mothers Are the 'Shock Absorbers' of Our Society," *New York
Times*, October 14, 2020.

17. De Benedictis, "'Feral' Parents."

18. Briggs, *How All Politics*; Patricia Hill Collins, *Black Feminist Thought: Knowledge,
Consciousness, and the Politics of Empowerment*, 2nd ed. (New York: Routledge, 2002).

19. Jennifer Nash, "The Political Life of Black Motherhood," *Feminist Studies* 44,
no. 3 (2018): 699–712.

20. Das, *Early Motherhood*; Faircloth, "Intensive Fatherhood?"; Jensen, *Parenting the Crisis*; Ellie Lee, "Introduction," in Lee et al., *Parenting Culture Studies*, 1–22;
Orgad, *Heading Home*; Valerie Palmer-Mehta and Sherianne Shuler, "'Devil Mammas' of Social Media: Resistant Maternal Discourses in Sanctimommy," in *Mediated Moms: Contemporary Challenges to the Motherhood Myth*, ed. Heather. L. Hundley
and Sara E. Hayden (New York: Peter Lang, 2016), 221–245; Thomson et al., *Making
Modern Mothers*; Wilson and Yochim, *Mothering through Precarity*.

21. Lee, "Introduction."

22. Wilson and Yochim, *Mothering through Precarity*.

23. Susan Braedley and Meg Luxton, *Neoliberalism and Everyday Life* (Montreal:
McGill-Queen's University Press, 2010). See also Catherine Rottenberg's discus-
sion of parents' investment in their children as human capital: Rottenberg, *Rise of
Neoliberal Feminism*.

24. Larry Elliott, "Each Generation Should Be Better Off than Their Parents?
Think Again," *Guardian*, February 14, 2016, http://www.theguardian.com/business
/2016/feb/14/economics-viewpoint-baby-boomers-generation-x-generation-rent
-gig-economy.

25. John H. Goldthrope, "Social Class Mobility in Modern Britain: Changing
Structure, Constant Process," *Journal of the British Academy* 4 (2016): 96.

26. Livingstone and Blum-Ross, *Parenting for a Digital Future*.

27. Das, *Early Motherhood*; Wilson and Yochim, *Mothering through Precarity*; Cooper, *Cut Adrift*; Orgad, *Heading Home*; Rose, *Mothers*; Thomson et al., *Making Modern Mothers*; Villalobos, *Motherload*.

28. Jo Swinson, "It's Astonishing How Quickly Confidence Evaporates on Maternity Leave," guest post, *Mumsnet*, October 16, 2014, https://www.mumsnet.com/Talk/guest_posts/2210769-Guest-post-Jo-Swinson-Its-astonishing-how-quickly-confidence-evaporates-on-maternity-leave.

29. Wilson and Yochim, *Mothering through Precarity*, 39.

30. Elias, Gill, and Scharff, *Aesthetic Labour*.

31. Susan Douglas and Meredith W. Michaels, *The Mommy Myth: The Idealization of Motherhood and How It Has Undermined All Women* (New York: Free Press, 2004).

32. Douglas and Michaels, *Mommy Myth*, 229.

33. McRobbie, "Notes on the Perfect."

34. Sherry Vevan, "The Confident Mother," accessed January 21, 2020, http://theconfidentmother.co.uk/read-a-sample-chapter/.

35. Meredith Ethington, "How to Become the Sorry-Not-Sorry Mom," *Perfection Pending*, accessed January 21, 2020, http://www.perfectionpending.net/2015/03/06/how-to-become-the-sorry-not-sorry-mom.

36. The Authentic Mom, "Motherhood: We Know What It's SUPPOSED to Be. . . . Now Let's Talk about What It's REALLY Like," accessed January 21, 2020, http://www.theauthenticmom.com.

37. Douglas and Michaels, *Mommy Myth*, 4.

38. Suzanna D. Walters and Laura Harrison, "Not Ready to Make Nice: Aberrant Mothers in Contemporary Culture," *Feminist Media Studies* 14, no. 1 (2014): 47; Jo Littler, "Mothers Behaving Badly: Chaotic Hedonism and the Crisis of Neoliberal Social Reproduction," *Cultural Studies* 34, no. 4 (2020): 499–520.

39. For example, Maressa Brown, "These Parenting Coronavirus Memes and Tweets Prove You Are Not Alone," *Parents*, March 18, 2020, https://www.parents.com/news/best-parenting-coronavirus-memes; Dafna Lemish and Nelly Elias, "'We Decided We Don't Want Children. We Will Let Them Know Tonight': Parental Humor on Social Media in a Time of Coronavirus Pandemic," *International Journal of Communication* 14 (2020): 5261–5287.

40. Heike Roth, Caroline Homer, and Jennifer Fenwick, "'Bouncing Back': How Australia's Leading Women's Magazines Portray the Postpartum 'Body,'" *Women and Birth* 25, no. 3 (2012): 128–134.

41. Lesley Husbands, "Blogging the Maternal: Self-Representations of the Pregnant and Postpartum Body," *Atlantis: Critical Studies in Gender, Culture and Social Justice* 32, no. 2 (2008): 77.

42. Linda Singh, "Instagram Affordances among Post-pregnant Body Advocates" (master's diss., Malmö University, Sweden, 2019).

43. Kennedy previously led the introduction of the so-called feminist dating app Bumble to the UK. See Phoebe Luckhurst, "Tinder Co-founder Whitney Wolfe on Bumble: Her New Feminist Dating App That Lets Women Make the First Move," *Evening Standard*, August 28, 2015, https://www.standard.co.uk/lifestyle/london-life/tinder-co-founder-whitney-wolfe-on-bumble-her-new-feminist-dating-app-that-lets-women-make-the-first-a2923011.html.

44. Phoebe Luckhurst, "Peanut: The Parenting App That's About to Give

Mumsnet a Run for Its Money," *Evening Standard*, February 9, 2017, https://www
.standard.co.uk/lifestyle/london-life/peanut-the-parenting-app-thats-about-to
-give-mumsnet-a-run-for-its-money-a3462306.html.

45. For example, Elizabeth Oates, "Is Motherhood Stealing Your Identity?," *EO*,
April 9, 2019, https://www.elizabethoates.com/is-motherhood-stealing-your
-identity; Christi Straub, "How to Embrace Motherhood without Losing Your
Identity," *Famous at Home*, July 2, 2018, https://www.joshuastraub.com/2018/07/02
/embrace-motherhood-without-losing-identity; Keyona, "Mom Life Stole My
Identity: 5 Ways to Rediscover Yourself after Motherhood," *Professional Momma*,
accessed February 19, 2021, https://www.professionalmomma.com/how-to
-rediscover-yourself-afer-motherhood.

46. Rebecca Asher, *Shattered: Modern Motherhood and the Illusion of Equality* (New
York: Vintage, 2012), 6.

47. Das, *Early Motherhood*; Tasha Dubriwny, "Mommy Blogs and the Disruptive
Possibilities of Transgressive Drinking," in Hundley and Hayden, *Mediated Moms*,
203–220; Sarah Pedersen, "The Good, the Bad and the 'Good Enough' Mother on
the UK Parenting Forum Mumsnet," *Women's Studies International Forum* 59 (2016):
32–38; Orgad, *Heading Home*; Palmer-Mehta and Shuler, "'Devil Mammas'"; Wilson and Yochim, *Mothering through Precarity*.

48. See, for example, Rosalind Gill, Yvonne Ehrstein, and Jo Littler, "The Af-
fective Life of Neoliberalism: Constructing (Un)Reasonableness on Mumsnet," in
Neoliberalism in Context: Governance, Subjectivity and Knowledge, ed. Simon Dawes and
Marc Lenormand (Basingstoke, UK: Palgrave Macmillan, 2019), 195–213.

49. Ranjana Das, "Speaking about Birth: Visible and Silenced Narratives in Online Discussions of Childbirth," *Social Media + Society* 3, no. 4 (2017): 6; see also Das,
Early Motherhood.

50. Wilson and Yochim, *Mothering through Precarity*, 175, 41.

51. Ahmed, *Promise of Happiness*.

52. Jo Littler, "The Rise of the 'Yummy Mummy': Popular Conservatism and
the Neoliberal Maternal in Contemporary British Culture," *Communication, Culture
and Critique* 6, no. 2 (2013): 233.

53. Karin Eldor, "Raising Boys in the #MeToo Era? The CEO of Peanut, a
Tinder-Like App for Moms, Shares Three Tips," *Forbes*, May 12, 2018, https://www
.forbes.com/sites/karineldor/2018/05/12/raising-boys-in-the-metoo-era-the-ceo-of
-peanut-a-tinder-like-app-for-moms-shares-three-tips.

54. The ad can be seen here: Helen Toomey Hesk (@helenhesk), @Bodenclothing
#marketingfail wear it like a Mum," Twitter, November 19, 2017, https://twitter
.com/helenhesk/status/932325935289905152.

55. Kathryn Jezer-Morton, "Online Momming in the 'Perfectly Imperfect'
Age," *The Cut*, April 10, 2019, https://www.thecut.com/2019/04/online-moms
-mommyblogs-instagram.html.

56. Shani Orgad and Kate Baldwin, "'How Any Woman Does What They Do Is
Beyond Comprehension': Meghan Markle and the Masking of Maternal Labours,"
Women's Studies in Communication 44, no. 2 (2021), http://eprints.lse.ac.uk/108552/.

57. Orgad and Baldwin, "'How Any Woman,'" drawing on Collins, *Black Feminist Thought*; Dorothy E. Roberts, "Punishing Drug Addicts Who Have Babies: Women of Color, Equality and the Right of Privacy," *Harvard Law Review* 104 (1991): 1441–1442; Hortense J. Spillers, "Mama's Baby, Papa's Maybe: An American Grammar Book," *Diacritics* 17, no. 2 (1987): 64–81.

58. Nefertiti Austin, *Motherhood So White: A Memoir of Race, Gender, and Parenting in America* (Naperville, IL: Sourcebooks, 2019); Dawn Marie Dow, *Mothering While Black* (Oakland: University of California Press, 2019); Dani McClain, "As a Black Mother, My Parenting Is Always Political," *The Nation*, March 27, 2019, https:// www.thenation.com/article/black-motherhood-family-parenting-dani-mcclain; Dasia Moore, "Being a Protective Black Mom Isn't a Parenting Choice—It's the Only Choice," *Quartz*, December 20, 2019, https://qz.com/1765439/why-black -moms-cant-be-helicopter-parents; Imani Perry, *Breathe: A Letter to My Sons* (Boston: Beacon, 2019).

59. Jennifer Nash, "Black Maternal Aesthetics," *Theory and Event* 22, no. 3 (2019): 551–575.

60. Moore, "Being a Protective Black Mom."

61. Ethington, "Sorry-Not-Sorry Mom."

62. Wilson and Yochim, *Mothering through Precarity*, 100.

63. See, for example, Sheryl G. Ziegler, "How to Let Go of Working-Mom Guilt," *Harvard Business Review*, September 4, 2020, https://hbr.org/2020/09/how -to-let-go-of-working-mom-guilt; Julie Relevant, "Coronavirus and Mom Guilt: 8 Things You Need to Let Go Of," Thrive Global, April 23, 2020, https://thrive global.com/stories/coronavirus-mom-guilt-8-things-you-need-to-let-go-of.

64. Liz Matheis, "Mama, Take Care of Yourself during COVID-19," *Psychology Today*, April 1, 2020, https://www.psychologytoday.com/gb/blog/special-matters /202004/mama-take-care-yourself-during-covid-19, emphasis added.

65. Kelly Wallace, "A 'Confidence Code' for Girls: 5 Ways to Build Up Our Daughters," CNN, May 21, 2018, https://edition.cnn.com/2018/05/21/health/girls -confidence-code-parenting/index.html.

66. Cerys Howell, "I Deleted My Baby Apps When I Realised How Much They Fetishise Motherhood," *Guardian*, August 2, 2017, https://www.theguardian .com/commentisfree/2017/aug/02/baby-apps-fetishise-motherhood-postnatal -depression.

67. Banet-Weiser, "'Confidence You Can Carry!'"

68. Banet-Weiser, "'Confidence You Can Carry!'"; Rebecca Hains, *Growing Up with Girl Power: Girlhood on Screen and in Everyday Life* (New York: Peter Lang, 2012); Ofra Koffman and Rosalind Gill, "'The Revolution Will Be Led by a 12-Year-Old Girl': Girl Power and Global Biopolitics," *Feminist Review* 105, no. 1 (2013): 83–102; Ofra Koffman, Shani Orgad, and Rosalind Gill, "Girl Power and 'Selfie Humanitarianism,'" *Continuum: Journal of Media and Cultural Studies* 29, no. 2 (2015): 157–168; Rosie Walters, "Reading Girls' Participation in Girl Up as Feminist: Club Members' Activism in the UK, USA and Malawi," *Gender and Development* 26, no. 3 (2018): 477–493, https://policy-practice.oxfam.org.uk/publications

/reading-girls-participation-in-girl-up-as-feminist-club-members-activism-in-the
-620589.

69. Banet-Weiser, "'Confidence You Can Carry!'"

70. See also Rosalind Gill and Ana S. Elias, "'Awaken Your Incredible': Love Your Body Discourses and Postfeminist Contradictions," *International Journal of Media and Cultural Politics* 10, no. 2 (2014): 184.

71. Gill and Elias, "'Awaken Your Incredible.'"

72. Sigal Barak-Brandes and Einat Lachover, "Branding Relations: Mother–Daughter Discourse on Beauty and Body in an Israeli Campaign by Dove," *Communication, Culture and Critique* 9, no. 3 (2016): 379–394.

73. Kelly Wallace, "The Ripple Effects on Girls When Moms Struggle with Body Image," *CNN*, June 7, 2017, https://edition.cnn.com/2017/06/07/health/body -image-moms-impact-daughters/index.html.

74. Claudia Rankine cited in Nash, "Black Maternal Aesthetics," 562 ("Black excellence"); Serena Williams, "Letter to My Mom," Reddit, September 19, 2017, https://www.reddit.com/user/serenawilliams/comments/714c1b/letter_to_my _mom.

75. Nash, "Black Maternal Aesthetics," 566, citing Daphne A. Brooks, "Suga Mama, Politicized," *The Nation*, November 30, 2006, https://www.thenation.com /article/archive/suga-mama-politicized.

76. Asher, *Shattered*.

77. American Girl, "We Believe in Creating Girls of Strong Character," accessed April 28, 2021, https://www.americangirl.com/shop/ag/who-we-are.

78. Anna Bull and Kim Allen, "Introduction: Sociological Interrogations of the Turn to Character," *Sociological Research Online* 23, no. 2 (2018): 392–398.

79. American Girl, *The Care and Keeping of Us*, accessed April 28, 2021, https:// www.americangirl.com/shop/ag/advice-library/the-care-and-keeping-of-us-dgd70.

80. Gill and Elias, "'Awaken Your Incredible,'" 184.

81. Wilson and Yochim, *Mothering through Precarity*, 40.

82. Nancy J. Chodorow, *The Reproduction of Mothering* (Berkeley: University of California Press, 1978); Luise Eichenbaum and Susie Orbach, *What Do Women Want? Exploding the Myth of Dependency* (Glasgow: Fontana/Collins, 1983).

83. For example, Kathleen Hassan, "Coaching," accessed April 28, 2021, http:// kathleenhassan.com/coaching.

Five. Confidence without Borders

1. Alyssa Bailey, "Meghan Markle Told South African Women 'I Am Here with You as Your Sister' in Powerful Speech," *Elle*, September 23, 2019, https://www.elle .com/culture/celebrities/a29188564/meghan-markle-nyanga-speech.

2. Cited in Bailey, "Meghan Markle Told"; Sophie Bateman, "Meghan Markle Gives Powerful Feminist Speech in South Africa," *Newshub*, September 24, 2019, https://www.newshub.co.nz/home/entertainment/2019/09/meghan-markle -gives-powerful-feminist-speech-in-south-africa.html; Katie Nicholl, "Meghan

Markle Has a Feminist Focus in South Africa," *Vanity Fair*, September 24, 2019, https://www.vanityfair.com/style/2019/09/meghan-markle-south-africa-female -leaders-feminism; Hannah Moran, "Meghan Markle Gives First Speech about Being 'a Woman of Colour' on Royal Tour in South Africa," *Evoke*, September 24, 2019, https://evoke.ie/2019/09/24/showbiz/gossip/meghan-markle-speech-south -africa; Amy Mackelden, "Meghan Markle Just Gave an Empowering and Emotional Speech on the Royal Tour," *Harper's Bazaar*, September 23, 2019, https:// www.harpersbazaar.com/celebrity/latest/a29189403/meghan-markle-speech -transcript-royal-tour-africa.

3. Jo Littler, "'I Feel Your Pain': Cosmopolitan Charity and the Public Fashioning of the Celebrity Soul," *Social Semiotics* 18, no. 2 (2008): 237–251.

4. Robert Mendick and Hannah Furness, "Arch Meets Archie: Duke and Duchess of Sussex Introduce Their Son to Desmond Tutu," *Telegraph*, September 25, 2019, https://www.telegraph.co.uk/royal-family/2019/09/25/archie-meets -archbishop-desmond-tutu-prince-harry-meghan-markle.

5. See also chapter 3, n36, and (for Brown) chapter 2.

6. Terina Allen, "This Is How Confident Women Embrace Their Power," *Forbes*, September 24, 2019, https://www.forbes.com/sites/terinaallen/2019/09/24 /this-is-how-confident-women-embrace-their-power.

7. Monique Jessen, "Here's How to Get Meghan Markle's 'Justice' Bracelet She Wore in South Africa—for Just \$35!," *People*, September 23, 2019, https://people .com/royals/meghan-markle-prince-harry-justice-bracelet-just-35-dollars.

8. Orgad and Baldwin, "How Any Woman."

9. See Anna Brech, "Angelina Jolie Shares a Lesson in Emotional Resilience," *Stylist*, 2019, https://www.stylist.co.uk/people/angelina-jolie-emotional -strength-brad-pitt-divorce/290569; Katie O'Malley, "Angelina Jolie Opens Up about Not Feeling 'Safe' and 'Free of Harm' in Recent Years," *Elle*, October 1, 2019, https://www.elle.com/uk/life-and-culture/culture/a29319141/angelina -jolie-maleficent-not-feeling-safe-free; Alicia Adejobi, "Angelina Jolie Admits She's 'Vulnerable' but Has 'More Fight' Following Brad Pitt Divorce," *Metro*, September 9, 2019, https://metro.co.uk/2019/09/09/angelina-jolie-admits -vulnerable-fight-following-brad-pitt-divorce-10713746.

10. Raka Shome, "'Global Motherhood': The Transnational Intimacies of White Femininity," *Critical Studies in Media Communication* 28, no. 5 (2011): 390.

11. Shome, "'Global Motherhood,'" 390. Regarding feminist ethical capitalism initiatives, see Lisa A. Daily, "We Bleed for Female Empowerment: Mediated Ethics, Commodity Feminism, and the Contradictions of Feminist Politics," *Communication and Critical/Cultural Studies* 16, no. 2 (2019): 140–158.

12. Rachael McLennan, "'A New Wrinkle': Age, Race and Writing Meghan Markle," *Women's Studies International Forum* 85 (2021): 102454, https://doi.org/10.1016/j .wsif.2021.102454.

13. Roland Barthes, *Mythologies* (New York: Hill and Wang, 1973), 116.

14. Mimi Thi Nguyen, *The Gift of Freedom: War, Debt, and Other Refugee Passages* (Durham, NC: Duke University Press, 2012).

15. Raka Shome, "Thinking Culture and Cultural Studies—from/of the Global South," *Communication and Critical/Cultural Studies* 16, no. 3 (2019): 196–218.

16. Shome, "Thinking Culture," 198, 203.

17. Shome, "Thinking Culture," 204.

18. Daily, "We Bleed for Female Empowerment"; Karin Gwin Wilkins and Florencia Enghel, "The Privatization of Development through Global Communication Industries: Living Proof?," *Media, Culture and Society* 35, no. 2 (2013): 165–181; Lisa Ann Richey and Stefano Ponte, *Brand Aid: Shopping Well to Save the World* (Minneapolis: University of Minnesota Press, 2011).

19. Michael K. Goodman and Christine Barnes, "Star/Poverty Space: The Making of the 'Development Celebrity,'" *Celebrity Studies* 2, no. 1 (2011): 72.

20. Daily, "We Bleed for Female Empowerment"; Richey and Ponte, *Brand Aid*; Shani Orgad and Kaarina Nikunen, "The Humanitarian Makeover," *Communication and Critical/Cultural Studies* 12, no. 3 (2015): 229–251.

21. Lilie Chouliaraki, *The Ironic Spectator: Solidarity in the Age of Post-humanitarianism* (Cambridge: Polity, 2013); Kate Nash, "Global Citizenship as Show Business: The Cultural Politics of Make Poverty History," *Media, Culture and Society* 30, no. 2 (2008): 167–181; Shani Orgad, "Visualizers of Solidarity: Organizational Politics in Humanitarian and International Development NGOs," *Visual Communication* 12, no. 3 (2013): 295–314; Richey and Ponte, *Brand Aid*; Anne Vestergaard, "Humanitarian Branding and the Media: The Case of Amnesty International," *Journal of Language and Politics* 7, no. 3 (2008): 471–493; Kalpana Wilson, "'Race,' Gender and Neoliberalism: Changing Visual Representations in Development," *Third World Quarterly* 32, no. 2 (2011): 315–331.

22. Wilkins and Enghel, "Privatization of Development."

23. Daily, "We Bleed for Female Empowerment"; Angharad Valdivia, "Holding Up Half the Sky: Global Narratives of Girls at Risk and Celebrity Philanthropy," *Girlhood Studies* 11, no. 3 (2018): 84–100; Srila Roy, "Precarity, Aspiration and Neoliberal Development: Women Empowerment Workers in West Bengal," *Contributions to Indian Sociology* 53, no. 3 (2019): 392–421.

24. Littler, "'I Feel Your Pain'"; Wilkins and Enghel, "Privatization of Development."

25. Wilkins and Enghel, "Privatization of Development."

26. Chouliaraki, *Ironic Spectator*; Elizabeth McAlister, "Soundscapes of Disaster and Humanitarianism: Survival Singing, Relief Telethons, and the Haiti Earthquake," *Small Axe* 39 (2012): 22–38; Shani Orgad, *Media Representation and the Global Imagination* (Cambridge: Polity, 2012).

27. Orgad, *Media Representation*, 78. For the new "post-humanitarian" paradigm, see Chouliaraki, *Ironic Spectator*.

28. Koffman and Gill, "'Revolution.'"

29. Shome, *Diana and Beyond*, 114.

30. Koffman, Orgad, and Gill, "Girl Power," 159.

31. Koffman and Gill, "'Revolution,'" 86.

32. "Girl Effect," Wikipedia, accessed March 29, 2021, https://en.wikipedia.org/wiki/Girl_Effect.

33. Sylvia Chant and Caroline Sweetman, "Fixing Women or Fixing the World? 'Smarteconomics,' Efficiency Approaches, and Gender Equality in Development," *Gender and Development* 20, no. 3 (2012): 521; Walters, "Reading Girls' Participation," 480, drawing on Jason Hickel, "The 'Girl Effect': Liberalism, Empowerment, and the Contradictions of Development," *Third World Quarterly* 35, no. 8 (2014): 1356.

34. Mimi Thi Nguyen, "The Biopower of Beauty: Humanitarian Imperialisms and Global Feminisms in an Age of Terror," *Signs* 36, no. 2 (2011): 371–372; Walters, "Reading Girls' Participation."

35. Wilson, "'Race,' Gender and Neoliberalism," 324.

36. Based on Wilson, "'Race,' Gender and Neoliberalism."

37. "Girl Up," Facebook, 2014, cited in Koffman, Orgad, and Gill, "Girl Power," 161.

38. Koffman, Orgad, and Gill, "Girl Power," 162.

39. Girl Up 2013, "11 Days of Action, Day 2: Tweet It Out 2013," cited in Koffman, Orgad, and Gill, "Girl Power," 162.

40. Orgad and Nikunen, "Humanitarian Makeover."

41. Orgad and Nikunen, "Humanitarian Makeover," 241.

42. Walters, "Reading Girls' Participation."

43. Walters, "Reading Girls' Participation," 486.

44. Walters, "Reading Girls' Participation," 486.

45. Nehal Jain, "What Being a Girl Up Teen Advisor Means to Me," *Girl Up*, June 19, 2016, accessed December 9, 2020, https://www.girlup.org/what-being-a -girl-up-teen-advisor-means/#sthash.Ukc6yLPI.dpbs.

46. Koffman, Orgad, and Gill, "Girl Power," 157.

47. Stephen Wearing, Mary Mostafanezhad, Nha Nguyen, Truc Ha Thanh Nguyen, and Matthew McDonald, "'Poor Children on Tinder' and Their Barbie Saviours: Towards a Feminist Political Economy of Volunteer Tourism," *Leisure Studies* 37, no. 5 (2018): 500–514.

48. Wearing et al., "'Poor Children on Tinder,'" 5.

49. ME to WE, "Me to We Travel," accessed April 28, 2021, https://travel .metowe.com/en-CA.

50. Wearing et al., "'Poor Children on Tinder.'"

51. Emma Martins, "Do You Know the Benefits of Volunteering Abroad?," *Go Volunteer Abroad*, September 2, 2019, https://www.govolunteerabroad.org/blog /benefits-of-volunteering-abroad.

52. GVI, "Volunteer Abroad," https://www.gvi.co.uk/volunteer-abroad.

53. In recent years, some of these testimonials have come under increasing fire for presenting simplified images that deprive their global South subjects of their agency and dignity, decontextualize their misery, and perpetuate the white-savior complex and misleading stereotypes of the developing world as a theater of tragedy and disaster. See, for example, the Norwegian Students' and Academics' International Assistance Fund (SAIH, https://saih.no/english); the Instagram parody account Barbie Savior, https://www.instagram.com/barbiesavior; SAIH Norway, "How to Get More Likes on Social Media," YouTube, November 7, 2017, https://

www.youtube.com/watch?v=7c9mwY3iiMI&t=22s; Malaka Gharib, "Woman's Instagram Post about Kenyan Child Ignites Fury," NPR, March 22, 2018, https:// www.npr.org/sections/goatsandsoda/2018/03/22/596002482/womans-instagram -post-about-kenyan-child-ignites-fury; Wearing et al., "'Poor Children on Tinder.'"

54. Shome, *Diana and Beyond*, 114.

55. Banet-Weiser, "'Confidence You Can Carry!'"

56. Daily, "We Bleed for Female Empowerment."

57. Daily, "We Bleed for Female Empowerment," 149.

58. Daily, "We Bleed for Female Empowerment," 150.

59. Marks and Spencer, "Love Your Boobs and Recycle Your Bra," last modified August 8, 2019, https://corporate.marksandspencer.com/media/press-releases /5c2f8d617880b21084450f5e/love-your-boobs-and-recycle-your-bra.

60. Sophie Gallagher, "Meet the Entrepreneur Taking Hundreds of Bras from London to Edinburgh to Help Women in Africa," *Huffington Post*, April 13, 2018, https://www.huffingtonpost.co.uk/entry/a-volunteer-is-driving-hundreds-of-bras -from-london-to-edinburgh-to-help-women-in-africa_uk_5acf2fa8e4b064876 77732ce.

61. Daily, "We Bleed for Female Empowerment."

62. Nguyen, "Biopower of Beauty."

63. Lupton, *Data Selves*.

64. ME to WE Shop, https://shop.metowe.com/en-CA/?_ga=2.29042876.10032 92150.1619620707-340351977.1619620707; ME to WE, "Welcome to ME to WE: Our Story," emphasis added.

65. ME to WE Shop, accessed December 9, 2020, https://ca.shop.metowe.com /products/unstoppable-rafiki-bracelet-by-sofia-carson?_ga=2.257283019.1318425864 .1571573683-824697089.1568964898.

66. South African scholar Pamila Gupta offers a radically different reading of the relationship that can be created between commodities, female confidence, and solidarity. See Pamila Gupta, "Fields of Marigold: Makers and Wearers of Luxury African Beaded Necklaces," in *African Luxury: Aesthetics and Politics*, ed. Mehita Iqani and Simidele Dosekun (Bristol, UK: Intellect, 2020), 109–122. Drawing on her ethnographic work about Marigold beaded necklaces that are produced in an almost exclusively female cooperative in Bulawayo, Zimbabwe, and sold in Johannesburg, South Africa, Gupta argues that these crafted luxury items embody "new forms of African feminine self-making, empowerment, and community" (Simidele Dosekun and Mehita Iqani, "The Politics and Aesthetics of Luxury in Africa," in Iqani and Dosekun, *African Luxury*, 10). Gupta argues that in the cases that she has studied, female confidence and empowerment derive very different meanings from those associated with purchasing jewelry and other commodities as a way to help empower communities in the global South. For Gupta, the Marigold necklaces, which are sold exclusively in Johannesburg, allow for the creation of affective binds that tie their female makers and wearers—a very different relationship between producer and consumer from that which is invited by the examples we discussed above. Unlike the commodities that circulate between and across the global South

and the global North within deeply unequal power relations, the Marigold beaded necklaces are a product of "artisanal labour" that "reminds us of Africa's role as a serious player in neoliberal global markets" (Gupta, "Fields of Marigold," 109). The Marigold necklace, Gupta writes, "allows its wearers to temporarily step out of the abstractions of capitalism where one is accordingly embedded in the impersonal relations of the market, and the commodity chain of anonymous purchases" (Gupta, "Fields of Marigold," 118). Admittedly, the commodities that Gupta studies belong to a very different context from that of the popular feminist commodity activism. However, her hopeful reading of these commodities serves as a valuable account of the meaningful possibilities that can be opened up by and through commodities, for women's confidence, empowerment, and solidarity.

67. Communicate Staff, "Which Is the Latest Brand to Celebrate Saudi Women?," May 15, 2018, https://old.communicateonline.me/more/campaigns-3/which-is-the-latest-brand-to-celebrate-saudi-women/.

68. EverydayMe Arabia, "#WeAreTheGenerationOfFirsts," YouTube, May 3, 2018, https://www.youtube.com/watch?v=6CQtueie-rY; Communicate Staff, "Which Is the Latest Brand."

69. Nguyen, "Biopower of Beauty," 367.

70. Authors' translation from Arabic. "#WeAreTheGenerationOfFirsts."

71. Nguyen, "Biopower of Beauty," 374.

72. Madawi al-Rasheed, "Saudi Women Can Now Travel without Consent—but This Progress Is Fragile," *Guardian*, August 2, 2019, https://www.theguardian.com/commentisfree/2019/aug/02/saudi-arabia-women-travel-consent-rights-feminist-movement.

73. Madawi al-Rasheed, *A Most Masculine State: Gender, Politics and Religion in Saudi Arabia* (Cambridge: Cambridge University Press, 2013); al-Rasheed, "Saudi Women Can."

74. Al-Rasheed, "Saudi Women Can."

75. Roy, "Precarity, Aspiration."

76. Roy, "Precarity, Aspiration," 395.

77. Roy, "Precarity, Aspiration," 417–418.

78. Peter Redifeld, "Doctors, Borders, and Life in Crisis," *Cultural Anthropology* 20, no. 3 (2005): 331, cited in Nguyen, "Biopower of Beauty," 368.

Conclusion

1. Michel Foucault, *Power-Knowledge: Selected Interviews and Other Writings, 1972–1977*, ed. Colin Gordon (Brighton, UK: Harvester Press, 1980).

2. Cruikshank, "Revolutions Within"; Davies, *Happiness Industry*; Rose, *Inventing Ourselves*.

3. Rosalind Gill, "Postfeminist Media Culture: Elements of a Sensibility," *European Journal of Cultural Studies* 10, no. 2 (2007): 147–166; McRobbie, *Aftermath of Feminism*; Yvonne Tasker and Diane Negra, *Interrogating Postfeminism: Gender and the Politics of Popular Culture* (Durham, NC: Duke University Press, 2007).

4. Laura Thompson and Ngaire Donaghue, "The Confidence Trick: Competing Constructions of Confidence and Self-Esteem in Young Australian Women's Discussions of the Sexualisation of Culture," *Women's Studies International Forum* 47 (2014): 23–35.

5. Scharff, *Repudiating Feminism*; Elisabeth Kelan, *Performing Gender at Work* (London: Palgrave Macmillan, 2009); McRobbie, *Aftermath of Feminism*; Elias, Gill, and Scharff, *Aesthetic Labour*; Gill, "Postfeminist Media Culture."

6. Gill and Orgad, "Confidence Cult(ure)."

7. Anne-Marie Slaughter, "Why Women Still Can't Have It All," *Atlantic*, July/August 2012; McRobbie, "Feminism, the Family"; Catherine Rottenberg, "Happiness and the Liberal Imagination: How Superwoman Became Balanced," *Feminist Studies* 40, no. 1 (2014): 144–168.

8. Ahmed, *Promise of Happiness*.

9. Gill, "Post-postfeminism?"

10. Emily Nussbaum, "On 'Shrill' and 'Better Things,' Women Stop Being Good Sports," *New Yorker*, March 11, 2019, https://www.newyorker.com/magazine/2019/03/18/on-shrill-and-better-things-women-stop-being-good-sports.

11. Vernon, *Unashamed*; Beauty and the Muse, http://www.beautyandthemuse.net.

12. Yomi Adegoke and Elizabeth Uviebinené, *Slay in Your Lane: The Black Girl Bible* (London: Fourth Estate, 2019). Following the success of *Slay in Your Lane*, in 2020 the book's authors published a sequel titled *Loud Black Girls*, a collection of essays from twenty Black British writers focused on Black girls today.

13. Adegoke and Uviebinené, *Slay in Your Lane*, 2.

14. Adegoke and Uviebinené, *Slay in Your Lane*, 118.

15. It Gets Better Project, "'Cripping Up Sex with Eva' Educator Isn't Afraid to Go There," YouTube, February 28, 2020, https://www.youtube.com/watch?v=5GcGoyq2dLk; Eva Sweeney, *Queers on Wheels: The Essential Guide for the Physically Disabled GLBTQ Community* (Pasadena, CA: CreateSpace, 2004).

16. "A Conversation with Eva Sweeney," Queer Disability Project, October 26, 2019, https://www.queerdisabilityproject.org/blog/a-conversation-with-eva-sweeney.

17. Audre Lorde, *A Burst of Light and Other Essays* (Mineola, NY: Ixia Press, 1988). For critiques of the appropriation and stripping of self-care of its radical political meanings, see Sara Ahmed, "Selfcare as Warfare," *Feministkilljoys*, August 25, 2014, https://feministkilljoys.com/2014/08/25/selfcare-as-warfare; Jordan Kisner, "The Politics of Conspicuous Displays of Self-Care," *New Yorker*, March 14, 2017, http://www.newyorker.com/culture/culture-desk/the-politics-of-selfcare; André Spicer, "'Self-Care': How a Radical Feminist Idea Was Stripped of Politics for the Mass Market," *Guardian*, August 21, 2019, http://www.theguardian.com/commentisfree/2019/aug/21/self-care-radical-feminist-idea-mass-market.

18. Harvard University, "Anti-racism Resources," https://projects.iq.harvard.edu/antiracismresources/bipoc/selfcare. In another example, an article in *The Conversation* is titled "Grief Is a Direct Impact of Racism," and though it follows the

familiar listicle format, its "Eight Ways to Support Yourself" locate intersectional oppressions as "acts of trauma and violence" that require safe spaces, community, intergenerational communication, and activism for change. See Roberta K. Timothy, "Grief Is a Direct Impact of Racism: Eight Ways to Support Yourself," *The Conversation*, May 3, 2018, https://theconversation.com/grief-is-a-direct-impact -of-racism-eight-ways-to-support-yourself-91750.

19. Shine (https://www.theshineapp.com/); The Nap Ministry (https://thenap ministry.wordpress.com/about/); Therapy for Black Girls (https://therapyforblack girls.com/).

20. Walters and Harrison, "Not Ready to Make Nice"; Ruth Cain, "'Just What Kind of Mother Are You?': Neoliberal Guilt and Privatised Maternal Responsibility in Recent Domestic Crime Fiction," in *We Need to Talk about Family: Essays on Neoliberalism, the Family and Popular Culture*, ed. Roberta Garrett, Tracey Jensen, and Angie Voela (Cambridge: Cambridge Scholars, 2016), 289–313; Littler, "Mothers Behaving Badly."

21. Lisa Lerer and Jennifer Medina, "The 'Rage Moms' Democrats Are Counting On," *New York Times*, August 17, 2020, https://www.nytimes.com/2020/08/17 /us/politics/democrats-women-voters-anger.html.

22. Julia Llewellyn Smith, "Politicians Beware—'Rage Mums' Are the New and Furious 'Worcester Woman,'" *Daily Telegraph*, August 24, 2020, https://www .telegraph.co.uk/women/politics/politicians-beware-rage-mums-new-furious -worcester-woman/.

23. Us for Them, accessed April 30, 2021, https://usforthem.co.uk.

24. Lerer and Medina, "'Rage Moms,'" note that the activism of rage moms in the US is diffuse and multiracial; as far as age is concerned, Patty Murray, the senator who coined the term, admitted she was more of a "rage nana."

25. Lapis Communication, "Be 100 Ragl (Worth 100 Men)," accessed April 30, 2021, https://www.lapis-communications.com/case-studies/be-100-ragl -worth-100-men.

26. In the context of this website, the word "Khateera" is used to denote a bold and audacious woman.

27. Gerrick D. Kennedy, "A Night at the Church of Lizzo, Pop Music's Patron Saint of Self-Care," *Los Angeles Times*, October 19, 2019, https://www.latimes.com /entertainment-arts/music/story/2019-10-19/lizzo-hollywood-palladium-concert -review; Allison P. Davis, "It's Just a Matter of Time Till Everybody Loves Lizzo as Much as She Loves Herself," *The Cut*, February 3, 2019, https://www.thecut.com /2019/02/lizzo-flute-pop-star.html.

28. Lizzo, "Truth Hurts," on *Lizzo, Cuz I Love You (Deluxe)*, 2017.

29. Samantha Irby, "Time Entertainer of the Year: Lizzo," *Time*, 2019, https:// time.com/entertainer-of-the-year-2019-lizzo.

30. Alanna Vagianos, "Lizzo Loves Being 'a Fat B***h,'" *Huffington Post*, April 29, 2019, https://www.huffingtonpost.co.uk/entry/lizzo-fat-bitch-v-magazine_n_5cc71 9cae4b04eb7ff996526.

31. Cited in Irby, "Time Entertainer."

32. Vagianos, "Lizzo Loves."

33. McRobbie, "Notes on the Perfect."

34. Gerrick D. Kennedy, "100% Her Year: How Lizzo Became the One Thing We All Loved in 2019," *Los Angeles Times*, December 11, 2019, https://www.latimes.com/entertainment-arts/music/story/2019-12-11/lizzo-2019-artist-year.

35. Catherine Connell, "Fashionable Resistance: Queer 'Fa(t)shion' Blogging as Counterdiscourse," *Women's Studies Quarterly* 41, nos. 1/2 (2012): 213.

36. Cited in Davis, "It's Just a Matter."

37. Cited in Davis, "It's Just a Matter."

38. Justin Enriquez, "Lizzo Sends a Message by Posing NUDE with Half of Her Body Covered in American Flag as She Thanks Fans for Voting," *Daily Mail*, November 3, 2020, https://www.dailymail.co.uk/tvshowbiz/article-8910165/Lizzo-sends-message-posing-NUDE-half-body-covered-American-flag-thanks-fans-voting.html.

39. Janelle Hobson, "Black Beauty and Digital Spaces: The New Visibility Politics," *Ada: A Journal of Gender, New Media and Technology* 10, no. 10 (2016), https://adanewmedia.org/2016/10/issue10-hobson.

40. Based on Tanisha Ford, *Liberated Threads: Black Women, Style, and the Global Politics of Soul* (Chapel Hill: University of North Carolina Press, 2016), 73.

41. Hobson, "Black Beauty."

42. Cited in Davis, "It's Just a Matter."

43. Cited in Davis, "It's Just a Matter."

44. Cited in Davis, "It's Just a Matter."

45. Irby, "Time Entertainer."

46. Cited in Kennedy, "100% Her Year."

47. Ehrenreich, *Natural Causes*.

48. Ronald Purser, *McMindfulness* (London: Repeater, 2019).

bibliography

Adegoke, Yomi, and Elizabeth Uviebinené. *Slay in Your Lane: The Black Girl Bible*. London: Fourth Estate, 2019.

Ahmed, Sara. *The Cultural Politics of Emotion*. London: Routledge, 2004.

Ahmed, Sara. *The Promise of Happiness*. Durham, NC: Duke University Press, 2010.

Aiello, Giorgia, and Katy Parry. *Visual Communication: Understanding Images in Media Culture*. London: Sage, 2020.

Allen, Kim, and Anna Bull. "Following Policy: A Network Ethnography of the UK Character Education Policy Community." *Sociological Research Online* 23, no. 2 (2018): 438–458.

Allen, Terina. "This Is How Confident Women Embrace Their Power." *Forbes*, September 24, 2019. https://www.forbes.com/sites/terinaallen/2019/09/24 /this-is-how-confident-women-embrace-their-power.

al-Rasheed, Madawi. *A Most Masculine State: Gender, Politics and Religion in Saudi Arabia*. Cambridge: Cambridge University Press, 2013.

al-Rasheed, Madawi. "Saudi Women Can Now Travel without Consent—but This Progress Is Fragile." *Guardian*, August 2, 2019. https://www.theguardian .com/commentisfree/2019/aug/02/saudi-arabia-women-travel-consent -rights-feminist-movement.

Appignanesi, Lisa. *Mad, Bad and Sad: A History of Women and the Mind Doctors from 1800 to the Present*. London: Virago, 2009.

Asher, Rebecca. *Shattered: Modern Motherhood and the Illusion of Equality*. New York: Vintage, 2012.

Austin, Nefertiti. *Motherhood So White: A Memoir of Race, Gender, and Parenting in America*. Naperville, IL: Sourcebooks, 2019.

Bailey, Alyssa. "Meghan Markle Told South African Women 'I Am Here with You as Your Sister' in Powerful Speech." *Elle*, September 23, 2019. https://www.elle.com/culture/celebrities/a29188564/meghan-markle-nyanga-speech.

Baker, Joanne. "Claiming Volition and Evading Victimhood: Post-feminist Obligations for Young Women." *Feminism and Psychology* 20, no. 2 (2010): 186–204.

Banerji, Mahika. "A Take on *The Subtle Art of Not Giving a Fuck*: Male Chauvinist as Hell." *Feminism in India*, April 13, 2018. https://feminisminindia.com/2018/04/13/the-subtle-art-of-not-giving-a-fuck-review.

Banet-Weiser, Sarah. "Am I Pretty or Ugly? Girls and the Market for Self-Esteem." *Girlhood Studies* 7, no. 1 (2014): 83–101.

Banet-Weiser, Sarah. "'Confidence You Can Carry!': Girls in Crisis and the Market for Girls' Empowerment Organizations." *Continuum: Journal of Media and Cultural Studies* 29, no. 2 (2015): 182–193.

Banet-Weiser, Sarah. *Empowered: Popular Feminism and Popular Misogyny*. Durham, NC: Duke University Press, 2018.

Banet-Weiser, Sarah. "'Free Self-Esteem Tools?': Brand Culture, Gender, and the Dove Real Beauty Campaign." In *Commodity Activism: Cultural Resistance in Neoliberal Times*, edited by Roopali Mukherjee and Sarah Banet-Weiser, 39–56. New York: New York University Press, 2012.

Banet-Weiser, Sarah. "'Ruined' Lives: Mediated White Male Victimhood." *European Journal of Cultural Studies* 24, no. 1 (2021): 60–80.

Barak-Brandes, Sigal, and Einat Lachover. "Branding Relations: Mother–Daughter Discourse on Beauty and Body in an Israeli Campaign by Dove." *Communication, Culture and Critique* 9, no. 3 (2016): 379–394.

Barker, Meg-John, Rosalind Gill, and Laura Harvey. *Mediated Intimacy: Sex Advice in Media Culture*. Cambridge: Polity, 2018.

Barr, Sabrina. "Love Island Criticised as New Figures Reveal Impact of Reality TV on Body Image." *Independent*, June 3, 2019. https://www.independent.co.uk/life-style/health-and-families/love-island-2019-mental-health-body-image-reality-tv-itv-a8940856.html.

Barthes, Roland. *Mythologies*. Translated by Annette Lavers. New York: Hill and Wang, 1973.

Bateman, Sophie. "Meghan Markle Gives Powerful Feminist Speech in South Africa." *Newshub*, September 24, 2019. https://www.newshub.co.nz/home/entertainment/2019/09/meghan-markle-gives-powerful-feminist-speech-in-south-africa.html.

Beilock, Sian Leah. "How Women Can Banish Self-Doubt at Work." *Financial*

Times, February 6, 2019. https://www.ft.com/content/d154b5a0-287a
-11e9-9222-7024d72222bc.

Bem, Sandra L. "The Measurement of Psychological Androgyny." *Journal of Consulting and Clinical Psychology* 42, no. 2 (1974): 155–162.

Bennett, Catherine. "Is Impostor Syndrome Just for Women? There Are Some Men I Can Think Of . . ." *Guardian*, December 16, 2018. https://www
.theguardian.com/commentisfree/2018/dec/16/is-impostor-syndrome-just
-for-women-there-are-some-men-i-can-think-of.

Berlant, Lauren. *Cruel Optimism*. Durham, NC: Duke University Press, 2011.

Binkley, Sam. "Governmentality and Lifestyle Studies." *Sociology Compass* 1, no. 1 (2007): 111–126.

Binkley, Sam. *Happiness as Enterprise: An Essay on Neoliberal Life*. New York: State University of New York Press, 2015.

Birmingham LGBT. "On Body Confidence in the Bedroom." *Diva*, April 5, 2019. https://divamag.co.uk/2019/04/05/on-body-confidence-in-the-bedroom.

Blackman, Lisa. "Self-Help, Media Cultures and the Production of Female Psychopathology." *European Journal of Cultural Studies* 7, no. 2 (2004): 219–236.

Blum, Linda M., and Nena F. Stracuzzi. "Gender in the Prozac Nation: Popular Discourse and Productive Femininity." *Gender and Society* 18, no. 3 (2004): 269–286.

Boltanski, Luc, and Eve Chiapello. *The New Spirit of Capitalism*. London: Verso, 2007.

Bordo, Susan. *Unbearable Weight: Feminism, Western Culture, and the Body*. Berkeley: University of California Press, 1993.

Bottrell, Dorothy. "Responsibilised Resilience? Reworking Neoliberal Social Policy Texts." *M/C Journal* 16, no. 5 (2013). https://doi.org/10.5204/mcj.708.

Braedley, Susan, and Meg Luxton. *Neoliberalism and Everyday Life*. Montreal: McGill-Queen's University Press, 2010.

Bratich, Jack, and Sarah Banet-Weiser. "From Pick-Up Artists to Incels: Con(fidence) Games, Networked Misogyny, and the Failure of Neoliberalism." *International Journal of Communication* 13 (2019): 5003–5027.

Briggs, Laura. *How All Politics Became Reproductive Politics: From Welfare Reform to Foreclosure to Trump*. Oakland: University of California Press, 2017.

Brockes, Emma. "Yes, I Do Give a Sh*t about These Sweary Book Covers." *Guardian*, February 7, 2019. https://www.theguardian.com/commentisfree/2019
/feb/07/emma-brockes-self-help-books.

Bröckling, Ulrich. "Gendering the Enterprising Self: Subjectification Programs and Gender Differences in Guides to Success." *Distinktion* 11 (2005): 7–23.

Brotheridge, Chloe. *Brave New Girl: Seven Steps to Confidence*. London: Michael Joseph, 2019.

Broughton, Ellie. "Move Over Mindfulness: It's Time for 'Finefulness.'" *Guardian*, February 20, 2019. https://www.theguardian.com/books/2019/feb/20
/move-over-mindfulness-its-time-for-finefulness-self-help.

Brown, Brené. "Courage over Comfort: Rumbling with Shame, Accountability,

and Failure at Work." *Brené Brown* (blog), March 13, 2018. https://brenebrown
.com/articles/2018/03/13/courage-comfort-rumbling-shame-accountability
-failure-work.

Brown, Brené. "Leading from Hurt versus Leading from Heart." *Brené Brown* (blog),
December 4, 2018. https://brenebrown.com/articles/2018/12/04/leading
-from-hurt-versus-leading-from-heart.

Brown, Helen Gurley. *Sex and the Single Girl*. New York: B. Geis Associates, 1962.

Brown, Wendy. *Undoing the Demos: Neoliberalism's Stealth Revolution*. Cambridge,
MA: MIT Press, 2015.

Bull, Anna, and Kim Allen. "Introduction: Sociological Interrogations of the Turn
to Character." *Sociological Research Online* 23, no. 2 (2018): 392–398.

Burkeman, Oliver. *The Antidote*. Edinburgh: Canongate, 2012.

Burman, Erica. "(Re)Sourcing the Character and Resilience Manifesto: Suppressions and Slippages of (Re)Presentation and Selective Affectivities." *Sociological Research Online* 23, no. 2 (2018): 130–151.

Butler, Judith. *Excitable Speech: A Politics of the Performative*. New York: Routledge, 1997.

Butler, Judith. *Gender Trouble: Feminism and the Subversion of Identity*. New York:
Routledge, 1990.

Butler, Judith. *The Psychic Life of Power: Theories in Subjection*. Stanford, CA: Stanford
University Press, 1997.

Cain, Ruth. "The Court of Motherhood: Affect, Alienation and Redefinitions
of Responsible Parenting." In *Regulating Family Responsibilities*, edited by Jo
Bridgeman and Heather Keating, 67–90. Farnham, UK: Ashgate, 2011.

Cain, Ruth. "'Just What Kind of Mother Are You?': Neoliberal Guilt and Privatised Maternal Responsibility in Recent Domestic Crime Fiction." In *We
Need to Talk about Family: Essays on Neoliberalism, the Family and Popular Culture*,
edited by Roberta Garrett, Tracey Jensen, and Angie Voela, 289–313. Cambridge: Cambridge Scholars, 2016.

Calkin, Sydney. "'Tapping' Women for Post-crisis Capitalism: Evidence from the
2012 World Development Report." *International Feminist Journal of Politics* 17,
no. 4 (2015): 611–629.

Carlin, Barbara A., Betsy D. Gelb, Jamie K. Belinne, and Latha Ramchand. "Bridging the Gender Gap in Confidence." *Business Horizons* 61 (2018): 765–774.

Cederström, Carl, and Andre Spicer. *The Wellness Syndrome*. Cambridge: Polity,
2014.

Chant, Sylvia, and Caroline Sweetman. "Fixing Women or Fixing the World?
'Smarteconomics,' Efficiency Approaches, and Gender Equality in Development." *Gender and Development* 20, no. 3 (2012): 517–529.

Chassany, Anne-Sylvaine. "Christine Lagarde Shows How to Deal with Imposter
Syndrome." *Financial Times*, July 9, 2019. https://www.ft.com/content
/13720bc4-a16e-11e9-a282-2df48f366f7d.

Chatzidakis, Andreas, Jamie Hakim, Jo Littler, Catherine Rottenberg, and Lynne
Segal. "From Carewashing to Radical Care: The Discursive Explosions of
Care during Covid-19." *Feminist Media Studies* 20, no. 6 (2020): 889–895.

"Cheesy Tunes to Help You Get Your Sweat On." *Evening Standard* (London), September 16, 2019.

Chen, Angus. "Invisibilia: How Learning to Be Vulnerable Can Make Life Safer." NPR, June 17, 2016. https://www.npr.org/sections/health-shots/2016/06 /17/482203447/invisibilia-how-learning-to-be-vulnerable-can-make-life-safer.

Chodorow, Nancy J. *The Reproduction of Mothering.* Berkeley: University of California Press, 1978.

Chouliaraki, Lilie. *The Ironic Spectator: Solidarity in the Age of Post-humanitarianism.* Cambridge: Polity, 2013.

Chunn, Louise. "Women Are at Breaking Point Because of Workplace Stress: Wellbeing Survey from Cigna." *Forbes,* March 26, 2019. https://www.forbes .com/sites/louisechunn/2019/03/26/women-are-at-breaking-point-because -of-workplace-stress-wellbeing-survey-from-cigna.

Clarke, John. "A Sense of Loss? Unsettled Attachments in the Current Conjuncture." *New Formations: A Journal of Culture/Theory/Politics* 96, no. 1 (2019): 132–146.

Clough, Patricia Ticineto, and Jean Halley, eds. *The Affective Turn: Theorizing the Social.* Durham, NC: Duke University Press, 2007.

Collins, Patricia Hill. *Black Feminist Thought: Knowledge, Consciousness, and the Politics of Empowerment.* 2nd ed. New York: Routledge, 2002.

Connell, Catherine. "Fashionable Resistance: Queer 'Fa(t)shion' Blogging as Counterdiscourse." *Women's Studies Quarterly* 41, nos. 1/2 (2012): 209–224.

Cooper, Marianne. *Cut Adrift: Families in Insecure Times.* Oakland: University of California Press, 2014.

Couldry, Nick. "Theorising Media as Practice." *Social Semiotics* 14, no. 2 (2004): 115–132.

Craig, Maxine Leeds. *Ain't I a Beauty Queen? Black Women, Beauty, and the Politics of Race.* New York: Oxford University Press, 2020.

Cruikshank, Barbara. "Revolutions Within: Self-Government and Self-Esteem." *Economy and Society* 22, no. 3 (1993): 327–344.

Cruikshank, Barbara. *The Will to Empower: Democratic Citizens and Other Subjects.* Ithaca, NY: Cornell University Press, 1999.

Cuddy, Amy. "Your Body Language May Shape Who You Are." TED Talk, June 2012, 19:33. https://www.ted.com/talks/amy_cuddy_your_body_language _may_shape_who_you_are?language=en.

Daily, Lisa A. "We Bleed for Female Empowerment: Mediated Ethics, Commodity Feminism, and the Contradictions of Feminist Politics." *Communication and Critical/Cultural Studies* 16, no. 2 (2019): 140–158.

Darvell, Marcia, and Ahmed Elsharkawy. *Eating Disorders, Body Image and the Media.* London: British Medical Association, 2000.

Das, Ranjana. *Early Motherhood in Digital Societies: Ideals, Anxieties and Ties of the Perinatal.* London: Routledge, 2020.

Das, Ranjana. "Speaking about Birth: Visible and Silenced Narratives in Online Discussions of Childbirth." *Social Media + Society* 3, no. 4 (2017): 1–11.

Davies, William. *The Happiness Industry: How the Government and Big Business Sold Us Well-Being*. London: Verso, 2015.

Davis, Allison P. "It's Just a Matter of Time Till Everybody Loves Lizzo as Much as She Loves Herself." *The Cut*, February 3, 2019. https://www.thecut.com/2019/02/lizzo-flute-pop-star.html.

Day, Elizabeth. *How to Fail: Everything I've Ever Learned from Things Going Wrong*. London: HarperCollins, 2019.

De Benedictis, Sara. "'Feral' Parents: Austerity Parenting under Neoliberalism." *Studies in the Maternal* 4, no. 2 (2012): 1–21.

De Benedictis, Sara, Bridget Conor, and Rosalind Gill. "Feminist Gloss." Unpublished manuscript.

De Benedictis, Sara, and Shani Orgad. "The Escalating Price of Motherhood: Aesthetic Labour in Popular Representations of 'Stay-at-Home' Mothers." In Elias, Gill, and Scharff, *Aesthetic Labour*, 101–116.

De Lauretis, Teresa. *Technologies of Gender: Essays on Theory, Film, and Fiction*. Basingstoke, UK: Macmillan, 1989.

Diebner, Rachel, Elizabeth Silliman, Kelly Ungerman, and Maxence Vancauwenberghe. "Adapting Customer Experience in the Time of Coronavirus." McKinsey and Company, April 2, 2020. https://www.mckinsey.com/business-functions/marketing-and-sales/our-insights/adapting-customer-experience-in-the-time-of-coronavirus.

Dosekun, Simidele, and Mehita Iqani. "The Politics and Aesthetics of Luxury in Africa." In *African Luxury: Aesthetics and Politics*, edited by Mehita Iqani and Simidele Dosekun, 3–16. Bristol, UK: Intellect, 2020.

Douglas, Susan. *Where the Girls Are: Growing Up Female with the Mass Media*. Harmondsworth, UK: Penguin, 1994.

Douglas, Susan, and Meredith W. Michaels. *The Mommy Myth: The Idealization of Motherhood and How It Has Undermined All Women*. New York: Free Press, 2004.

Dow, Dawn Marie. *Mothering While Black*. Oakland: University of California Press, 2019.

Dowling, Emma. *The Care Crisis: What Caused It and How Can We End It?* London: Verso, 2021.

Drenten, Jenna, and Lauren Gurrieri. "Social Media, the 'Bikini Bridge' and the Viral Contagion of Body Ideals." *The Conversation*, December 3, 2017. https://theconversation.com/social-media-the-bikini-bridge-and-the-viral-contagion-of-body-ideals-87262.

Drucker, Ali. "What *Shrill* Can Teach Us about the Bare-Minimum Boyfriend." *The Cut*, March 27, 2019. https://www.thecut.com/2019/03/what-shrill-can-teach-us-about-the-bare-minimum-boyfriend.html.

Dua, Taylor. "Vulnerability Is a Key Component of Management Say PwC Execs Talking Diversity and Inclusion." *The Drum*, July 16, 2019. https://www.thedrum.com/news/2019/07/16/vulnerability-key-component-management-say-pwc-execs-talking-diversity-and-inclusion.

Dubriwny, Tasha. "Mommy Blogs and the Disruptive Possibilities of Transgressive

Drinking." In *Mediated Moms: Contemporary Challenges to the Motherhood Myth*, edited by Heather L. Hundley and Sara Hayden, 203–220. New York: Peter Lang, 2015.

Duffy, Brooke Erin. *(Not) Getting Paid to Do What You Love: Gender, Social Media, and Aspirational Work*. New Haven, CT: Yale University Press, 2019.

Du Gay, Paul. *Consumption and Identity at Work*. London: Sage, 1996.

Duggan, Lisa. "The New Homonormativity: The Sexual Politics of Neoliberalism." In *Materializing Democracy: Toward a Revitalized Cultural Politics*, edited by Russ Castronovo and Dana D. Nelson, 175–194. Durham, NC: Duke University Press, 2012.

Dunham, Lena. *Not That Kind of Girl: A Young Woman Tells You What She's "Learned."* London: HarperCollins, 2015.

Egan, Danielle. *Becoming Sexual: A Critical Appraisal of the Sexualization of Girls*. Cambridge: Polity, 2013.

Ehrenreich, Barbara. *Bright-Sided: How Positive Thinking Is Undermining America*. New York: Macmillan, 2010.

Ehrenreich, Barbara. *Natural Causes: Life, Death and the Illusion of Control*. London: Granta, 2018.

Eichenbaum, Luise, and Susie Orbach. *What Do Women Want? Exploding the Myth of Dependency*. Glasgow: Fontana/Collins, 1983.

Eldor, Karin. "Raising Boys in the #MeToo Era? The CEO of Peanut, a Tinder-Like App for Moms, Shares Three Tips." *Forbes*, May 12, 2018. https://www.forbes .com/sites/karineldor/2018/05/12/raising-boys-in-the-metoo-era-the-ceo-of -peanut-a-tinder-like-app-for-moms-shares-three-tips.

Elias, Ana Sofia. "Beautiful Body, Confident Soul: Young Women and the Beauty Labour of Neoliberalism." PhD diss., King's College London, 2016.

Elias, Ana Sofia, and Rosalind Gill. "Beauty Surveillance: The Digital Self-Monitoring Cultures of Neoliberalism." *European Journal of Cultural Studies* 21, no. 1 (2017): 59–77.

Elias, Ana Sofia, Rosalind Gill, and Christina Scharff. *Aesthetic Labour: Rethinking Beauty Politics in Neoliberalism*. London: Palgrave Macmillan, 2017.

Elliott, Larry. "Each Generation Should Be Better Off Than Their Parents? Think Again." *Guardian*, February 14, 2016. http://www.theguardian.com/business /2016/feb/14/economics-viewpoint-baby-boomers-generation-x-generation -rent-gig-economy.

Evans, Adrienne, and Sarah Riley. *Technologies of Sexiness: Sex, Identity, and Consumer Culture*. Oxford: Oxford University Press, 2015.

Fahs, Breanne. "Dreaded 'Otherness': Heteronormative Patrolling in Women's Body Hair Rebellions." *Gender and Society* 25, no. 4 (2011): 451–472.

Faircloth, Charlotte. "Intensive Fatherhood? The (Un)Involved Dad." In *Parenting Culture Studies*, edited by Ellie Lee, Jennie Bristow, Charlotte Faircloth, and Jan Macvarish, 184–199. London: Palgrave Macmillan, 2014.

Favaro, Laura. "'Just Be Confident Girls!': Confidence Chic as Neoliberal Governmentality." In Elias, Gill, and Scharff, *Aesthetic Labour*, 283–299.

Favaro, Laura. "Transnational Technologies of Gender and Mediated Intimacy." PhD diss., City, University of London, 2017.

Favaro, Laura, and Rosalind Gill. "'Emasculation Nation Has Arrived': Sexism Rearticulated in Online Responses to Lose the Lads' Mags Campaign." *Feminist Media Studies* 16, no. 3 (2016): 379–397.

Favaro, Laura, and Rosalind Gill. "'Pump Up the Positivity': Neoliberalism, Affective Entrepreneurship and the Victimhood/Agency Debate." In *Re-writing Women as Victims: From Theory to Practice*, edited by María José Gámez Fuentes, Sonia Núñez Puente, and Emma Gómez Nicolau, 154–165. London: Routledge, 2019.

Ford, Tanisha. *Liberated Threads: Black Women, Style, and the Global Politics of Soul.* Chapel Hill: University of North Carolina Press, 2016.

Forkert, Kirsten. *Austerity as Public Mood: Social Anxieties and Social Struggles.* London: Rowman and Littlefield, 2017.

Foster, Dawn. *Lean Out.* London: Repeater, 2016.

Foucault, Michel. *The Birth of Biopolitics: Lectures at the Collège de France, 1978–1979.* Translated by Graham Burchell. London: Springer, 2008.

Foucault, Michel. *Power-Knowledge: Selected Interviews and Other Writings, 1972–1977.* Edited by Colin Gordon. Brighton, UK: Harvester Press, 1980.

Foucault, Michel. *Technologies of the Self: A Seminar with Michel Foucault.* Edited by Luther H. Martin, Huck Gutman, and Patrick H. Hutton. London: Tavistock, 1988.

Foucault, Michel. *The Use of Pleasure.* Vol. 2 of *The History of Sexuality.* Translated by Robert Hurley. Harmondsworth, UK: Penguin, 1987.

Fraser, Nancy. "Feminism, Capitalism and the Cunning of History." *New Left Review* 56 (2009): 97–117.

Friedan, Betty. *The Feminine Mystique.* 1963; repr., London: Penguin, 2000.

Friedli, Lynne, and Robert Stearn. "Positive Affect as Coercive Strategy: Conditionality, Activation and the Role of Psychology in UK Government Workfare Programmes." *Medical Humanities* 41, no. 1 (2015): 40–47.

Furedi, Frank. "Parental Determinism: A Most Harmful Prejudice." *Spiked*, May 21, 2012. https://www.spiked-online.com/2012/05/21/parental-determinism-a-most-harmful-prejudice.

Gaines, Alisha. *Black for a Day: White Fantasies of Race and Empathy.* Chapel Hill: University of North Carolina Press, 2017.

Gallagher, Sophie. "Meet the Entrepreneur Taking Hundreds of Bras from London to Edinburgh to Help Women in Africa." *Huffington Post*, April 13, 2018. https://www.huffingtonpost.co.uk/entry/a-volunteer-is-driving-hundreds-of-bras-from-london-to-edinburgh-to-help-women-in-africa_uk_5acf2fa8e4b06487677732ce.

Garrett, Roberta, Tracey Jensen, and Angie Voela, eds. *We Need to Talk about Family: Essays on Neoliberalism, the Family and Popular Culture.* Cambridge: Cambridge Scholars, 2016.

Gates, Melinda. "How Melinda Gates Learned to Overcome Fear." *Teen Vogue*, May

31, 2019. https://www.teenvogue.com/story/how-melinda-gates-learned-to
-overcome-fear.

Gates, Melinda. *The Moment of Lift: How Empowering Women Changes the World*. London: Blue Bird, 2019.

Gharib, Malaka. "Woman's Instagram Post about Kenyan Child Ignites Fury." NPR, March 22, 2018. https://www.npr.org/sections/goatsandsoda/2018 /03/22/596002482/womans-instagram-post-about-kenyan-child-ignites -fury.

Gill, Rosalind. "Beyond the 'Sexualisation of Culture' Thesis: An Intersectional Analysis of 'Sixpacks,' 'Midriffs' and 'Hot Lesbians' in Advertising." *Sexualities* 12, no. 2 (2009): 137–160.

Gill, Rosalind. "'Doing Her Best with What She's Got': Authorship, Irony, and Mediating Feminist Identities in Lena Dunham's *Girls*." In *Reading Lena Dunham's "Girls": Feminism, Postfeminism, Authenticity and Gendered Performance in Contemporary Television*, edited by Meredith Nash and Imelda Whelehan, 225–242. Basingstoke, UK: Palgrave Macmillan, 2017.

Gill, Rosalind. *Feeling Judged: Posting Perfect Lives on Social Media*. Cambridge: Polity, 2021.

Gill, Rosalind. *Gender and the Media*. Cambridge: Polity, 2007.

Gill, Rosalind. "Mediated Intimacy and Postfeminism: A Discourse Analytic Examination of Sex and Relationships Advice in a Women's Magazine." *Discourse and Communication* 3, no. 4 (2009): 345–369.

Gill, Rosalind. "Postfeminist Media Culture: Elements of a Sensibility." *European Journal of Cultural Studies* 10, no. 2 (2007): 147–166.

Gill, Rosalind. "Post-postfeminism? New Feminist Visibilities in Postfeminist Times." *Feminist Media Studies* 16, no. 4 (2016): 610–630.

Gill, Rosalind. "The Sexualisation of Culture?" *Social and Personality Psychology Compass* 6, no. 7 (2012): 483–498.

Gill, Rosalind. "Surveillance Is a Feminist Issue." In *Routledge Handbook of Contemporary Feminism*, edited by Tasha Oren and Andrea L. Press, 148–161. New York: Routledge, 2019.

Gill, Rosalind, and Ngaire Donaghue. "Resilience, Apps and Reluctant Individualism: Technologies of Self in the Neoliberal Academy." *Women's Studies International Forum* 54 (January–February 2016): 91–99.

Gill, Rosalind, Yvonne Ehrstein, and Jo Littler. "The Affective Life of Neoliberalism: Constructing (Un)Reasonableness on Mumsnet." In *Neoliberalism in Context: Governance, Subjectivity and Knowledge*, edited by Simon Dawes and Marc Lenormand, 195–213. Basingstoke, UK: Palgrave Macmillan, 2019.

Gill, Rosalind, and Ana S. Elias. "'Awaken Your Incredible': Love Your Body Discourses and Postfeminist Contradictions." *International Journal of Media and Cultural Politics* 10, no. 2 (2014): 179–188.

Gill, Rosalind, and Akane Kanai. "Affirmative Adverting and the Mediated Feeling Rules of Neoliberalism." In *Neoliberalism and the Media*, edited by Marian Meyers, 131–146. New York: Routledge, 2019.

Gill, Rosalind, and Shani Orgad. "The Amazing Bounce-Backable Woman: Resilience and the Psychological Turn in Neoliberalism." *Sociological Research Online* 23, no. 2 (2018): 477–495.

Gill, Rosalind, and Shani Orgad. "The Confidence Cult(ure)." *Australian Feminist Studies* 30, no. 86 (2015): 324–344.

Gill, Rosalind, and Shani Orgad. "Confidence Culture and the Remaking of Feminism." *New Formations* 91 (2017): 16–34.

Gillies, Val. "Childrearing, Class and the New Politics of Parenting." *Sociology Compass* 2/3 (2008): 1079–1095.

Gillies, Val, Rosalind Edwards, and Nicola Horsley. *Challenging the Politics of Early Intervention.* Bristol, UK: Policy Press, 2017.

Ginsburg, Faye, and Rayna Rapp. "Disability Worlds." *Annual Review of Anthropology* 42 (2013): 53–68.

Goffman, Erving. *Gender Advertisements.* New York: Harper and Row, 1979.

Goldberg, David T. "Neoliberalizing Race." *Macalester Civic Forum* 1, no. 1 (2007). http://digitalcommons.macalester.edu/maccivicf/vol1/iss1/14.

Goldfine, Jael. "The Rise of the Vulnerable Heroine." *Paper Magazine*, April 3, 2019. https://www.papermag.com/vulnerable-heroine-kesha-lady-gaga-beyonce-2633185821.html.

Goldman, Robert. *Readings Ads Socially.* London: Routledge, 1992.

Goldman, Robert, Deborah Heath, and Sharon L. Smith. "Commodity Feminism." *Critical Studies in Mass Communication* 8, no. 3 (1991): 333–351.

Goldthrope, John H. "Social Class Mobility in Modern Britain: Changing Structure, Constant Process." *Journal of the British Academy* 4 (2016): 89–111.

Goodman, Michael K., and Christine Barnes. "Star/Poverty Space: The Making of the 'Development Celebrity.'" *Celebrity Studies* 2, no. 1 (2011): 69–85.

Grensing-Popha, Lin. "Ways for Women to Build Confidence in the Workplace." *HR Daily Advisor*, August 2, 2018. https://hrdailyadvisor.blr.com/2018/08/02/ways-women-build-confidence-workplace.

Grose, Jessica. "Mothers Are the 'Shock Absorbers' of Our Society." *New York Times*, October 14, 2020.

Grossberg, Lawrence. "Cultural Studies in Search of a Method, or Looking for Conjunctural Analysis." *New Formations: A Journal of Culture/Theory/Politics* 96/97 (2019): 38–68.

Gupta, Pamila. "Fields of Marigold: Makers and Wearers of Luxury African Beaded Necklaces." In *African Luxury: Aesthetics and Politics*, edited by Mehita Iqani and Simidele Dosekun, 109–122. Bristol, UK: Intellect, 2020.

Hains, Rebecca. *Growing Up with Girl Power: Girlhood on Screen and in Everyday Life.* New York: Peter Lang, 2012.

Hall, Stuart. "The Spectacle of the 'Other.'" In *Representation: Cultural Representations and Signifying Practices*, edited by Stuart Hall, 223–279. London: Sage, 1997.

Hall, Stuart, Doreen Massey, and Mike Rustin, eds. *After Neoliberalism? The Kilburn Manifesto.* London: Lawrence and Wishart, 2015.

Hannah, Sophie. *How to Hold a Grudge: From Resentment to Contentment—the Power of Grudges to Transform Your Life*. London: Hodder and Stoughton, 2018.

Harris, Anita. *Future Girl: Young Women in the Twenty-First Century*. New York: Psychology Press, 2004.

Harvey, David. *A Brief History of Neoliberalism*. Oxford: Oxford University Press, 2005.

Harvey, Laura, and Rosalind Gill. "Spicing It Up: Sexual Entrepreneurs and the Sex Inspectors." In *New Femininities: Postfeminism, Neoliberalism and Subjectivity*, edited by Rosalind Gill and Christina Scharff, 52–67. London: Palgrave Macmillan, 2011.

Harvey-Jenner, Catriona. "11 Women Who Showed Us That Numbers Mean Nothing When It Comes to Body Confidence." *Cosmopolitan*, December 27, 2017. https://www.cosmopolitan.com/uk/body/health/g14469299/numbers-weight-sizes-mean-nothing-health-fitness-body-confidence.

Hazleden, Rebecca. "Love Yourself: The Relationship of the Self with Itself in Popular Self-Help Texts." *Journal of Sociology* 39, no. 4 (2003): 413–428.

Hearn, Alison. "Confidence Man: Breaking the Spell of Trump the Brand." *Soundings: A Journal of Politics and Culture* 66 (2017): 79–89.

Henderson, Meg, and Anthea Taylor. *Postfeminism in Context: The Australian Postfeminist Imaginary*. New York: Routledge, 2018.

Hobson, Janelle. "Black Beauty and Digital Spaces: The New Visibility Politics." *Ada: A Journal of Gender, New Media and Technology* 10, no. 10 (2016). https://adanewmedia.org/2016/10/issue10-hobson.

Hochschild, Arlie. "Emotion Work, Feeling Rules, and Social Structure." *American Journal of Sociology* 85, no. 3 (1979): 551–575.

Hochschild, Arlie, with Anne Machung. *The Second Shift: Working Families and the Revolution at Home*. New York: Penguin, 1989.

Hollis, Rachel. *Girl, Stop Apologizing: A Shame-Free Plan for Embracing and Achieving Your Goals*. New York: HarperCollins, 2019.

hooks, bell. *Black Looks: Race and Representation*. Boston: South End, 1992.

Hosie, Rachel. "How Women's Bodies Have Changed since 1957." *Independent*, March 16, 2017. https://www.independent.co.uk/life-style/health-and-families/womens-body-changes-since-1957-self-image-fashion-weight-health-sizes-positive-a7633036.html.

Hosie, Rachel. "Lingerie Brand Receives Backlash for Diverse Campaign but Refuses to Take It Down." *Independent*, March 15, 2017. https://www.independent.co.uk/life-style/fashion/livi-rae-lingerie-brand-diverse-campaign-backlash-refuse-take-down-response-a7630801.html.

Hoskins, Tansy E. *Stitched Up: The Anti-capitalist Book of Fashion*. London: Pluto, 2014.

Howell, Cerys. "I Deleted My Baby Apps When I Realised How Much They Fetishise Motherhood." *Guardian*, August 2, 2017. https://www.theguardian.com/commentisfree/2017/aug/02/baby-apps-fetishise-motherhood-postnatal-depression.

Husbands, Lesley. "Blogging the Maternal: Self-Representations of the Pregnant and Postpartum Body." *Atlantis: Critical Studies in Gender, Culture and Social Justice* 32, no. 2 (2008): 68–79.

Illouz, Eva. *Cold Intimacies: The Making of Emotional Capitalism*. Cambridge: Polity, 2007.

Illouz, Eva. *Saving the Modern Soul: Therapy, Emotions, and the Culture of Self-Help*. Berkeley: University of California Press, 2008.

Irby, Samantha. "Time Entertainer of the Year: Lizzo." *Time*, 2019. https://time .com/entertainer-of-the-year-2019-lizzo.

Jameson, Fredric. *Postmodernism, or, The Cultural Logic of Late Capitalism*. Durham, NC: Duke University Press, 1991.

Jane, Emma A. "'Your a Ugly, Whorish, Slut': Understanding E-bile." *Feminist Media Studies* 14, no. 4 (2014): 531–546.

Jankowski, Glen. "The Sexism of Men's Body Dissatisfaction Accounts." *Psychology of Women and Equalities Review* 2, no. 1 (2019): 38–54.

Jensen, Tracey. "Against Resilience." In *We Need to Talk about Family: Essays on Neoliberalism, the Family and Popular Culture*, edited by Roberta Garrett, Tracey Jensen, and Angie Voela, 76–94. Cambridge: Cambridge Scholars, 2016.

Jensen, Tracey. *Parenting the Crisis: The Cultural Politics of Parent-Blame*. Bristol, UK: Policy Press, 2018.

Jessen, Monique. "Here's How to Get Meghan Markle's 'Justice' Bracelet She Wore in South Africa—for Just $35!" *People*, September 23, 2019. https://people.com /royals/meghan-markle-prince-harry-justice-bracelet-just-35-dollars.

Jezer-Morton, Kathryn. "Online Momming in the 'Perfectly Imperfect' Age." *The Cut*, April 10, 2019. https://www.thecut.com/2019/04/online-moms -mommyblogs-instagram.html.

Kabeer, Naila. *The Power to Choose: Bangladeshi Women and Labour Supply Decision-Making in London and Dhaka*. New York: Verso, 2005.

Kadir, Shaira, and Joanna Tidy. "Gays, Gaze and Aunty Gok: The Disciplining of Gender and Sexuality in *How to Look Good Naked*." *Feminist Media Studies* 13, no. 2 (2011): 177–191.

Kafer, Alison. *Feminist, Queer, Crip*. Bloomington: Indiana University Press, 2013.

Kanai, Akane. *Gender and Relatability in Digital Culture*. London: Palgrave Macmillan, 2019.

Kanai, Akane, and Rosalind Gill. "Woke? Affect, Neoliberalism, Marginalised Identities and Consumer Culture." *New Formations: A Journal of Culture/ Theory/Politics* 102 (2020): 10–27.

"Katty Kay and Claire Shipman Launch 'Your Confidence Code' Online Course." *Elle*, October 22, 2020. https://www.elle.com/culture/books/a34452278 /confidence-code-katty-kay-claire-shipman.

Kay, Jilly Boyce, and Helen Wood. "Culture and Commoning in a Time of Coronavirus: Introduction to a *Cultural Commons* Special Section on COVID-19." *European Journal of Cultural Studies* 23, no. 4 (2020): 630–634. https://doi .org/10.1177%2F1367549420928360.

Kay, Katty, and Claire Shipman. *The Confidence Code for Girls: Taking Risks,*

Messing Up, and Becoming Your Amazingly Imperfect, Totally Powerful Self. New York: HarperCollins, 2018.

Kay, Katty, and Claire Shipman. *The Confidence Code: The Science and Art of Self-Assurance—What Women Should Know.* New York: HarperCollins, 2014.

Kay, Katty, and Claire Shipman. "Gender Discrimination Isn't Fair, but It's No Reason to Give Up on Self-Confidence." *Guardian,* April 30, 2014. https://www .theguardian.com/commentisfree/2014/apr/30/gender-discrimination-self -confidence-gap.

Kelan, Elisabeth. *Performing Gender at Work.* London: Palgrave Macmillan, 2009.

Kelly, Erin L., and Phyllis Moen. *Overload: How Good Jobs Went Bad and What We Can Do about It.* Princeton, NJ: Princeton University Press, 2020.

Kennedy, Gerrick D. "A Night at the Church of Lizzo, Pop Music's Patron Saint of Self-Care." *Los Angeles Times,* October 19, 2019. https://www.latimes.com /entertainment-arts/music/story/2019-10-19/lizzo-hollywood-palladium -concert-review.

Kennedy, Gerrick D. "100% Her Year: How Lizzo Became the One Thing We All Loved in 2019." *Los Angeles Times,* December 11, 2019. https://www.latimes .com/entertainment-arts/music/story/2019-12-11/lizzo-2019-artist-year.

Kleeman, Jenny. "SNL Producer and Film-Maker Are Latest to Accuse YouTube of Anti-LGBT Bias." *Guardian,* November 22, 2019. https://www.theguardian .com/technology/2019/nov/22/youtube-lgbt-content-lawsuit-discrimination -algorithm.

Koffman, Ofra, and Rosalind Gill. "'The Revolution Will Be Led by a 12-Year-Old Girl': Girl Power and Global Biopolitics." *Feminist Review* 105, no. 1 (2013): 83–102.

Koffman, Ofra, Shani Orgad, and Rosalind Gill. "Girl Power and 'Selfie Human-itarianism.'" *Continuum: Journal of Media and Cultural Studies* 29, no. 2 (2015): 157–168.

Kohrs, Kirsten, and Rosalind Gill. "Confident Appearing: Revisiting *Gender Adver-tisements* in Contemporary Culture." In *Routledge Handbook of Language, Gen-der, and Sexuality,* edited by Jo Angouri and Judith Baxter, 528–542. London: Routledge, 2021.

Lahad, Kinneret, and Michal Kravel-Trovi. "Happily-Ever After: Self-Marriage, the Claim of Wellness, and Temporal Ownership." *Sociological Review* 68, no. 3 (2020): 659–674. Published ahead of print, November 15, 2019. https://doi .org/10.1177%2F0038026119889479.

Lasch, Christopher. *The Culture of Narcissism: American Life in an Age of Diminishing Expectations.* New York: Norton, 1979.

Layard, Richard. *Happiness: Lessons from a New Science.* London: Penguin, 2011.

Lazar, Michelle M. "'Seriously Girly Fun!': Recontextualising Aesthetic Labour as Fun and Play in Cosmetics Advertising." In Elias, Gill, and Scharff, *Aesthetic Labour,* 51–66.

Lee, Ellie. "Introduction." In *Parenting Culture Studies,* edited by Ellie Lee, Jennie Bristow, Charlotte Faircloth, and Jan Macvarish, 1–22. London: Palgrave Macmillan, 2014.

Lee, Ellie, Jennie Bristow, Charlotte Faircloth, and Jan Macvarish, eds. *Parenting Culture Studies*. London: Palgrave Macmillan, 2014.

Lehmann, Christine. "'Self-Care' Urged for Women Caregivers amid Pandemic." WebMD, September 16, 2020. https://www.webmd.com/lung/news /20200916/self-care-urged-for-women-caregivers-amid-pandemic.

Lemke, Thomas. "'The Birth of Bio-politics': Michel Foucault's Lecture at the Collège de France on Neo-liberal Governmentality." *Economy and Society* 30, no. 2 (2001): 190–207.

Lerer, Lisa, and Jennifer Medina. "The 'Rage Moms' Democrats Are Counting On." *New York Times*, August 17, 2020. https://www.nytimes.com/2020/08/17 /us/politics/democrats-women-voters-anger.html.

Leung, Shirley. "Five Ways the Pandemic Can Ultimately Make the Workplace Better for Women." *Boston Globe*, November 6, 2020. https://www.boston globe.com/2020/11/06/magazine/five-ways-pandemic-can-ultimately-make -workplace-better-women.

Littler, Jo. *Against Meritocracy: Culture, Power and Myths of Mobility*. London: Rout-ledge, 2018.

Littler, Jo. "'I Feel Your Pain': Cosmopolitan Charity and the Public Fashioning of the Celebrity Soul." *Social Semiotics* 18, no. 2 (2008): 237–251.

Littler, Jo. "Mothers Behaving Badly: Chaotic Hedonism and the Crisis of Neolib-eral Social Reproduction." *Cultural Studies* 34, no. 4 (2020): 499–520.

Littler, Jo. "The Rise of the 'Yummy Mummy': Popular Conservatism and the Neoliberal Maternal in Contemporary British Culture." *Communication, Cul-ture and Critique* 6, no. 2 (2013): 227–243.

Livingstone, Sonia, and Alicia Blum-Ross. *Parenting for a Digital Future: How Hopes and Fears about Technology Shape Children's Lives*. Oxford: Oxford University Press, 2020.

Llewellyn Smith, Julia. "Politicians Beware—'Rage Mums' Are the New and Furious 'Worcester Woman.'" *Daily Telegraph*, August 24, 2020. https://www .telegraph.co.uk/women/politics/politicians-beware-rage-mums-new -furious-worcester-woman/.

Lorde, Audre. *A Burst of Light and Other Essays*. Mineola, NY: Ixia Press, 1988.

Lubiano, Wahneema. "Black Ladies, Welfare Queens, and State Minstrels: Ideolog-ical War by Narrative Means." In *Race-ing Justice, En-Gendering Power: Essays on Anita Hill, Clarence Thomas, and the Construction of Social Reality*, edited by Toni Morrison, 323–363. New York: Pantheon, 1992.

Luckhurst, Phoebe. "Peanut: The Parenting App That's About to Give Mumsnet a Run for Its Money." *Evening Standard*, February 9, 2017. https://www.standard .co.uk/lifestyle/london-life/peanut-the-parenting-app-thats-about-to-give -mumsnet-a-run-for-its-money-a3462306.html.

Luckhurst, Phoebe. "Tinder Co-founder Whitney Wolfe on Bumble: Her New Feminist Dating App That Lets Women Make the First Move." *Evening Stan-dard*, August 28, 2015. https://www.standard.co.uk/lifestyle/london-life

/tinder-co-founder-whitney-wolfe-on-bumble-her-new-feminist-dating-app
-that-lets-women-make-the-first-a2923011.html.

Lupton, Deborah. "Beyond the Quantified Self: The Reflexive Monitoring Self."
This Sociological Life, July 28, 2014. https://simplysociology.wordpress
.com/2014/07/28/beyond-the-quantified-self-the-reflexive-monitoring
-self.

Lupton, Deborah. *Data Selves: More-than-Human Perspectives*. Cambridge: Polity,
2019.

Lupton, Deborah. "Quantified Sex: A Critical Analysis of Sexual and Reproductive Self-Tracking Using Apps." *Culture, Health and Sexuality* 17, no. 4 (2015):
440–453.

Lupton, Deborah. "Self-Tracking Modes: Reflexive Self-Monitoring and Data Practices." Paper presented at Imminent Citizenships: Personhood and Identity
Politics in the Informatic Age workshop, August 27, 2014, Australian National University, Canberra.

Lupton, Deborah, and Gareth M. Thomas. "Playing Pregnancy: The Ludification
and Gamification of Expectant Motherhood in Smartphone Apps." *M/C Journal* 18, no. 5 (2015). https://doi.org/10.5204/mcj.1012.

Lynch, Meghan. "Blogging for Beauty? A Critical Analysis of Operation Beautiful."
Women's Studies International Forum 34, no. 6 (2011): 582–592.

Lyons, Margaret. "Review: The Find-Yourself Beauty of 'Shrill.'" *New York Times*,
March 14, 2019. https://www.nytimes.com/2019/03/14/arts/television/shrill
-review-hulu.html.

Mackelden, Amy. "Meghan Markle Just Gave an Empowering and Emotional
Speech on the Royal Tour." *Harper's Bazaar*, September 23, 2019. https://www
.harpersbazaar.com/celebrity/latest/a29189403/meghan-markle-speech
-transcript-royal-tour-africa.

Mackenzie, Cate. "How to Have a Healthy Summer Fling." *Psychologies*, August 26,
2019. https://www.psychologies.co.uk/summer.

Magladry, Madison. "Fitspiration or Fitsploitation: Postfeminism, Digital Media
and Authenticity in Women's Fitness Culture." PhD diss., Curtin University,
Australia, 2019.

Manson, Mark. *The Subtle Art of Not Giving a F*ck: A Counterintuitive Approach to Living a Good Life*. New York: HarperOne, 2016.

Marcus, George. *Ethnography through Thick and Thin*. Princeton, NJ: Princeton University Press, 1998.

Markle, Meghan. "HRH the Duchess of Sussex Introduces the September Issue
in Her Own Words." *Vogue*, July 29, 2019. https://www.vogue.co.uk/article
/meghan-markle-editors-letter-september-2019-issue.

Marshall, Elizabeth. "Schooling Ophelia: Hysteria, Memory and Adolescent Femininity." *Gender and Education* 19, no. 6 (2007): 707–728.

McAlister, Elizabeth. "Soundscapes of Disaster and Humanitarianism: Survival
Singing, Relief Telethons, and the Haiti Earthquake." *Small Axe* 39 (2012): 22–38.

McClain, Dani. "As a Black Mother, My Parenting Is Always Political." *The Nation*, March 27, 2019. https://www.thenation.com/article/black -motherhood-family-parenting-dani-mcclain.

McClintock, Anne. *Imperial Leather: Race, Gender and Sexuality in the Colonial Contest*. London: Routledge, 1995.

McGee, Micki. "Capitalism's Care Problem: Some Traces, Fixes, and Patches." *Social Text* 142 (2020): 39–65.

McGee, Micki. "Neurodiversity." *Contexts* 11, no. 3 (2012): 12–13.

McGee, Micki. *Self Help, Inc.: Makeover Culture in American Life*. Oxford: Oxford University Press, 2005.

McKee, Lyra. "Lyra McKee: A Letter to My 14-Year-Old Self." *Guardian*, April 19, 2019. https://www.theguardian.com/commentisfree/2019/apr/19/lyra -mckee-letter-gay-journalism-northern-ireland.

McKinsey and Company. *Women Matter, Time to Accelerate: Ten Years of Insights on Gender Diversity*. McKinsey and Company, October 2017. https://www .mckinsey.com/featured-insights/gender-equality/women-matter-ten-years -of-insights-on-gender-diversity.

McLennan, Rachael. "'A New Wrinkle': Age, Race and Writing Meghan Markle." *Women's Studies International Forum* 85 (2021): 102454. https://doi.org/10.1016 /j.wsif.2021.102454.

McNay, Lois. *Foucault and Feminism: Power, Gender and the Self*. Cambridge: Polity, 1992.

McNicholas Smith, Kate, and Imogen Tyler. "Lesbian Brides: Post-queer Popular Culture." *Feminist Media Studies* 17, no. 3 (2017): 315–331.

McRobbie, Angela. *The Aftermath of Feminism: Gender, Culture and Social Change*. London: Sage, 2009.

McRobbie, Angela. "Feminism, the Family and the New 'Mediated' Maternalism." *New Formations: A Journal of Culture/Theory/Politics* 80 (2013): 119–137.

McRobbie, Angela. "Notes on the Perfect: Competitive Femininity in Neoliberal Times." *Australian Feminist Studies* 30, no. 83 (2015): 3–20.

Mendick, Robert, and Hannah Furness. "Arch Meets Archie: Duke and Duchess of Sussex Introduce Their Son to Desmond Tutu." *Telegraph*, September 25, 2019. https://www.telegraph.co.uk/royal-family/2019/09/25/archie-meets -archbishop-desmond-tutu-prince-harry-meghan-markle.

Moore, Dasia. "Being a Protective Black Mom Isn't a Parenting Choice—It's the Only Choice." *Quartz*, December 20, 2019. https://qz.com/1765439/why-black -moms-cant-be-helicopter-parents.

Morad, Renee. "5 Ways Women Can Boost Their Confidence during the COVID-19 Pandemic." *NBC News*, October 28, 2020. https://www.nbcnews.com/know -your-value/feature/5-ways-women-can-boost-their-confidence-during -covid-19-ncna1245139.

Moran, Hannah. "Meghan Markle Gives First Speech about Being 'a Woman of Colour' on Royal Tour in South Africa." *Evoke*, September 24, 2019. https:// evoke.ie/2019/09/24/showbiz/gossip/meghan-markle-speech-south-africa.

Morris, Natalie. "The Underboob Bikini Is the Next Big Instagram Trend."

Metro, May 13, 2019. https://metro.co.uk/2019/05/13/underboob-bikini-next
-big-instagram-trend-9506261.

Morrissey, Helena. *A Good Time to Be a Girl: Don't Lean In, Change the System*. London: William Collins, 2018.

Morton, Katherine. "Emerging Geographies of Disciplining the Ageing Body: Practising Cosmetic Technologies in the Aesthetic Clinic." *Gender, Place and Culture* 22, no. 7 (2015): 1041–1057.

Mukherjee, Roopali. "Antiracism Limited: A Pre-history of Post-race." *Cultural Studies* 30, no. 1 (2016): 47–77.

Mukherjee, Roopali, and Sarah Banet-Weiser, eds. *Commodity Activism: Cultural Resistance in Neoliberal Times*. New York: New York University Press, 2012.

Mukherjee, Roopali, Sarah Banet-Weiser, and Herman Gray, eds. *Racism Postrace*. Durham, NC: Duke University Press, 2019.

Murphy, Meghan. "Femininity Is No Joke: On the #nomakeupselfie and #manupandmakeup." *Feminist Current*, March 21, 2014. https://www
.feministcurrent.com/2014/03/21/femininity-is-no-joke-nomakeupselfie-and
-manupandmakeup%E2%80%AC.

Murphy, Rewa. "(De)Constructing 'Body Love' Discourses in Young Women's Magazines." PhD diss., Victoria University of Wellington, 2013.

Murphy, Rewa, and Sue Jackson. "Bodies-as-Image? The Body Made Visible in Magazine Love Your Body Content." *Women's Studies Journal* 25, no. 1 (2011): 17–30.

Murray, Dara Persis. "Branding 'Real' Social Change in Dove's Campaign for Real Beauty." *Feminist Media Studies* 13, no. 1 (2012): 83–101.

Nafus, Dwan, and Jamie Sherman. "This One Does Not Go Up to 11: The Quantified Self Movement as an Alternative Big Data Practice." *International Journal of Communication* 8 (2014): 1784–1794.

Nakamura, Lisa. *Digitizing Race: Visual Cultures of the Internet*. Minneapolis: University of Minnesota Press, 2008.

Nash, Jennifer. "Black Maternal Aesthetics." *Theory and Event* 22, no. 3 (2019): 551–575.

Nash, Jennifer. "The Political Life of Black Motherhood." *Feminist Studies* 44, no. 3 (2018): 699–712.

Nash, Kate. "Global Citizenship as Show Business: The Cultural Politics of Make Poverty History." *Media, Culture and Society* 30, no. 2 (2008): 167–181.

Negra, Diane. *What a Girl Wants? Fantasizing the Reclamation of Self in Postfeminism*. London: Routledge, 2009.

Neustadt, Romi. *Get Over Your Damn Self: The No-BS Blueprint to Building a Life-Changing Business*. San Diego, CA: LiveFullOut Media, 2016.

Nguyen, Mimi Thi. "The Biopower of Beauty: Humanitarian Imperialisms and Global Feminisms in an Age of Terror." *Signs* 36, no. 2 (2011): 359–383.

Nguyen, Mimi Thi. *The Gift of Freedom: War, Debt, and Other Refugee Passages*. Durham, NC: Duke University Press, 2012.

Nicholl, Katie. "Meghan Markle Has a Feminist Focus in South Africa." *Vanity Fair*, September 24, 2019. https://www.vanityfair.com/style/2019/09
/meghan-markle-south-africa-female-leaders-feminism.

Nicholls, Dominic. "Army Chiefs Say Controversial 'Snowflake' Recruitment Campaign Was Most Successful in a Decade as New Series Is Launched." *Telegraph*, January 2, 2020. https://www.telegraph.co.uk/news/2020/01/02 /army-chiefs-say-controversial-snowflake-recruitment-campaign.

Nicholson, Rebecca. "Shrill Review—Taboo-Smashing Comedy Is a Big, Fat Delight." *Guardian*, December 15, 2019. https://www.theguardian.com/tv -and-radio/2019/dec/15/shrill-review-taboo-smashing-comedy-is-a-big -fat-delight-lindy-west.

Noble, Safiya. *Algorithms of Oppression: How Search Engines Reinforce Racism.* New York: New York University Press, 2018.

Nussbaum, Emily. "On 'Shrill' and 'Better Things,' Women Stop Being Good Sports." *New Yorker*, March 11, 2019. https://www.newyorker.com /magazine/2019/03/18/on-shrill-and-better-things-women-stop-being-good -sports.

O'Neill, Rachel. *Seduction: Men, Masculinity and Mediated Intimacy.* Cambridge: Polity, 2018.

Orgad, Shani. "The Cruel Optimism of *The Good Wife*: The Fantastic Working Mother on the Fantastical Treadmill." *Television and New Media* 18, no. 2 (2017): 165–183.

Orgad, Shani. *Heading Home: Motherhood, Work, and the Failed Promise of Equality.* New York: Columbia University Press, 2019.

Orgad, Shani. *Media Representation and the Global Imagination.* Cambridge: Polity, 2012.

Orgad, Shani. "Visualizers of Solidarity: Organizational Politics in Humanitarian and International Development NGOs." *Visual Communication* 12, no. 3 (2013): 295–314.

Orgad, Shani. "Working 9-to-5 Then 5-to-9: 'Hustle Culture' for Women during a Global Pandemic." LSE Blog, February 11, 2021. https://blogs.lse.ac.uk/medialse /2021/02/11/working-9-to-5-then-5-to-9-hustle-culture-for-women-during-a -global-pandemic/.

Orgad, Shani, and Kate Baldwin. "'How Any Woman Does What They Do Is Beyond Comprehension': Meghan Markle and the Masking of Maternal Labours." *Women's Studies in Communication* 44, no. 2 (2021). http://eprints.lse .ac.uk/108552/.

Orgad, Shani, and Sara De Benedictis. "The 'Stay-at-Home' Mother, Postfeminism and Neoliberalism: Content Analysis of UK News Coverage." *European Journal of Communication* 30, no. 4 (2015): 418–436.

Orgad, Shani, and Rosalind Gill. "Safety Valves for Mediated Female Rage in the #MeToo Era." *Feminist Media Studies* 19, no. 4 (2019): 596–603.

Orgad, Shani, and Kaarina Nikunen. "The Humanitarian Makeover." *Communication and Critical/Cultural Studies* 12, no. 3 (2015): 229–251.

Ouellette, Laurie. *Lifestyle TV.* New York: Routledge, 2016.

Palmer-Mehta, Valerie, and Sherianne Shuler. "'Devil Mammas' of Social Media: Resistant Maternal Discourses in Sanctimommy." In *Mediated Moms: Contem-*

porary Challenges to the Motherhood Myth, edited by Heather L. Hundley and Sara E. Hayden, 221–245. New York: Peter Lang, 2016.

Peck, Janice. "TV Talk Shows as Therapeutic Discourse: The Ideological Labor of the Televised Talking Cure." *Communication Theory* 5, no. 1 (1995): 58–81.

Pedersen, Sarah. "The Good, the Bad and the 'Good Enough' Mother on the UK Parenting Forum Mumsnet." *Women's Studies International Forum* 59 (2016): 32–38.

Pereira, Maria do Mar. *Power, Knowledge and Feminist Scholarship: An Ethnography of Academia.* London: Routledge, 2019.

Perry, Imani. *Breathe: A Letter to My Sons.* Boston: Beacon, 2019.

Petter, Olivia. "Missguided Celebrates Female 'Flaws' in Latest Campaign." *Independent*, May 10, 2018. https://www.independent.co.uk/life-style/fashion/missguided-female-flaws-imperfections-celebration-campaign-body-positivity-fashion-a8345176.html.

Piepzna-Samarasinha, Leah Lakshmi. *Care Work: Dreaming Disability Justice.* Vancouver, BC: Arsenal Pulp, 2018.

Pipher, Mary. *Reviving Ophelia: Helping You to Understand and Cope with Your Teenage Daughter.* New York: Penguin, 1995.

Potter, Jonathan. "Discourse Analysis and Constructionist Approaches: Theoretical Background." In *Handbook of Qualitative Research Methods for Psychology and the Social Sciences*, edited by J. Richardson, 125–140. Leicester, UK: British Psychological Society, 1996.

Puar, Jasbir. "Rethinking Homonationalism." *International Journal of Middle East Studies* 45, no. 2 (2013): 336–339.

Pulrang, Andrew. "Self-Help or Activism: A Fundamental Divide in the Disability Community." *Forbes*, February 23, 2020. https://www.forbes.com/sites/andrewpulrang/2020/02/23/self-help-or-activism-a-fundamental-divide-in-the-disability-community/.

Purser, Ronald. *McMindfulness.* London: Repeater, 2019.

Radner, Hilary. "Introduction: Queering the Girl." In *Swinging Single: Representing Sexuality in the 1960s*, edited by Hilary Radner and Moya Luckett, 1–36. Minneapolis: University of Minnesota Press, 1999.

Ramamurthy, Anandi, and Kalpana Wilson. "'An Act of Struggle in the Present': History, Education and Political Campaigning by South Asian Anti-imperialist Activists in Britain." In *Reflections on Knowledge, Learning and Social Movements: History's Schools*, edited by Aziz Choudry and Salim Vally, 149–168. Abingdon, UK: Routledge, 2017.

Ramamurthy, Anandi, and Kalpana Wilson. "Come and Join the Freedom-Lovers: Racism, Appropriation and Resistance in Advertising." In *Colonial Advertising and Commodity Racism*, edited by Wulf D. Hund, Michael Pickering, and Anandi Ramamurthy, 69–89. Zurich: Lit Verlag, 2013.

Rapping, Elayne. *The Culture of Recovery: Making Sense of the Self-Help Movement in Women's Lives.* Boston: Beacon, 1997.

Redifeld, Peter. "Doctors, Borders, and Life in Crisis." *Cultural Anthropology* 20, no. 3 (2005): 328–361.

Reid, Sharmadean. "How Can I Boost My Confidence at Work?" *Guardian*, March 5, 2018. https://www.theguardian.com/money/2018/mar/05/how-can-i-boost -my-confidence-at-work.

Rettberg, Jill W. *Seeing Ourselves through Technology: How We Use Selfies, Blogs and Wearable Devices to See and Shape Ourselves*. London: Springer, 2014.

Richey, Lisa Ann, and Stefano Ponte. *Brand Aid: Shopping Well to Save the World*. Minneapolis: University of Minnesota Press, 2011.

Riley, Sarah, Adrienne Evans, Emma Anderson, and Martine Robson. "The Gendered Nature of Self-Help." *Feminism and Psychology* 29, no. 1 (2019): 3–18.

Riley, Sarah, Adrienne Evans, and Martine Robson. *Postfeminism and Health*. London: Routledge, 2018.

Rimke, Heidi Marie. "Governing Citizens through Self-Help Literature." *Cultural Studies* 14, no. 1 (2000): 61–78.

Rinaldi, Karen. *It's Great to Suck at Something: The Unexpected Joy of Wiping Out and What It Can Teach Us about Patience, Resilience, and the Stuff That Really Matters*. New York: Atria, 2019.

Ringrose, Jessica, and Emma Renold. "Normative Cruelties and Gender Deviants: The Performative Effects of Bully Discourses for Girls and Boys in School." *British Educational Research Journal* 36, no. 4 (2010): 573–596.

Ritschel, Chelsea. "Nike Uses Plus-Size Mannequins in Store." *Independent*, June 5, 2019. https://www.independent.co.uk/life-style/nike-plus-size-mannequin -london-store-niketown-a8946196.html.

Roberts, Dorothy E. "Punishing Drug Addicts Who Have Babies: Women of Color, Equality and the Right of Privacy." *Harvard Law Review* 104 (1991): 1441–1442.

Robert Walters. "Empowering Women in the Workplace." Accessed January 14, 2020. https://www.robertwalters.co.uk/empowering-women/career-advice /top-tips-for-career-confidence.html.

Rodrigues, Sara. "Undressing Homogeneity: Prescribing Femininity and the Transformation of Self-Esteem in *How to Look Good Naked*." *Journal of Popular Film and Television* 40, no. 1 (2012): 42–51.

Rose, Jacqueline. *Mothers: An Essay on Love and Cruelty*. London: Faber and Faber, 2018.

Rose, Nikolas. *Governing the Soul: The Shaping of the Private Self*. London: Taylor and Francis/Routledge, 1990.

Rose, Nikolas. *Inventing Ourselves: Psychology, Power, Personhood*. Cambridge: Cambridge University Press, 1998.

Ross, Tim. "David Cameron Plans Parenting Classes for All Families." *Telegraph*, January 10, 2016. https://www.telegraph.co.uk/news/newstopics/eureferendum /12091327/David-Cameron-plans-parenting-classes-for-all-families.html.

Roth, Heike, Caroline Homer, and Jennifer Fenwick. "'Bouncing Back': How Australia's Leading Women's Magazines Portray the Postpartum 'Body.'" *Women and Birth* 25, no. 3 (2012): 128–134.

Rottenberg, Catherine. "Happiness and the Liberal Imagination: How Superwoman Became Balanced." *Feminist Studies* 40, no. 1 (2014): 144–168.

Rottenberg, Catherine. *The Rise of Neoliberal Feminism*. Oxford: Oxford University Press, 2018.

Rowe, Kristin Denise. "'I Love This Cotton Hair!': Black Women, Natural Hair, and Re(constructions) of Beauty." Master's thesis, Michigan State University, 2015.

Roy, Srila. "Precarity, Aspiration and Neoliberal Development: Women Empowerment Workers in West Bengal." *Contributions to Indian Sociology* 53, no. 3 (2019): 392–421.

Salter, Philip. "Don't Stress: This Female Entrepreneur Has a New App Boosting Sleep, Calm and Confidence." *Forbes*, April 5, 2018. https://www.forbes.com /sites/philipsalter/2018/04/05/dont-stress-this-female-entrepreneur-has-a -new-app-boosting-sleep-calm-and-confidence.

Sandberg, Sheryl. *Lean In: Women, Work, and the Will to Lead*. New York: W. H. Allen, 2013.

Sandberg, Sheryl, and Adam Grant. *Option B: Facing Adversity, Building Resilience, and Finding Joy*. London: W. H. Allen, 2017.

Saujani, Reshma. *Brave, Not Perfect*. London: HQ, 2019.

Scharff, Christina. "The Psychic Life of Neoliberalism: Mapping the Contours of Entrepreneurial Subjectivity." *Theory, Culture and Society* 33, no. 6 (2016): 107–122.

Scharff, Christina. *Repudiating Feminism: Young Women in a Neoliberal World*. Farnham, UK: Ashgate, 2013.

Sender, Katherine. *The Makeover: Reality Television and Reflexive Audiences*. New York: New York University Press, 2012.

Seppälä, Emma. "What Bosses Gain by Being Vulnerable." *Harvard Business Review*, December 11, 2014. https://hbr.org/2014/12/what-bosses-gain-by-being -vulnerable.

Seyfert, Robert. "Beyond Personal Feelings and Collective Emotions: Toward a Theory of Social Affect." *Theory, Culture and Society* 29, no. 6 (2012): 27–46.

Shome, Raka. *Diana and Beyond: White Femininity, National Identity, and Contemporary Media Culture*. Champaign: University of Illinois Press, 2014.

Shome, Raka. "'Global Motherhood': The Transnational Intimacies of White Femininity." *Critical Studies in Media Communication* 28, no. 5 (2011): 388–406.

Shome, Raka. "Thinking Culture and Cultural Studies—from/of the Global South." *Communication and Critical/Cultural Studies* 16, no. 3 (2019): 196–218.

Showalter, Elaine. *The Female Malady: Women, Madness, and English Culture, 1830–1980*. New York: Pantheon, 1985.

Showalter, Elaine. "Ophelia, Gender and Madness." British Library, March 15, 2016. https://www.bl.uk/shakespeare/articles/ophelia-gender-and-madness.

Singh, Linda. "Instagram Affordances among Post-pregnant Body Advocates." Master's diss., Malmö University, Sweden, 2019.

Slaughter, Anne-Marie. *Unfinished Business: Women, Men, Work, Family*. London: Oneworld Publications, 2015.

Sobande, Francesca. "'We're All in This Together': Commodified Notions of Connection, Care and Community in Brand Responses to COVID-19." *European Journal of Cultural Studies* 23, no. 6 (2020): 1033–1037. Published ahead of print, June 22, 2020. https://doi.org/10.1177%2F1367549420932294.

Sobande, Francesca. "Woke-Washing: 'Intersectional' Femvertising and Branding 'Woke' Bravery." *European Journal of Marketing* 54, no. 11 (2019): 2723–2745. https://doi.org/10.1108/EJM-02-2019-0134.

Son, Hugh. "New Goldman CEO's Advice to Help Remake a Wall Street Titan: Be Vulnerable." *CNBC*, July 27, 2018. https://www.cnbc.com/2018/07/27/goldman -sachs-ceo-explains-how-to-be-more-effective-be-vulnerable.html.

Sonninen, Lotta. *The Little Book of Bad Moods*. London: Bloomsbury, 2018.

Soukup, Ruth. *Do It Scared: Finding the Courage to Face Your Fears, Overcome Adversity, and Create a Life You Love*. Grand Rapids, MI: Zondervan, 2019.

"'Speak Your Truth. Follow Your Wild Heart': How Brené Brown Learned to Cope with Cruelty Online." *Vogue*, August 21, 2019. https://www.vogue.co.uk /arts-and-lifestyle/article/brene-brown-writes-for-vogue.

Spillers, Hortense J. "Mama's Baby, Papa's Maybe: An American Grammar Book." *Diacritics* 17, no. 2 (1987): 64–81.

Squire, Corinne. "Empowering Women? The Oprah Winfrey Show." In *Feminist Television Criticism: A Reader*, edited by Charlotte Brunsdon, Julie D'Acci, and Lynn Spigel, 98–113. Oxford: Oxford University Press, 1997.

Squires, Catherine R. *The Post-racial Mystique: Media and Race in the Twenty-First Century*. New York: New York University Press, 2014.

Sunim, Haemin. *Love for Imperfect Things: How to Accept Yourself in a World Striving for Perfection*. London: Penguin, 2019.

Sweeney, Eva. *Queers on Wheels: The Essential Guide for the Physically Disabled GLBTQ Community*. Pasadena, CA: Create Space, 2004.

Swidler, Ann. "What Anchors Cultural Practices?" In *The Practice Turn in Contemporary Theory*, edited by Theodore R. Schatzki, Karin Knorr Cetina, and Eike von Savigny, 74–92. London: Routledge, 2001.

Tasker, Yvonne, and Diane Negra. *Interrogating Postfeminism: Gender and the Politics of Popular Culture*. Durham, NC: Duke University Press, 2007.

Tate, Shirley. "Black Beauty: Shade, Hair and Anti-racist Aesthetics." *Ethnic and Racial Studies* 30, no. 2 (2007): 300–319.

Taylor, Stephanie, and Susan Luckman. *The New Normal of Working Lives: Critical Studies in Contemporary Work and Employment*. London: Palgrave Macmillan, 2018.

Thompson, Laura, and Ngaire Donaghue. "The Confidence Trick: Competing Constructions of Confidence and Self-Esteem in Young Australian Women's Discussions of the Sexualisation of Culture." *Women's Studies International Forum* 47 (2014): 23–35.

Thompson, Wanna. "How White Women on Instagram Are Profiting Off Black Women." *Paper Magazine*, November 14, 2018. https://www.papermag.com /white-women-blackfishing-instagram-2619714094.html.

Thomson, Rachel, Mary Jane Kehily, Lucy Hadfield, and Sue Sharpe. *Making Modern Mothers*. Bristol, UK: Policy Press, 2011.

Tolentino, Jia. "The Gig Economy Celebrates Working Yourself to Death." *New Yorker*, March 22, 2017. https://www.newyorker.com/culture/jia-tolentino /the-gig-economy-celebrates-working-yourself-to-death.

Tyler, Imogen. "Pregnant Beauty: Maternal Femininities under Neoliberalism." In *New Femininities: Postfeminism, Neoliberalism and Subjectivity*, edited by Rosalind Gill and Christina Scharff, 21–36. Hampshire, UK: Palgrave Macmillan, 2011.

Tyler, Imogen. *Revolting Subjects: Social Abjection and Resistance in Neoliberal Britain*. New York: Zed Books, 2013.

Tyler, Melissa. "Managing between the Sheets: Lifestyle Magazines and the Management of Sexuality in Everyday Life." *Sexualities* 7, no. 1 (2004): 81–106.

Vagianos, Alanna. "Lizzo Loves Being 'a Fat B***h.'" *Huffington Post*, April 29, 2019. https://www.huffingtonpost.co.uk/entry/lizzo-fat-bitch-v-magazine_n_5cc71 9cae4b04eb7ff996526.

Valdivia, Angharad. "Holding Up Half the Sky: Global Narratives of Girls at Risk and Celebrity Philanthropy." *Girlhood Studies* 11, no. 3 (2018): 84–100.

Valenti, Lauren. "Selena Gomez on Acne, Mental Health, and Her Day-to-Night Make-Up Strategy." *Vogue*, September 4, 2020. https://www.vogue.co.uk /beauty/article/selena-gomez-beauty-secrets-skincare-makeup.

Valenti, Lauren. "Watch Liv Tyler Do Her 25-Step Beauty and Self-Care Routine." *Vogue*, July 25, 2019. https://www.vogue.com/article/liv-tyler -beauty-skin-self-care-secrets-tricks-techniques.

van Noord, Maria. *Self Esteem for Women: Proven Techniques and Habits to Grow Your Self Esteem, Assertiveness and Confidence in Just 60 Days*. Self-published, 2018.

Vernon, Leah. *Unashamed: Musings of a Fat, Black Muslim*. Boston: Beacon, 2019.

Vestergaard, Anne. "Humanitarian Branding and the Media: The Case of Amnesty International." *Journal of Language and Politics* 7, no. 3 (2008): 471–493.

Villalobos, Ana. *Motherload: Making It All Better in Insecure Times*. Oakland: University of California Press, 2014.

Wallace, Kelly. "A 'Confidence Code' for Girls: 5 Ways to Build Up Our Daughters." *CNN*, May 21, 2018. https://edition.cnn.com/2018/05/21/health/girls -confidence-code-parenting/index.html.

Wallace, Kelly. "The Ripple Effects on Girls When Moms Struggle with Body Image." *CNN*, June 7, 2017. https://edition.cnn.com/2017/06/07/health/body -image-moms-impact-daughters/index.html.

Walters, Helen. "Vulnerability Is the Birthplace of Innovation, Creativity and Change: Brené Brown at TED2012." *TED Blog*, March 2, 2012. https://blog.ted .com/vulnerability-is-the-birthplace-of-innovation-creativity-and-change -brene-brown-at-ted2012.

Walters, Rosie. "Reading Girls' Participation in Girl Up as Feminist: Club Members' Activism in the UK, USA and Malawi." *Gender and Development* 26, no. 3 (2018): 477–493. https://policy-practice.oxfam.org.uk/publications /reading-girls-participation-in-girl-up-as-feminist-club-members-activism -in-the-620589.

Walters, Suzanna D., and Laura Harrison. "Not Ready to Make Nice: Aberrant

Mothers in Contemporary Culture." *Feminist Media Studies* 14, no. 1 (2014): 38–55.

Warner, Michael. "Introduction: Fear of a Queer Planet." *Social Text* 29 (1991): 3–17.

Wearing, Stephen, Mary Mostafanezhad, Nha Nguyen, Truc Ha Thanh Nguyen, and Matthew McDonald. "'Poor Children on Tinder' and Their Barbie Saviours: Towards a Feminist Political Economy of Volunteer Tourism." *Leisure Studies* 37, no. 5 (2018): 500–514.

West, Caroline. "The Lean In Collection: Women, Work, and the Will to Represent." *Open Cultural Studies* 2, no. 1 (2018): 430–439. https://doi.org/10.1515/culture-2018-0039.

Wetherell, Margaret. "Trends in the Turn to Affect: A Social Psychological Critique." *Body and Society* 21, no. 2 (2015): 139–166.

Wetherell, Margaret, and David Beer. "The Future of Affect Theory: An Interview with Margaret Wetherell." *Theory, Culture and Society*, October 15, 2014. https://www.theoryculturesociety.org/the-future-of-affect-theory-an-interview-with-margaret-wetherall.

Wheeler, Kathryn. "How to Rebuild Confidence Post-lockdown." Happiful, June 5, 2020. https://happiful.com/how-to-rebuild-confidence-post-lockdown.

Whitehead, Joanna. "New Mothercare Campaign Encourages Mothers to Feel Confident about Their Bodies." *Independent*, February 25, 2019. https://www.independent.co.uk/life-style/health-and-families/mothercare-body-confidence-proud-mums-campaign-birth-pregnancy-a8792406.html.

Whiteman, Julie. "Enduring Notions of Heterosexuality: A Study in Contemporary Sex and Relationships." PhD thesis, University of Birmingham, 2020. https://etheses.bham.ac.uk/id/eprint/10412/7/Whiteman2020PhD.pdf.

Widdows, Heather. *Perfect Me*. Princeton, NJ: Princeton University Press, 2018.

Wilkins, Karin Gwin, and Florencia Enghel. "The Privatization of Development through Global Communication Industries: Living Proof?" *Media, Culture and Society* 35, no. 2 (2013): 165–181.

Williams, Patrick. "The Importance of Being Courageously Vulnerable at Work." *Forbes*, August 29, 2018. https://www.forbes.com/sites/forbescoachescouncil/2018/08/29/the-importance-of-being-courageously-vulnerable-at-work.

Williams, Raymond. *The Long Revolution: An Analysis of the Democratic, Industrial, and Cultural Changes Transforming Our Society*. New York: Columbia University Press, 1961.

Williams, Ruth. "Eat, Pray, Love: Producing the Female Neoliberal Spiritual Subject." *Journal of Popular Culture* 47, no. 3 (2014): 613–633.

Williams, Serena. "Letter to My Mom." Reddit, September 19, 2017. https://www.reddit.com/user/serenawilliams/comments/714c1b/letter_to_my_mom.

Wilson, Julie A., and Emily Chivers Yochim. *Mothering through Precarity: Women's Work and Digital Media*. Durham, NC: Duke University Press, 2017.

Wilson, Kalpana. "'Race,' Gender and Neoliberalism: Changing Visual Representations in Development." *Third World Quarterly* 32, no. 2 (2011): 315–331.

Winch, Alison. *Girlfriends and Postfeminist Sisterhood*. London: Palgrave Macmillan, 2013.

Wong, Alice. *Disability Visibility: First-Person Stories from the Twenty-First Century*. New York: Vintage, 2020.

Wood, Rachel. "Look Good, Feel Good: Sexiness and Sexual Pleasure in Neoliberalism." In Elias, Gill, and Scharff, *Aesthetic Labour*, 317–332.

Wynn, Aiden. "Confidence at Work: Why Are We All Feeling So Down on Ourselves at the Moment?" *Stylist*. Accessed November 5, 2020. https://www.stylist.co.uk/life/careers/confidence-at-work-wfh-uncertainty/442157.

Zarya, Valentina. "The World's Most Successful Women Share Their Best Career Advice." *World Economic Forum*, October 5, 2017. https://www.weforum.org/agenda/2017/10/the-worlds-most-successful-women-share-their-best-career-advice.

Zemler, Emily. "20 Strong Women Who Kick Ass on TV." *Elle*, March 21, 2018. https://www.elle.com/culture/movies-tv/g19496038/20-strongest-women-on-tv.

index

45–48; women blamed for lack of, 31, 50–52. *See also* "love your body" (LYB) messages

body confidence industrial complex, 31, 34–36

body positivity, 1–2, 14, 32, 36, 155–156; mainstream versions of, 40, 44, 76

Bold Type, The (TV show), 39–40

Bolsonaro, Jair, 7

Boohoo brand sweatshops, 44–45

Bordo, Susan, 46

Born Free Africa, 135

Boston Globe, 69

Boston Women's Health Book Collective, 160

Braedley, Susan, 105

"brand aid," 128

Bratich, Jack, 7

Brave, Not Perfect (Saujani), 64

breathing, 88

Breslin, Dawn, 10

Bridges, Ruby, 161

British Medical Association, 33

Brown, Brené, 4, 68, 72–74, 125

Brown, Helen Gurley, 14

Brown, Wendy, 16

Bull, Anna, 102

Burkeman, Oliver, 93

"Bye Bitch" (Lizzo), 156–157

Cain, Ruth, 102

Call to Courage, The (Brown), 72

Cameron, David, 102

Campaign for Body Confidence, 105

Canada, 33, 86

capitalism, 11–12, 15–17, 21, 45, 66; "emotional," 17; "ethical," 138; global market, 128, 129; normalizing struggle within, 66–69; patriarchal, 69, 126–127, 144; philanthrocapitalism, 27, 126, 129–130, 141; racial, 157

Cardi B, 112

Care and Keeping of Us: A Sharing Collection for Girls and Their Moms, The, 121, 123

Care and Keeping of You: The Body Book for Girls, The, 120

"carewashing," 44, 84, 173n51

Care Work: Dreaming Disability Justice (Piepzna-Samarasinha), 33

Carson, Sofia, 137, *137*

celebrities, 1–2, 9, 63, 145, 161; anti-self-help texts, 92–93; Black mothers, 112–113; and body confidence, 31, 38, 41–44; and international development, 124–128; and mothering, 108, 112–113; and philanthrocapitalism, 27, 124–128, 130, 141–142; and relationship confidence, 82, 84, 92–93; vulnerability, turn to, 4, 70, 149–150, 154–159

character, turn to, 17, 102, 119–120

Charles, Prince, 41

"choice," 15

class, 8, 13, 17, 86, 90, middle-classness, 36, 59, 75, 87, 100–101, 133, 149; middle-class parents, 104, 111–113; working-class parents, 102; working-class women, 152, class-based analyses, 13–14, 104

class inequalities, 1, 7–8, 105

Clinique advertisement, 21, 22

CNN, 114–115

Collins, Patricia Hill, 112

colonialism, 126–128, 130, 133, 137, 139, 142; logics of, 27, 40, 87

commodity, body confidence as, 35–36, 171n18

commodity activism/cause marketing, 35, 128, 135–138, 171n18

"commodity feminism," 20, 44

confidence: as affective regime, 22–23; as beyond debate, 3–4, 32; coaching, 60–61; as cultural formation (dispositif), 18, 28, 144, 154; cultural prominence of, 4–5, 31–32; movement as representation of, 21, 169n81; as Northern and Western phenomenon, 24–25; one-size-fits-all message, 7, 144–145; as progressive political project, 5–6; Taylorization of, 92. *See also* confidence cult(ure)

"Confidence Coalition," 116

Confidence Code, The (Kay and Shipman), 2, 10, 26, 57, 61–63, 100

Confidence Code for Girls: Taking Risks, Messing Up, and Becoming Your Amazingly Imperfect, Totally Powerful Self, The (Kay and Shipman), 100–101, 115, 119, 123

emotional capitalism, 17
"emotional style," 15
emotions, "core," 72, 74
"empowerment workers," 140–141
endorphins, 88
Engelbert, Cathy, 60
Ensler, Eve, 136
entrepreneurialism, language of, 16, 78,
    130–131, 133–134
Estéreo, Bomba, 1

Facebook, 40
facing forward, as synonym for confidence,
    21
*Failosophy: A Handbook for When Things Go
    Wrong* (Day), 97–98
failure: embracing, 73, 92–98; role-
    modeling through mothering, 115–117
fat activism, 32, 34, 148–149, *149*, 156; plus-
    size bloggers, 34, 172n35. *See also* Lizzo
Fa(t)shion February, 156
fat talk, 50–51
Favaro, Laura, 80
feeds, 90
"feeling rules," 19, 23
femininity, 13, 20, 42, 49, 53, 65, 89, 107–108,
    111–112, 130
feminism: aestheticized version of, 147;
    "commodity," 20, 44; "corporate 1%,"
    75; "faux," 37, 38; feminist T-shirt as pol-
    itics, 45; friendships between women
    as, 81–82; history of erased, 146; indi-
    vidualistic reconstruction of, 6–8, 98;
    influence on confidence cult(ure), 5–6,
    32; and mothering, 107–108; neoliberal
    remaking of, 6, 159–160; not mentioned
    in feminist books, 96; as "obvious,"
    7–8; popular, 2, 45, 81, 108, 143, 145–147;
    reframing of in mothering context,
    122–123; remaking of, 145–147; second-
    wave, 30; and therapeutic culture, 13;
    visibility of, 2, 20, 81, 143. *See also* post-
    feminist discourses
"femvertising," 1, 31, 37
Fenty brand, 8
Fenwick, Jennifer, 108

film, 29–30, 56–58
fitness culture, 54
Fiverr, 67–68
Florrick, Alicia, 58
Floyd, George, 4, 8, 44, 61, 71, 72, 113
Flynn, Gillian, 95
Forbes, 125
Foster, Dawn, 75
Foucault, Michel, 11, 18–19, 144
France, 177n14
Freud, Sigmund, 11
Friedan, Betty, 14
Friedli, Lynn, 17

Gaines, Alisha, 44
Gates, Bill, 70
Gates, Melinda, 70, 71–72, 74, 126
Gender Advertisements (Goffman), 21
Geox (Respira) shoes ad, 169n81
*Get Over Your Damn Self: The No-BS Blueprint
    to Building a Life-Changing Business* (Neu-
    stadt), 64
Getty Images, 20–21, 38, 59, 61, 168n78
Gevinson, Tavi, 21, 22
Gifts of Imperfection, The (Brown), 72
gig economy, 68
Gill, Rosalind, 21, 130
Gillette ad, 53
Girl, Stop Apologizing (Hollis), 2, 26, 64–67,
    70
Girl Effect, 130
girls: confidence products for, 100, 116,
    119–121, *120, 121*; "crisis" of, 100–101, 115–116,
    119; education, in global South, 124,
    131–132, 137–138, 140, 145; as focus of gov-
    ernment campaigns, 106; girl power and
    confidence culture, 129–135; and "ideal
    victim" discourse of NGOs, 130; market
    for empowerment, 100–101, 115–116; par-
    ents as underlying market, 101–105; white,
    middle-class in "crisis," 100–101
Girls Who Code, 64
Girl Up campaign, 131–133
Glamour, 81, 98
global market capitalism, 128–129
"global motherhood," 126–127

Index   233

fidence discourses and technologies, 127; girl power and confidence culture, 129–135; "global mother" role, 126; global North as consumer, 130–131; humanitarian aid, criticisms of, 128–129; privatization of foreign aid, 128; privileging in, 127, 129, 134, 137; voluntourism industry, 133–135. *See also* global South

"intersectionality disclaimer," 97

invisibilization, 32, 45

Irby, Samantha, 159

Irish Republican Army (IRA), 8–9

"it gets better" movement, 9, 96–97

Itsines, Kayla, 85

Jameson, Fredric, 89

Jamil, Jameela, 125

Jezer-Morton, Kathryn, 112

Jolie, Angelina, 125, 126

Joseph, Gillian, 131

journaling, 91, 93, 121, 151

Jubilee Centre, 102

"Justice" bracelet, 125

Justice Desk (human rights organization), 124

"Just Not Sorry" (Google add-on), 51

Kabul Beauty School, 139

Kafer, Alison, 9

Kaling, Mindy, 56

Kanai, Akane, 16–17

Kay, Katty, 2, 26, 57, 63, 100–101, 115

KeepOnBeingYou movement, 38–39, *39*

Kennedy, Michelle, 109

Khateera (digital content platform), *153*, 153–154

Koffman, Ofra, 130, 131

Kohrs, Kirsten, 21

Lachover, Einat, 117

Lady Leshurr, 149

Lagarde, Christine, 63

Lasch, Christopher, 84

Late Night (comedy film), 56, 58–59, 73

"law of attraction," 161

Lawrence, Iska, 43

Layard, Richard, 13

Lean Cuisine, 37

Lean In (Sandberg), 2, 58, 63, 65–66, 146, 150

"Lean In Collection," 20–21, 59, 61, 168n78

LeanIn.org, 20, 58, 176n3

Lean In: Women, Work, and the Will to Lead (Sandberg), 26, 57, 58–61

Lee, Ellie, 104

Lerer, Lisa, 152

lesbians, 8, 82–83, 148, 151. *See also* queer (LGBTQ+) people

"Letter to My Mom" (Williams), 118–119, 122–123

LGBTQ+ people. *See* queer (LGBTQ+) people

lifestyle media, 15, 77

linguistic "reprogramming," 121

LinkedIn, 4, 61, 67, 71

Little Book of Bad Moods, The, 78, 93

Littler, Jo, 152

Living Proof campaign, 129

Lizzo, 1, 4, 143, 154–159, *157*

Lorde, Audre, 150, 151

L'Oréal, 34, *41*, 41–42, 88

Lovato, Demi, 1, 82

Love Island (reality show), 31

"love your body" (LYB) messages, 10, 23, 54; commercial campaigns, 26, 31, 37–40; "faux feminism," 37, 38; and international development, 135; monochrome space in ads, 41, *41*; and motherhood, 105; toxic beauty standards in, 45–48. *See also* body confidence; confidence imperative

Lupton, Deborah, 85

Luxton, Meg, 105

madness, 13

magazines, 10, 39–40, 76–77, 81, 83

magical thinking, 90

"Make a Plan, Make a Difference" campaign, 102–103, *103*

Manson, Mark, 78, 94

Marc Jacobs ad, 42, 52

Margulies, Julianna, 67

Marie Claire, 81

Markle, Meghan, 74, 124–127, 184n36

Marks and Spencer (M&S), 135

Martell, Katie, 37–38

Martin, Trayvon, 113

Roy, Srila, 140
Rustin, Mike, 15

Sandberg, Sheryl, 2, 20–21, 26, 57, 58–61, 63, 65, 68, 100, 146; vulnerability expressed by, 70–72
Saudi Arabia, 138–140
Saujani, Reshma, 64
Scarlet fashion magazine, 39–40
Scharff, Christina, 16
Schumer, Amy, 29–30, 39
"security work," 103–104
seduction "community-industry," 7
self: "belabored," 12; extension of, 88; gendered technology of, 19–20, 143, 144; labor vs. improvement, 63; obligation to work on, 18, 26–28, 57, 61, 168n78; practices of as historically and culturally specific, 18; as rational and calculating, 16; self-tracking/reflexive monitoring, 85, 91–92, 104; surveillance of, 46–47; technology of, 10, 22–23; unfixing/untethering of, 15
self-actualization, 12
self-care: apps, 77–78, 84–92; and the confidence cult, 83–92; inspirational messages, 83–84; working on confidence as, 15
self-esteem, 2, 11, 24, 26, 145, 148, 151; and body confidence, 30, 32–33, 35, 171n18; Dove project, 35; and international development, 128, 134; and mothering, 100, 106, 114, 116–117; as political at level of self, 16; and relationships, 80; and workplace, 59–60. *See also* body confidence
self-governing subjects, 15; mothers as, 104, 113–114, 122
self-help, 11; anti-self-help, 78, 92–98; neoliberalization of, 14–15; parenting books, 106–107; rise of, 13–15; "sweary self-help," 93
Self-Help, Inc. (McGee), 14
"selfie gaze," 47, 131
"self-made woman," 71
self-marriage, 77
self-monitoring, 18, 64, 85, 146; and mothering, 101, 104–105, 113–115, 118, 122–123

self-policing, 65, 75, 88; of mothering, 104, 113–114
self-tracking, 136–137
Seligman, Martin, 13
Sender, Katherine, 15
Sex Education (TV show), 150, 151
sexual confidence, 76–77, 95, 98; "aberrant" mothers, 108; and disability, 151; heterosexual women, 79–80; lesbian and bisexual women, 82–83; as new sexy, 78–80; "sexual entrepreneurs," 78–79; sexuality as work, 78–80. *See also* relationships, confident
"shadowbanning," 45
Shape of a Mother, The (website), 108
Shipman, Claire, 2, 26, 57, 63, 100–101, 115
Shome, Raka, 87, 126–128
Showalter, Elaine, 13
Shrill (TV show), 84, 148
"Shwopping," 135–136
"side hustle," 68
"Simply Complicated" (Lovato), 82
Sincero, Jean, 2
Sinclair, Emma, 136
sisterhood, 124–126
Slaughter, Anne-Marie, 146
Slay in Your Lane: The Black Girl Bible (Adegoke and Uviebinené), 148–150
Smalls For All, 135–136
Smart Girl's Guide: Knowing What to Say, A, 120–121
Smart Girl's Guide: Liking Herself, A, 120
Smart Works, 125
Smedley, Jen, 117–118
Smith, Julia Llewellyn, 152
Smith, Keri, 93
Smith, Sharon, 20
Sm'touha Menni (YouTube satirical series), 153–154
social abjection, 23
social justice, 43–44, 143, 159
social media, 2; and body confidence messaging, 33–34; hashtags, 31; "mamasphere," 104–105; "mommy blogs," 106–108, 113–114; online hate, 34;

CPSIA information can be obtained
at www.ICGtesting.com
Printed in the USA
LVHW011328200322
713909LV00013B/1496

9 781478 017608